When Children Refuse School

When Children Refuse School

A COGNITIVE-BEHAVIORAL THERAPY APPROACH

SECOND EDITION

Therapist Guide

Christopher A. Kearney • Anne Marie Albano

OXFORD
UNIVERSITY PRESS

2007

OXFORD
UNIVERSITY PRESS

Oxford University Press, Inc., publishes works that further
Oxford University's objective of excellence
in research, scholarship, and education.

Oxford   New York
Auckland   Cape Town   Dar es Salaam   Hong Kong   Karachi
Kuala Lumpur   Madrid   Melbourne   Mexico City   Nairobi
New Delhi   Shanghai   Taipei   Toronto

With offices in
Argentina   Austria   Brazil   Chile   Czech Republic   France   Greece
Guatemala   Hungary   Italy   Japan   Poland   Portugal   Singapore
South Korea   Switzerland   Thailand   Turkey   Ukraine   Vietnam

Copyright © 2007 by Oxford University Press, Inc.

Published by Oxford University Press, Inc.
198 Madison Avenue, New York, New York 10016

www.oup.com

Library of Congress Cataloging-in-Publication Data
Kearney, Christopher A.
When children refuse school : a cognitive-behavioral therapy approach :
therapist guide / Christopher A. Kearney and Anne Marie Albano.—
2nd ed.
p. cm.—(Treatments that work)
Includes bibliographical references.
ISBN: 978-0-19-530830-3
1. School phobia.   2. Cognitive therapy for children.
I. Albano, Anne Marie.   II. Title.   III. Series.
[DNLM: 1. Phobic Disorders—therapy.   2. Child Behavior Disorders—
therapy.   3. Cognitive Therapy.   4. Schools.   WM178 K24w 2007]
RJ506.S33W4544 2007
618.92'89142—dc22
2006032825

3 5 7 9 8 6 4 2

Printed in the United States of America
on acid-free paper

About Treatments *ThatWork*™

Stunning developments in healthcare have taken place over the last several years, but many of our widely accepted interventions and strategies in mental health and behavioral medicine have been brought into question by research evidence as not only lacking benefit, but perhaps, inducing harm. Other strategies have been proven effective using the best current standards of evidence, resulting in broad-based recommendations to make these practices more available to the public. Several recent developments are behind this revolution. First, we have arrived at a much deeper understanding of pathology, both psychological and physical, which has led to the development of new, more precisely targeted interventions. Second, our research methodologies have improved substantially, such that we have reduced threats to internal and external validity, making the outcomes more directly applicable to clinical situations. Third, governments around the world and healthcare systems and policymakers have decided that the quality of care should improve, that it should be evidence based, and that it is in the public's interest to ensure that this happens (Barlow, 2004; Institute of Medicine, 2001).

Of course, the major stumbling block for clinicians everywhere is the accessibility of newly developed evidence-based psychological interventions. Workshops and books can go only so far in acquainting responsible and conscientious practitioners with the latest behavioral healthcare practices and their applicability to individual patients. This new series, Treatments-*ThatWork*™, is devoted to communicating these exciting new interventions to clinicians on the frontlines of practice.

The manuals and workbooks in this series contain step-by-step detailed procedures for assessing and treating specific problems and diagnoses. But this series also goes beyond the books and manuals by providing ancillary materials that will approximate the supervisory process in assisting practitioners in the implementation of these procedures in their practice.

In our emerging healthcare system, the growing consensus is that evidence-based practice offers the most responsible course of action for the health professional. All behavioral healthcare clinicians deeply desire to provide the best possible care for their patients. In this series, our aim is to close the dissemination and information gap and make that possible.

This Therapist guide and the companion workbook for parents address the treatment of children and teenagers who refuse school, including not only youth who are absent from class but those who attend school under substantial duress. School refusal is a common problem facing parents and educators, with up to 28% of American school-aged youths refusing school at some time. It can significantly affect a child's well-being and a family's ability to function. Cognitive Behavioral Therapy has shown to be effective in treating a broad range of school refusal behavior. This comprehensive guide outlines four complete treatment packages tailored to each of the main reasons that children refuse school. These treatments are child-based, parent-based, or family-based depending on the child's reasons for refusing school, but the goal of each module is full-time return to school and successful integration into the classroom.

David H. Barlow, Editor-in-Chief,
Treatments *ThatWork*™
Boston, Massachusetts

Contents

Chapter 1   Introductory Information for Therapists   *1*

Chapter 2   Assessment   *19*

Chapter 3   Consultation Session and General Treatment
Session Procedures   *41*

Chapter 4   Children Refusing School to Avoid School-Related
Stimuli That Provoke Negative Affectivity   *61*

Chapter 5   Children Refusing School to Escape Aversive Social
and/or Evaluative Situations   *109*

Chapter 6   Children Refusing School for Attention   *155*

Chapter 7   Children Refusing School for Tangible Rewards
Outside of School   *201*

Chapter 8   Slip and Relapse Prevention   *247*

References   *267*

About the Authors   *271*

Chapter 1 | *Introductory Information for Therapists*

Background Information and Purpose of This Program

The treatment program presented in this guide is designed for youths with primary school refusal behavior. The treatment program is based on a functional model of school refusal behavior that classifies youths on the basis of what reinforces absenteeism. For children who refuse school to avoid school-based stimuli that provoke negative affectivity, we use child-based psychoeducation, somatic control exercises, gradual reintroduction (exposure) to the regular classroom setting, and self-reinforcement. This treatment package is designed to reduce unpleasant physiological symptoms, expose a child to various school-related items and situations, and gradually increase attendance.

For children who refuse school to escape aversive social and/or evaluative situations, we use child-based psychoeducation, somatic control exercises, cognitive restructuring, gradual reintroduction (exposure) to the regular classroom setting, and self-reinforcement. This treatment package is similar to the first functional condition but includes cognitive restructuring because many youths who escape aversive social and/or evaluative situations at school are older and more cognitively advanced. Social skills training with role-play may apply to this function as well. This treatment package is designed to reduce social and performance anxiety in key school-related situations, build or refine social/coping skills, and gradually increase attendance.

For youths who refuse school to pursue attention from significant others, parent-based treatment includes modifying parent commands, establishing regular daily routines, developing rewards for attendance and punishments for nonattendance, reducing excessive reassurance-seeking behavior, and engaging in forced school attendance under certain conditions. This treatment package relies on parent-based techniques to re-establish parental control via contingency management. Gradual return to school is emphasized as well.

For youths who refuse school to pursue tangible rewards outside of school, family-based treatment includes contingency contracts, communication skills training, escorting a child to school and from class to class, and peer refusal skills training. This treatment package relies on family-based techniques to increase incentives for school attendance, curtail social and other activities as a result of nonattendance, and improve problem-solving, negotiation, and communication skills. Supervision and gradual return to school are emphasized as well.

The first two treatment packages are primarily child-based. In contrast, the third treatment package is primarily parent-based and the fourth treatment package is primarily family-based. Although the specific treatment packages are quite different in their components, key goals of each are to reintroduce a child to the academic setting and achieve full-time school attendance with minimal distress.

Problem Focus

School refusal behavior refers to child-motivated refusal to attend school and/or difficulties remaining in classes for an entire day. Problematic absenteeism from school has been defined historically in many ways. For example, labels such as truancy (delinquent absenteeism), school phobia (fear-based absenteeism), and school refusal (anxiety-based absenteeism) are commonly used but *do not represent all youths with trouble attending school.* "School refusal behavior" is thus an overarching or umbrella construct that represents a child's inability to maintain age-appropriate functioning vis-à-vis school attendance or adaptive coping to school-related stressors. Specifically, school refusal behavior refers to youths aged 5 to 17 years who:

■ Are completely absent from school for periods of time

■ Attend but then leave school during the day or skip certain classes

- Arrive late to school (chronic tardiness)

- Attend school following intense morning misbehaviors, such as temper tantrums or refusal to move, designed to induce absenteeism

- Display unusual distress during school days that leads to pleas for future nonattendance directed to parents or others

School refusal behavior is thus a dimensional construct that includes youths who miss long periods of school as well as those who rarely miss school but who attend under substantial duress. In addition, many youths with school refusal behavior show highly fluctuating attendance patterns. A youth may, for example, skip school entirely on Monday, arrive late to school on Tuesday, attend school Wednesday morning but not Wednesday afternoon, attend school Thursday, and attend school Friday under duress because of an important examination that day.

We have found that initial school refusal behavior often remits spontaneously, so *substantial* school refusal behavior is defined as cases lasting at least 2 weeks or a shorter time with significant interference in a family's daily functioning. *Acute school refusal behavior* refers to cases lasting 2 weeks to 1 calendar year, having been a problem for a majority of that time. *Chronic school refusal behavior* refers to cases lasting more than 1 calendar year and, therefore, across at least two academic years.

Our definition of school refusal behavior excludes certain cases that may be outside the scope of this therapist guide. Primary *exclusionary* criteria include the presence of:

- Legitimate physical illness such as asthma that makes school attendance highly problematic

- School withdrawal, when a parent deliberately keeps a child home from school

- Familial or societal conditions that predominate a child's life, such as homelessness or running away to avoid maltreatment

- Psychiatric conditions or other difficulties *primary* to school refusal behavior, such as academic failure, learning disorder, depression, bipolar disorder, hyperactivity, conduct disorder, psychosis, developmental disorder, substance abuse, and lack of motivation

- Profound family dysfunction such as extreme permissiveness and little parental supervision

- School-based verbal or physical threats or poor academic climate, including bullying, student–teacher conflict, inattention to a child's curricular needs, or other legitimate concern

Up to 28% of American school-aged youths refuse school at some time, though the problem is considerably more prevalent in certain schools and geographical areas. In addition, many children show internalizing and externalizing disorders with school refusal behavior as a key element. School refusal behavior is generally seen equally in boys and girls and among families of various socioeconomic status. Most children with school refusal behavior are aged 10 to 13 years, but the problem also peaks at ages 5 to 6 and 14 to 15 years as children enter new schools. However, youths may show school refusal behavior at any age.

A hallmark of school refusal behavior is *heterogeneity:* dozens of presenting behaviors typify this population. Common internalizing problems include general and social anxiety, social withdrawal, depression, fear, fatigue, and somatic complaints (especially stomachaches, headaches, nausea, and tremors). Common externalizing problems include temper tantrums (including crying, screaming, flailing), verbal and physical aggression, reassurance-seeking, clinging, refusal to move, noncompliance, and running away from school or home. Many youths display a combination of internalizing and externalizing problems.

School refusal behavior has severe short- and long-term consequences if left untreated. Short-term consequences include significant child stress, declining academic status, social alienation, increased risk of legal trouble, family conflict, severe disruption in a family's daily functioning, potential child maltreatment and lack of supervision, and financial expense. Long-term consequences include economic deprivation from a lessened chance of attending college, occupational and marital problems, substance abuse and criminal behavior, and poor psychosocial functioning, often involving anxiety and depression. Risk for these problems increases the longer a child is out of school. School refusal behavior is thus a common but vexing problem faced by educators and health and mental health professionals.

Alternative, traditional treatments for school refusal behavior are outlined in a later section. A key drawback of these approaches, however, is that they do not apply well to *all* cases of school refusal behavior. In contrast, our treatment program *is* designed to cover all cases of school refusal behavior by arranging commonly used therapeutic techniques tailored to a client's individual characteristics.

Common therapeutic techniques in clinical child psychology and in this guide include essentials of systematic desensitization, cognitive restructuring, self-reinforcement, modeling and role-play, contingency management, contingency contracting, and communication skills training, among others. A full review of the well-demonstrated effectiveness of these techniques for youths with psychopathology is outside the scope of this guide (see Mash & Barkley, 2006). In addition, a review of the substantial general effectiveness of these techniques for youths with school refusal behavior and related conditions has been presented elsewhere (see Kearney, 2001, 2005).

The procedures in this guide have also been tested within the specific context of a functional, prescriptive model of school refusal behavior. Relevant research includes preliminary, uncontrolled work as well as a controlled study of prescriptive and nonprescriptive treatment (Chorpita, Albano, Heimberg, & Barlow, 1996; Kearney, 2002a; Kearney, Pursell, & Alvarez, 2001; Kearney & Silverman, 1990, 1999). The latter study indicated that a key measure in the functional model (School Refusal Assessment Scale-Revised) (see chapter 2) could accurately predict which prescriptive or tailored treatments would be effective for a particular case of school refusal behavior and which nonprescriptive treatments would be ineffective for a particular case of school refusal behavior.

Although the procedures in this guide have been shown to be highly useful for youths with psychopathology and school refusal behavior, the functional model remains in development. As such, we encourage clinicians to utilize our guidelines with appropriate caution. In addition, clinicians should consider recommending adjunctive treatments such as medication, family therapy, or educational interventions for learning disorders or classroom misbehavior as appropriate and necessary.

Cognitive-Behavior Therapy for Youths With School Refusal Behavior

The procedures in this guide are generally cognitive-behavioral in nature. The primary aims are to modify cognitions (where appropriate) and behaviors to enhance full-time school attendance without distress. Some procedures in this guide may be closely related to a family systems perspective as well. These include contingency contracting and communication skills training, but a behavioral, problem-solving emphasis is also laden upon these techniques. Clinicians who utilize the procedures in this guide will likely find them most familiar and useful if their training, experience, and background are derived from a cognitive-behavioral perspective.

Cognitive-Behavior Therapy Model of School Refusal Behavior

The primary cognitive-behavior therapy model presented in this guide is a functional one. Many behaviors characterize children who refuse school, which has led to poor consensus about conceptualizing, classifying, assessing, and treating this population. *We believe, therefore, that therapists should focus on the few maintaining variables in addition to the many forms of school refusal behavior.* Children generally refuse school for one or more of the following reasons, or *functions:*

■ To avoid school-related objects and situations (stimuli) that provoke negative affectivity (symptoms of dread, anxiety, depression, and somatic complaints)

■ To escape aversive social and/or evaluative situations at school

■ To receive or pursue attention from significant others outside of school

■ To obtain or pursue tangible rewards outside of school

The first two functions refer to children who refuse school for negative reinforcement, or to get away from something unpleasant at school. Common examples of school-related *objects* that children avoid are buses, fire alarms, gymnasia, playgrounds, hallways, and classroom items. Common examples of school-related *social situations* that children avoid are interactions with teachers, principals, and verbally or physically aggressive peers. Common examples of school-related *evaluative situations* that children avoid are tests, recitals, athletic performances, speaking or writing in front of others, or walking into class with others present.

The latter two functions refer to children who refuse school for positive reinforcement, or to pursue someone or something attractive outside of school. Many younger children refuse school to force parents to acquiesce to demands for physical closeness and extra attention. This function is sometimes linked to separation anxiety. In addition, older children and adolescents often refuse school for tangible rewards such as watching television at home, sleeping, playing sports, shopping, gambling, engaging in social parties with friends, and using substances. For these children, missing school is simply more fun than attending school. Therapists may be more apt to receive referrals for positively reinforced than negatively reinforced school refusal behavior. However, any type of school refusal behavior can be quite debilitating.

Some children, perhaps as many as a third, refuse school for two or more functions. For example, some children are initially upset about school activities and try to remain home to avoid them. These children may then realize the attractiveness of staying home and thus refuse school for negative and positive reinforcement. Conversely, some children miss school for long periods of time for positive reinforcement, but later must return to school and face new classes, teachers, and peers. This may provoke anxiety and lead to school refusal behavior for negative reinforcement as well.

Children who refuse school for multiple reasons generally require a more complex treatment strategy than children who refuse school for one reason. This strategy will likely involve a combination of treatment approaches and an extended timeframe. A combined-treatment strategy for these children is crucial as well because those who refuse school for multiple reasons have likely been out of school for a long period of time. This chronic situation tends to be resistant to a single treatment approach. *Because children often refuse school for more than one reason, read the parts of this guide that apply most to your client as well as other parts that may be relevant.*

The treatment program described in this guide has the benefit of covering all youths with school refusal behavior, not simply those with anxiety-based conditions. Procedures arranged in this guide also represent well-tested techniques commonly used by clinical child psychologists. These techniques are carefully arranged by function to tailor treatment to the particular characteristics of a given child and follow a specific assessment process (see chapter 2).

An important caveat to this treatment program is that the procedures may not fully apply to youths with extreme symptomatology, comorbid diagnoses, marital or familial dysfunction, or physical illness or handicap. In cases of intense anxiety, depression, attention-deficit/hyperactivity disorder, or psychosis, for example, psychiatric consultation is particularly recommended. In addition, the treatment techniques may be less suited for youths whose primary behavior problem is not school refusal behavior or whose school refusal behavior is based on legitimate threat or complaint. Many of the procedures described here will be more useful if highly problematic comorbid situations are initially addressed and if parents and school officials are properly prepared to engage in extensive treatment. Pretreatment considerations are discussed in more depth in chapter 3.

Our procedures are generally delineated for prototypical cases of school refusal behavior. As a result, you may find some changes to be necessary for your particular case. Unforeseen circumstances always arise, and we have therefore tried to incorporate a sense of flexibility into these procedures. In similar fashion, you should be flexible when utilizing these procedures. For example, some cases of school refusal behavior take less time to resolve than what is described here, but other cases take more time. You should use this guide as just that—a guide—and be innovative when addressing this fascinating and often unpredictable population.

As the therapist, you can adjust the procedures in this therapist guide to your own style, a child's cognitive-developmental status, relevant family issues that arise, and other pertinent factors. In general, however, this program is based on a cognitive-behavioral/family systems approach. If you are not familiar with this approach, then additional readings, training, and structured supervision may benefit you and your clients. This applies to all aspects of this guide, and especially to the cognitive restructuring techniques in chapter 5.

Furthermore, do not "blend" this approach with others, such as adding a psychodynamic formulation or other theoretical orientation. This will serve to confuse children and parents and strays from the empirical basis for the program and its procedures. In addition, do not use these procedures in a group format. Although flexibility when using this guide is encouraged, increasingly greater deviation from its procedures may be correlated with diminishing benefits.

Alternative Treatments

Traditional treatments used by mental health professionals and educators for school refusal behavior have been single in nature and primarily include:

■ Psychodynamic therapies to increase distance between a parent and child to reduce separation anxiety and/or improve a child's self-esteem in the classroom

■ Behavioral treatments based on systematic desensitization for children with a specific phobia of some school-related item

■ Forced school attendance

■ Family-based treatment techniques such as communication skills training and written/oral contracts among family members

■ Antidepressant and anxiolytic medication

■ Inpatient or residential programs to address youths with chronic school refusal behavior

These single treatments work well for some, but not all, children with school refusal behavior. For example, therapies designed to increase parent–child distance and improve child self-esteem may work best for young children with separation anxiety and an enmeshed family structure. However, these treatments are less effective for older children and adolescents without these problems. In addition, systematic desensitization is effective for children fearful of a specific school-related item. However, this scenario applies only to a minority of those who refuse school. Forced school attendance may work well for young children or those who have just started refusing school, but it does not work well for older children or those with chronic attendance problems. Family-based techniques such as communication skills training and contracting require much verbal input from all family members. Therefore, young children may not be able to contribute. Medication works well for some but not all children, serious side effects may occur, and parents often do not prefer this treatment approach. Finally, inpatient or residential programs are variably effective, more directed toward chronic cases, and heavily dependent on level of parent support.

Because these different treatments work well only some of the time, a clear need exists to develop a thorough and comprehensive assessment and treatment approach for youths with school refusal behavior. This approach should address *all* youths with primary school refusal behavior, be easily implemented by therapists, and have effective therapeutic components. An overview of our prescriptive approach designed to meet these criteria is presented next.

Prescriptive Assessment and Treatment Approach for School Refusal Behavior

We have developed *a prescriptive approach* for assessing and treating all youths with primary school refusal behavior. We believe that four groups of youths with school refusal behavior can be based on the reasons (or maintaining variables or functions) why children refuse school. Again, these reasons include avoidance of school-related stimuli that provoke negative affectivity, escape from aversive social and/or evaluative situations, pursuit of attention, and pursuit of tangible rewards outside of school.

Descriptive and experimental functional analytical procedures discussed in chapter 2 may be used to conceptualize a particular child and assign him to one or more functional groups. *When a child's school refusal behavior has been assigned to one of these basic groups, then a specific treatment approach may be prescribed.* These treatment approaches differ depending on the group. If a child refuses school for more than one reason, then a combination of treatments is prescribed. Overall, we believe that a prescriptive approach to treatment is the best strategy for addressing many different types of children with school refusal behavior. A brief overview of specific treatments per function was presented at the beginning of this chapter.

Specific Information for a Particular Case of School Refusal Behavior

Because school refusal behavior is often surrounded by many related problems, clinicians may be concerned about whether this therapist guide is indeed appropriate. In this section, we provide some questions you could raise during the screening process. The answers may give you a good idea as to whether our guide will be useful.

What If a Child Has Just Started Refusing to Attend School?

The answer to this question may be crucial for deciding whether to use this guide. If a child's school refusal behavior has occurred sporadically for less than 2 weeks, then the problem is likely to end soon (*self-corrective school refusal behavior*). In this case, you may ask the family to call back in 1 week if the problem persists or schedule an appointment for 1 week later. In many instances, this appointment will turn out to be unnecessary because the child returned to school on his own.

The procedures in this guide might still be appropriate for brand-new cases, however, if school refusal behavior has been occurring every day for at least 1 week *and* is severe enough to create substantial family conflict or a serious disruption in a family's daily functioning. In this case, and in cases where a child has refused school for more than 2 weeks, the procedures in this guide will be more applicable and useful.

What Is the Child's Primary Behavior Problem?

A description of a child's primary behavior problem is integral to the screening process and may help you decide if our procedures are warranted. Parents may struggle with this question, so ask whether competing behaviors are more severe than school refusal behavior. In essence, identify differential diagnoses or other problems that may explain a child's presenting symptoms:

- For children refusing school to avoid school-based stimuli that provoke negative affectivity, common differential diagnoses or problems include panic disorder and agoraphobia, generalized anxiety disorder, specific phobia, and depression and suicidal behavior.

- For children refusing school to escape aversive social and/or evaluative situations, common differential diagnoses or problems include social anxiety disorder and depression and suicidal behavior.

- For children refusing school for attention, common differential diagnoses or problems include separation anxiety disorder, oppositional defiant disorder, or noncompliance in response to most parent commands.

- For children refusing school for tangible rewards, common differential diagnoses or problems include conduct-disordered behavior (e.g., stealing, fire-setting, aggression), substance abuse, and lack of motivation in many situations.

Note that any problem listed above could apply to any function of school refusal behavior. The disorders most commonly associated with each function are listed here. In addition, other problems could apply to any function, including attention-deficit/hyperactivity disorder, learning disorder or academic failure, and pervasive developmental disorders.

If these behaviors are primary to school refusal behavior, then our therapist guide may be only partially useful. We say "partially useful" because addressing school refusal behavior is sometimes the first step toward resolving other primary behaviors. This is so because missing school is often an urgent problem and one that parents want to initially address. For example, many parents of defiant children wish to start treatment by focusing on compliance to commands to attend school. In cases where the first step to an overall treatment plan is returning a child to school, the procedures described in this guide may be helpful.

Many parents are "in the dark" or confused and upset by their child's problems, and are thus unable to provide detailed information about primary behaviors. In addition, a common parental mistake is to emphasize external (e.g., breaking curfew, not doing homework) and not internal (e.g., anxiety, depression) behavior problems. Scheduling a formal assessment session and asking more focused questions at that time may thus be appropriate. In the meantime, contact others (following consent) who can provide more insightful information. Examples include educational, medical, and other mental health professionals familiar with your case.

What Other Factors Might Explain School Refusal Behavior?

In many cases of school refusal behavior, other factors or variables instigate or explain the problem. The exclusionary criteria mentioned earlier may provide some guidelines for screening questions. For example, is a child's school refusal behavior a direct result of medical problems such as asthma, pain, insomnia, diabetes, infection, or sensorimotor handicap? If this is possible, then refer the family for a medical examination. In addition, be sure to consult with a medical doctor as necessary and appropriate throughout treatment.

Another competing explanation for school refusal behavior is *school withdrawal*, where a parent deliberately keeps a child home from school. Because parents often wish to maintain the status quo in this situation, cases of school withdrawal are not often seen by therapists. However, one should be aware of likely scenarios just in case. Common reasons for school withdrawal include parental anxiety and need for a "safety" person, utilizing the child as a supplemental economic source (e.g., for work or babysitting), disguising child maltreatment, parental fears of a child being kidnapped at school by an estranged spouse, peer-related safety issues, and complaints about the quality or appropriateness of a teacher or school. In cases of school withdrawal, intervention with the parents and/or others is probably necessary and may not involve the procedures described here.

The presence of primary familial or systemic problems also diminishes the utility of this guide. For example, if a child is constantly running away from home and missing school to avoid sexual maltreatment, then resuming school attendance is not the immediate concern. In addition, many children miss school because their families have been ejected from their home. In these cases, a broader approach to treatment is clearly needed.

What Is the Child's Age?

Knowing the child's age is important for three reasons. First, some parents will refer to treatment children less than 5 years old for refusing to attend preschool or other activities. This problem is probably related to school refusal behavior in older children, but our guide is not meant to address preschoolers. If you use this guide for very young children, you will have to significantly adapt the discussed procedures and use them with substantial caution.

Second, a child's age may be an important, but not always accurate, predictor of why he is refusing to attend school. In general, children aged 5 to 11 years tend to refuse school to avoid general negative affectivity and/or to receive attention. Conversely, adolescents aged 12 to 17 years tend to refuse school to escape aversive social or evaluative situations and/or to obtain tangible rewards outside of school. Although exceptions are common, and many children refuse school for multiple reasons, knowing a child's age may help you devise an initial hypothesis about the function of school refusal behavior. Then, more specific questions can be asked in formal assessment (see chapter 2).

Third, knowing a child's age may give you an early idea about treatment direction. For example, therapies that rely more on verbal content, such as cognitive therapy, may be more appropriate for adolescents than younger children. Conversely, forced school attendance is much easier to implement for a 6-year-old than a 16-year-old. Again, exceptions are common, but knowing a child's age and cognitive level of functioning will help you formulate an efficient and effective treatment plan.

Is the Child's School Refusal Behavior Extremely Severe?

Our guide may not apply to extremely severe cases of school refusal behavior. These cases most likely involve (1) extreme levels of negative affectivity such that any approach to school is almost impossible, (2) severe delinquent behavior, and/or (3) school absence longer than one calendar year. In these cases, alternative treatments may be necessary. In cases of extreme anxiety, for example, pharmacotherapy may be used initially to control physical anxiety symptoms and ease exposure to school. In cases of severe delinquent behavior, residential or inpatient treatment may help control explosive behaviors or establish some pattern of school attendance before outpatient therapy with family members. Alternative school programs may also be explored in cases of extended absence. These include part-time, night, credit by examination, independent study, homebound, and vocational programs.

What If Your Model Does Not Fit My Case?

If our definition or prescriptive approach to school refusal behavior does not fit your case, then other procedures would, of course, be more appropriate. However, many procedures in this guide can be directed toward non-school refusal behaviors. For example, somatic control exercises, exposure-based practices, and cognitive restructuring procedures apply to those with general or social anxiety. In addition, contingency management and contracting procedures apply to family conflict or children with noncompliance. However, the procedures described in this guide are designed to specifically address children with primary school refusal behavior.

Youths on Medication

The procedures in this guide may still be used if youths are currently medicated for conditions directly related to school refusal behavior, such as anxiety or depression, or conditions perhaps unrelated to school refusal behavior, such as attention-deficit/hyperactivity or bipolar disorder. Ongoing consultation with the prescribing physician or psychiatrist is strongly recommended during assessment and treatment. In many cases, treatment must be expanded to accommodate comorbid psychiatric conditions. However, the procedures in this guide can be woven into an expanded treatment protocol.

Outline of This Therapist Guide

This therapist guide is designed to provide you with an *outline* of our prescriptive approach for assessing and treating school refusal behavior in children. Not all procedures are discussed with as much depth as possible, of course, but the most crucial information is given to guide your clinical process. Chapter 2 describes our recommended assessment and treatment assignment procedures. Chapter 3 describes aspects of a consultation session, including suggestions for summarizing assessment results and making treatment recommendations to a family. Chapter 3 also contains important points to consider for each treatment phase.

Chapters 4 through 7 describe prescriptive treatment packages for each function of school refusal behavior. Sample dialogue, troubleshooting recommendations, and discussions of special circumstances are also included. Chapter 4 discusses prescriptive treatment procedures for children refusing school to avoid school-based stimuli that provoke negative affectivity. Chapter 5 discusses prescriptive treatment procedures for children refusing school to escape aversive social and/or evaluative situations. Chapter 6 discusses prescriptive treatment procedures for children refusing school for attention. Chapter 7 discusses prescriptive treatment procedures for children refusing school for tangible rewards. Finally, chapter 8 discusses issues related to slips and relapse prevention as well as recommendations for youths with chronic school refusal behavior.

Chapters 4 through 8 also contain a detailed discussion of special topics pertinent to treating youths with school refusal behavior. Although these topics have been linked to those functions in which they are likely most applicable, we recommend that you read each one. Chapter 4 includes special topics on medicating children with severe distress, home schooling, when to keep a child home from school, a child who will not ride the school bus, children who are distressed on Sunday evenings, and methods for gradually increasing school attendance time. Chapter 5 includes special topics on panic attacks, extracurricular activities, perfectionism, being teased, and attending gym class.

Chapter 6 includes special topics on parents skipping work to be home with a child, a child home from school during the day, and coming to school late in the morning. Chapter 7 includes special topics on 504 and individualized education plans, alternative school placements, calling the police, and problems getting out of bed. Chapter 8 also includes a discussion of special circumstances such as parents leaving for work before a child goes to school, multiple children in a family refusing school, children with developmental disorders, and children referred to the legal system for nonattendance. Other general suggestions in chapter 8, such as those for children starting a new school, are included as well.

Use of the Parent Workbook and Self-Directed Book

The clinical procedures in this guide are also described in a parent workbook. Parents who use the workbook are strongly urged to do so in conjunction with a qualified therapist. We recommend you give your clients a copy of the parent workbook. In doing so, they can be more prepared for the assessment and treatment process and ideally more motivated to complete therapeutic homework assignments. We also suggest, in case your clients have specific questions, that you become familiar with our descriptions of assessment and treatment procedures in the parent workbook.

A self-directed book designed for parents of youths with subclinical forms of school refusal behavior is also available (Kearney, 2007). *Getting Your Child to Say "Yes" to School: A Guide for Parents of Youth with School Refusal Behavior* outlines many of the procedures discussed in this guide and the parent workbook and may be especially useful as a reference for clients who complete treatment. The book is arranged by function and may be referred to by children and parents following treatment to help prevent relapse. A book designed for educators who address youths with school refusal behavior is also forthcoming. This book may be useful for clinicians who consult regularly with school personnel regarding cases of school refusal behavior.

Chapter 2 *Assessment*

This chapter provides an overview of our recommended assessment process for youths with school refusal behavior. The overall purpose of formally assessing a child with school refusal behavior is to obtain answers to three critical questions:

What Is the Behavior Problem?

Pinpoint exactly what school refusal behaviors are present (see chapter 1 for common examples) as well as severity of the behaviors. With respect to the latter, discover how often a child is actually attending school and, if not, what she is doing during the daytime. In anxiety-based cases, determine which components—behavioral avoidance, cognitive distortions, and/or physiological reactions—are most problematic. In addition, a history of school refusal behavior over the past days, weeks, and months would be helpful. Obtaining such a history should come from different sources such as the child, parents, and educational, medical, and mental health professionals as appropriate so different perspectives on the problem can be understood and synthesized.

During this process, other important variables can be identified as well. For example, the context in which school refusal behavior is occurring should become clearer. Several immediate factors might affect school refusal behavior and the treatment process. These include crises, personality and cultural variables, medical or developmental problems, comorbid problems, school variables (e.g., level of support from school officials, school violence and demographics), parental attitude and disciplinary style, family member perspectives and motivation, and family stressors and resources, among others. Other, more peripheral influences may also become evident, such as family conflict and other dynamics, divorce, inadequate academic performance, poor peer relations, parental psychopathology, religion, nutrition, finances, and employment and education status, among others. Finally, initial discussions about the behavior problem will help you establish rapport with family members, a process crucial for maintaining compliance to later treatment.

What Is Maintaining School Refusal Behavior?

You should also pinpoint variables that maintain school refusal behavior; in essence, what is the major function of school refusal behavior for the child? During initial formal assessment, probe whether school refusal behavior is largely maintained by child factors or factors related to parents or other family members. For example, is the family fairly cohesive and healthy but has a child with a specific anxiety problem? Or, is one parent or family member inadvertently or deliberately rewarding a child's school refusal behavior via attention, sympathy, or bribes? A detailed procedure for identifying the maintaining variables of school refusal behavior follows later in this chapter.

What Is the Best Treatment for School Refusal Behavior?

This is the most important question that must be answered by the end of formal assessment. Assessing the source of reward for school refusal behavior will help you form a hypothesis about its function that can be confirmed using other methods. Remember that the function of school refusal behavior is a major part of our prescriptive model and will serve as the basis for assigning treatment. In this chapter, a method is presented for linking specific functions with different prescriptive treatments.

The Importance of Assessing School Refusal Behavior via Functional Analysis

Different methods are available for assessing school refusal behavior and its maintaining variables. For example, one could use an open-ended clinical approach and interview, but the presence of many different presenting behaviors can be overwhelming. In addition, one could use a strict diagnostic approach, but many children with school refusal behavior present with several comorbid (or no) diagnoses. What can be done, therefore, to efficiently and effectively assess this population and answer the questions raised above?

A good strategy for formally assessing children with school refusal behavior is functional analysis. Specifically, descriptive and experimental functional analyses can be done efficiently and effectively to identify what maintains school refusal behavior and how it should be treated. We offer here a clear, simple, and efficient step-by-step process for conducting a functional analysis for children with school refusal behavior. This will give you a straightforward approach for getting to the heart of a particular case of school refusal behavior.

The Assessment Session and Recommended Forms of Assessment

This section is divided into two parts. The first part describes procedures to help answer the first question raised above: What is the behavior problem? This part discusses interviews, child self-report measures, and parent and teacher checklists pertinent to this population. The second part describes procedures, based on functional analysis, to help answer the second and third questions raised above: What is maintaining, and what is the best treatment for, school refusal behavior? This part discusses (1) descriptive procedures such as questionnaires to initially identify maintaining variables of school refusal behavior, and (2) experimental procedures in the form of observations to confirm the presence of these maintaining variables. A discussion then follows about choosing prescriptive treatment.

Procedures to Assess the Behavior Problem

Interview

When assessing a behavior problem, most therapists use some type of interview. Reliable and valid semistructured interviews based on systematic clinical observation are available, including the *Anxiety Disorders*

Interview Schedule for DSM-IV: Child and Parent Versions (ADIS for DSM-IV: C/P) (Silverman & Albano, 1996). The ADIS for DSM-IV: C/P has child and parent versions that assess for various diagnostic problems. As such, information can be obtained about many different problems, and the major difficulties confronting a child with school refusal behavior can be identified. In fact, the ADIS for DSM-IV: C/P has a special section on school refusal-related problems that can help you address the questions raised above. In addition, hierarchies from the interview may be useful when implementing some of the treatment procedures in this guide.

Many therapists prefer, of course, to rely on a less structured approach in accordance with their own clinical style. If you do, some suggestions are provided here for what might be asked during your interview (in addition, of course, to many other questions you will want to ask regarding your particular case). Although the following questions are aimed toward parents, answers should come from as many individuals (including the child) as you deem relevant to your case:

How often does your child refuse school *specifically* because she is generally distressed or upset about school? Follow-up questions:

- Is your child upset about school more than most children her age?

- What school-related objects or situations does she avoid (especially the bus, classroom items, transitions between classes/activities, playground, cafeteria, gymnasium, hallway, fire alarm)?

- Has your child told you of recent negative life events, or have you noticed she has suddenly changed her behavior in any way?

- Has your child expressed to you or have you noticed any specific emotions or physical symptoms about going to school? What are they?

- Do these problems occur every day or primarily on school days?

How often does your child refuse school *specifically* because she wants to escape social and/or evaluative situations at school? Follow-up questions:

- Does your child try to escape these situations more than most children her age?

- What specific social or evaluative situations does she stay away from (especially writing or speaking in front of others, meeting new people, interacting with peers, performing during recitals, tests, athletic contests, or being in or approaching groups of people)?

- Has your child told you of recent negative social or evaluative events, or have you noticed she has suddenly changed her social behavior in any way?

- Has your child expressed to you or have you noticed any specific emotions or physical symptoms about interacting in social or evaluative situations? What are they?

- Do these problems occur primarily in all social or evaluative situations or primarily in those situations related to school?

How often does your child refuse school *specifically* because she wants to get attention from you or a significant other? Follow-up questions:

- Does your child show this attention-seeking behavior more than most children her age?

- What specific behaviors does your child do to get attention from you (especially clinging, reassurance-seeking, refusal to move, tantrums, telephone calls, protests, verbal demands for attention, guilt-inducing behavior, or running away from school to get to you)?

- Has your child told you of recent negative life events, or have you noticed she has suddenly changed her behavior toward you in any way?

- Has your child expressed to you or have you noticed any specific emotions or physical symptoms about interacting with you or being away from you? What are they?

- Do these problems occur in most daily situations or primarily in school-related situations?

How often does your child refuse school *specifically* because she wants to pursue tangible rewards from some source outside of school? Follow-up questions:

- Does your child pursue tangible rewards outside of school more than most children her age?

- What specific things does she leave school to pursue (especially spending time with friends, substance use, watching television or playing games at home, riding a bicycle, or attending shopping centers or casinos)?

- Has your child told you of recent negative life or school events, or have you noticed she has suddenly changed her behavior in any way?

- Has your child expressed to you or have you noticed any specific emotions she has about being in or leaving school? What are they?

- Does your child's pursuit of tangible rewards occur in many daily situations or primarily when school is in session?

Does your child refuse school for a combination of reasons that we just discussed? If so, which reasons are most prominent?

As a general rule in cases of school refusal behavior, interview the child before the parents. In many of these cases, the child has already been labeled a "disruptive influence" or been blamed by parents and school officials for the problems at hand. Sometimes this is accurate and sometimes not. Interviewing the child first has several advantages. First, you will convey that the child's input is taken as seriously and valuably as her parent's input. This helps build your rapport and credibility with the child.

Second, interviewing the child first allows you to emphasize that you will not "gang up" with the parents against the child. Disabusing the notion that you are another authority figure who will try to make the child attend school must often be a top priority during assessment and early treatment. However, you will have to make clear at some point that school attendance is an essential treatment goal. In doing so, explain that you will help facilitate everyone's, including the child's, *reasonable* points of view. Third, this interviewing order allows you to immediately discuss confidentiality with the child and types of information you must report to others. Conveying these messages early in treatment is important for all children and perhaps especially for children refusing school to pursue tangible rewards.

Self-Report Measures

Several child self-report measures are available and pertinent to children with school refusal behavior. Many of these measures are specific to internalizing problems, however, and may not completely cover all relevant behaviors such as acting-out problems. For these latter problems, reliance on parent and teacher reports is recommended. Useful child self-report measures for assessing school refusal behavior include the following:

■ Negative Affect Self-Statement Questionnaire (NASSQ) (Ronan, Kendall, & Rowe, 1994). The NASSQ is a measure of self-statements reflective of general anxiety and depression. Separate versions have been developed for children (7 to 10 years; 14 items) and adolescents (11 to 15 years; 39 items). This measure may be most useful for assessing those who refuse school to avoid stimuli that provoke negative affectivity.

■ Children's Depression Inventory (CDI) (Kovacs, 1992). The CDI is a 27-item measure of recent depressive symptoms most pertinent for assessing children who refuse school for negative reinforcement or for knowing if depression is primary to school refusal behavior.

■ Revised Children's Manifest Anxiety Scale and State-Trait Anxiety Inventory for Children (RCMAS) (Reynolds & Paget, 1983) (STAIC) (Spielberger, 1973). These measures target general, situational, or physiological anxiety as well as worry and concentration difficulties. The measures are most pertinent for children who refuse school for negative reinforcement.

■ Fear Survey Schedule for Children-Revised (FSSCR) (Ollendick, 1983). The FSSCR is an 80-item measure of general fearfulness. Most children with school refusal behavior do not show specific fears, but this measure may be pertinent for those who do. Special attention should be paid to school-oriented items.

■ Daily Life Stressors Scale (DLSS) (Kearney, Drabman, & Beasley, 1993). The DLSS is a 30-item measure of distress a child experiences from common, everyday events. Special attention should be paid to morning and school-related events, especially for children refusing school for negative reinforcement and for attention.

- Social Anxiety Scale for Children-Revised (SASC-R) (La Greca & Stone, 1993). The SASC-R is a 22-item measure of negative social evaluation pertinent to children who escape aversive social/evaluative situations.

- The Multidimensional Anxiety Scale for Children (MASC) (Stallings & March, 1995). The MASC is a 45-item measure of physical anxiety, harm avoidance, and social and separation anxiety. The MASC is particularly useful for assessing children refusing school for negative reinforcement.

- Youth Self-Report (YSR) (Achenbach & Rescorla, 2001). The YSR is a 118-item measure that solicits child ratings of internalizing and externalizing behavior problems. The YSR is designed for 11–18-year-olds and is useful for all adolescents refusing school.

Parent and Teacher Measures

Parent and teacher measures are also available for obtaining information about various childhood behaviors and family factors. Each is pertinent to youths who refuse school, and primary ones include the following:

- Child Behavior Checklist (CBCL) (Achenbach & Rescorla, 2001) and Conners Parent Rating Scale (CPRS) (Conners, 1997). These measures solicit parent ratings of various internalizing and externalizing behavior problems related to nonattendance. These behaviors include anxiety, depression, somatic complaints, overactivity, aggression, noncompliance, demands for attention, and social problems, among others.

- Family Environment Scale (FES) (Moos & Moos, 1986). The FES is a 90-item measure of family dynamics such as cohesion, conflict, expressiveness, and independence. Several factors are related to functions of school refusal behavior (see Kearney & Silverman, 1995). In general, families of children who refuse school, compared to normative families, show less independence and greater conflict, detachment, and isolation.

- Teacher Report Form (TRF) (Achenbach & Rescorla, 2001) and Conners Teacher Rating Scale (CTRS) (Conners, 1997). These measures are similar in structure and scope to the CBCL and CPRS, respectively, but solicit ratings from teachers or school officials most familiar with a particular child.

Behavioral Observation

If possible, conduct a direct behavioral observation of the child's and family's morning activities. This observation might give you some additional information and questions to help define school refusal behavior and confirm the presence of certain maintaining variables. A sample protocol for conducting such an observation is presented here.

Procedures to Assess the Maintaining Variables of School Refusal Behavior

Once you have a good idea about the form of school refusal behavior, investigate the maintaining variables of the problem. As mentioned earlier, this is best accomplished via functional analysis. Such analysis can occur in two steps: descriptive and experimental. For this population, descriptive functional analysis involves soliciting child and parent ratings of why a child is refusing school. Experimental functional analysis involves direct observation of why a child is refusing school. These analyses can be synthesized to form a decision about which treatment should be assigned.

Descriptive Functional Analysis

A descriptive functional analysis of school refusal behavior may be best accomplished using the School Refusal Assessment Scale-Revised (SRAS-R) (Kearney, 2002b, 2006). The SRAS-R is a 24-item measure of the relative influence of the four functional conditions for school refusal be-

Behavioral Observation for School Refusal Behavior

Child's Name: _____ Date: _____

Needed: stopwatch, daily logbook forms

Instructions for the recorder:

Prior to the home visit, discuss the 0–10 rating scale with the child and parents. Describe in detail the constructs of negative affectivity (i.e., general negative mood including anxiety and depression) and noncompliance (i.e., refusal to comply with parental commands/requests). Distribute to each party a copy of the daily logbook form for review.

Schedule a time to meet with the family in their home setting on a school day. Determine the child's rising time (e.g., 6:30 A.M.) and schedule to arrive 15 minutes earlier. Using a stopwatch, record the amount of time the child resists activities that would serve to prepare him or her for school attendance. Specifically, record time in minutes taken for the following:

1. Verbal/physical resistance to rise from bed at the prespecified time.

Verbal/physical resistance in this situation is defined as any verbalization, vocalization, or physical behavior that serves to contradict school attendance. In this situation, such behaviors include (but are not limited to) verbal and physical noncompliance, clinging to bed, locking his or herself in a bedroom, or refusal to move.

2. Verbal/physical resistance to dressing, washing, and eating.

Verbal/physical resistance in this situation is defined as any verbalization, vocalization, or physical behavior that serves to contradict school attendance. In this situation, such behaviors include (but are not limited to) verbal and physical noncompliance, clinging, screaming, crying, throwing objects, aggressive behavior, locking oneself in a room, running away, or refusal to move.

3. Verbal/physical resistance to riding in a car or bus to school.

Verbal/physical resistance in this situation is defined as any verbalization, vocalization, or physical behavior that serves to contradict school attendance. In this situation, such behaviors include (but are not limited to) verbal and physical noncompliance, locking oneself in the car, screaming, crying, aggressive behavior, running away, or refusal to move.

4. Verbal/physical resistance to entering the school building.

Verbal physical resistance in this situation is defined as any verbalization, vocalization, or physical behavior that serves to contradict school attendance. In this situation, such behaviors include (but are not limited to) verbal and physical noncompliance, clinging, screaming, crying, aggressive behavior, running away, or refusal to move.

5. Record the child's rating of negative affectivity and the parent's rating of negative affectivity and noncompliance on the 0–10 scale (0 = *none*, 2 = *mild*, 4 = *moderate*, 6 = *marked*, 8 = *severe*, and 10 = *extreme*)

    a. In the middle of morning preparation activities, and
    b. Upon entering the school building (if applicable).

Contact the school attendance officer at the child's school to record any time missed during that school day. Complete all remaining sections of the recording sheet.

Recording Sheet for Behavioral Observation

Participants: _____

Date/Time: _____

1. Record total verbal/physical resistance time for rising from bed.

   Total Minutes: _____

2. Record total verbal/physical resistance time for dressing, washing, and eating.

   Total Minutes: _____

3. Record child rating of negative affectivity at midpoint of morning preparation activities.

   Negative Affectivity Rating: _____

4. Record parent rating of child's (a) negative affectivity and (b) noncompliance at midpoint of morning preparation activities.

   Negative Affectivity Rating: _____

   Noncompliance Rating: _____

5. Record total verbal/physical resistance time for riding in a car or bus to school.

   Total Minutes: _____

6. Record total verbal/physical resistance time for entering the school building.

   Total Minutes: _____

7. Record child rating of negative affectivity upon entering school building (if applicable).

   Negative Affectivity Rating: _____

8. Record parent rating of child's (a) negative affectivity and (b) noncompliance upon entering school building (if applicable).

   Negative Affectivity Rating: _____

   Noncompliance Rating: _____

9. Record total amount of time missed during the school day.

   Total Minutes: _____

10. Record total amount of resistance time plus time missed during the school day.

    Total Minutes: _____

11. Record total time between rising time and end of school day.

    Total Minutes: _____

12. Calculate percentage of resistance/missed time to total time (i.e., between rising time and end of school day).

    Percentage: _____

havior. Items are scored on a 0-to-6 scale from "never" to "always." Child (SRAS-C) and parent (SRAS-P) versions have been developed.

Six items are devoted to each function. Regarding the first function (negative affectivity), children and parents are generally asked how often a child refuses school because of bad feelings related to something at school. Regarding the second function (social/evaluative situations), children and parents are generally asked how often a child refuses school because of difficulties interacting with or performing before others at school. Regarding the third function (attention), children and parents are generally asked how often a child refuses school to spend time with parents. Regarding the fourth function (tangible rewards), children and parents are generally asked how often a child misses school to have more fun outside of school. Versions of the SRAS-R can be found in the appendix.

To conduct a descriptive functional analysis, ask the child and parent(s) to separately complete the SRAS-C and SRAS-P, respectively. This takes only a few minutes. Young children may need you to read the items for them. Ideally, SRAS-R ratings are obtained from the child, mother, and father if all are available.

Following completion of each questionnaire, derive item means for each function. On the SRAS-R-C and each SRAS-R-P, therefore, scores are added for:

- Items 1, 5, 9, 13, 17, and 21 (first function)
- Items 2, 6, 10, 14, 18, and 22 (second function)
- Items 3, 7, 11, 15, 19, and 23 (third function)
- Items 4, 8, 12, 16, 20, and 24 (fourth function)

These four total scores are then each divided by 6 (or number of items answered in each set). For example, if a child's total rating score across the:

- First item set was 18, then the item mean would be 3.00
- Second item set was 12, then the item mean would be 2.00
- Third item set was 36, then the item mean would be 6.00
- Fourth item set was 6, then the item mean would be 1.00

Do this separately for ratings from the child, mother, and father.

After this is done, compute the mean item scores per functional condition across all SRAS-R versions given. Assume, for example, that the:

- Child's mean item scores from the SRAS-C were: 3.00, 3.50, 6.00, and 0.50.

- Mother's mean item scores from the SRAS-P were: 4.00, 4.50, 5.50, and 1.00.

- Father's mean item scores from the SRAS-P were: 3.50, 4.50, 5.00, and 1.50.

In this case, therefore, the:

- Overall mean for the first function would be: 3.50 (3.00 + 4.00 + 3.50/3).

- Overall mean for the second function would be: 4.17 (3.50 + 4.50 + 4.50/3).

- Overall mean for the third function would be: 5.50 (6.00 + 5.50 + 5.00/3).

- Overall mean for the fourth function would be: 1.00 (0.50 + 1.00 + 1.50/3).

The highest-scoring function is considered to be the primary reason why a particular child is refusing school. Scores within 0.25 points of one another are considered equivalent (in one treatment study, scores within 0.50 points of one another were also considered equivalent). In this case, therefore, the highest-scoring function is the third one, or attention-seeking (5.50). However, these numbers also provide a *profile of related influences.* In this case, for example, the child may be somewhat refusing school for the first and second functions (i.e., avoidance of stimuli provoking negative affectivity and escape from aversive social and/or evaluative situations; 3.50 and 4.17). However, the relative influence of the fourth functional condition, tangible rewards, is low (1.00) and may not be a substantial factor. *Remember that these are hypotheses based on child and parent ratings.*

This process is the essence of descriptive functional analysis. Care should be taken, of course, to note inconsistencies between child/parent SRAS-R ratings and interview information. If discrepancies exist, discuss them with relevant family members. In some cases, a re-administration of the SRAS-R is warranted. If time is short or an experimental analysis cannot be conducted, then prescriptive treatment may be assigned on the basis of this descriptive procedure. This should be done with caution, however. Ideally, one should confirm the descriptive analysis by engaging in the procedures described next.

Experimental Functional Analysis

The key feature of experimental functional analysis is to observe child and family behavior under different circumstances. For example, you may suspect a child is refusing school to pursue parental attention. In this case, compare how the child behaves on the way to school when accompanied by his mother versus you or someone else. If a significant difference in the child's behavior exists (e.g., the child attends with no problem with his mother but displays tantrums with others), your hypothesis is supported about what maintains school refusal behavior (i.e., attention). Following are some sample scenarios you may use in your assessment.

If you suspect a child is refusing school to avoid school-related stimuli that provoke negative affectivity (i.e., dread, fear, anxiety, depression, somatic complaints), then compare the child's behavior when asked to attend school under regular circumstances with the child's behavior:

- When asked to attend school without certain circumstances present (e.g., no full-day attendance, physical education class, lunch with peers, playground)

- When asked to accompany you to an equally large building that resembles a school (e.g., an office building with similar busy activity)

If you suspect a child is refusing school to escape aversive social and/or evaluative situations, then compare the child's behavior when asked to attend school under regular circumstances with the child's behavior:

- When asked to attend school without certain circumstances present (e.g., no recitals, oral presentations, athletic performances, intense social interactions)

- When asked to attend school with no one or only a few people present

If you suspect a child is refusing school for attention, then compare the child's behavior when asked to attend school under regular circumstances with the child's behavior when:

- Her parents accompany the child to school and the classroom

- The child is allowed to contact her parents at any time during the school day and be picked up from school by the parents at any time

If you suspect a child is refusing school to pursue tangible rewards, then compare the child's behavior when asked to attend school under regular circumstances with the child's behavior when:

- Increased rewards are made available for attending school

- Outside activities are severely curtailed or punished as a result of missing school

Significant changes in a child's behavior between the status quo and the changed scenario indicates evidence for a certain function of school refusal behavior. Specific behaviors you should closely monitor include:

- Behavioral avoidance in the form of clinging, refusal to move, running away, and/or noncompliance to requests

- Physiological reactivity such as stomachaches, headaches, abdominal pain, tremors, and nausea/vomiting

- Cognitive distortions or verbalizations about discomfort related to school

- Sudden changes in internal or external behavior

- Pleas to end the observation and return home

- Increased family conflict, especially following curtailment of the child's social activities

- Significant changes in parental behavior

- Teacher reports of differences in the child's behavior at school

Should a formal behavioral observation not prove feasible, watch for key behaviors in the office setting that may confirm why a child refuses school. For example, a child who is tearful, passive, and withdrawn during assessment may refuse school due to dread of the academic setting. A child who seems anxious about interacting with those in the clinic may refuse school to escape aversive social and/or evaluative situations. A child who has difficulty separating from a parent to avoid speaking alone with the therapist may refuse school for parental attention. Finally, an older child who argues forcefully with her parents to resist changes in her social lifestyle may refuse school for tangible rewards outside of school. These initial hypotheses may need to be tested using additional formal assessment, however.

Assigning Prescriptive Treatment

At the completion of the descriptive and experimental functional analysis, prescriptive treatment is assigned. Prescriptive treatment is the assignment of individualized therapy based on a subtype of a disorder or problem. *With respect to school refusal behavior, prescriptive treatment is assigned on the basis of the primary function of absenteeism.*

Monitoring School Refusal Behavior on a Daily Basis

Following formal assessment, continue to monitor a child's daily school refusal behaviors and attendance. This will help you gauge familial compliance to homework assignments, increase family members' awareness of what is happening, and note whether positive or negative changes in behavior are occurring across time.

Specifically, ask your clients to provide ratings in daily logbooks, which are presented here. You may photocopy and distribute the logbooks or download multiple copies from the Treatments *ThatWork*™ Web site at www.oup.com/us/ttw. Logbooks for photocopying can also be found in the corresponding parent workbook. *Children and parents are asked to complete their logbooks separately.* This is done to examine differences in child and parent ratings and further convey to the child that her input will be considered as valuable as parental input. Ask parents not to influence their child's ratings even if the child seems not to take the task seriously or gives ratings quite different from the parents. Have parents remind their child to complete the forms each day. Tell the child to contact you as soon as possible if she has a question about what rating to give.

Ratings are made on a 0-to-10 scale ranging from 0 (*none*) to 10 (*extreme amount*). Ratings are made with respect to a child's anxiety (nervousness, tension), depression (sadness, unhappiness), and overall distress (general feelings of dread or being upset). In addition, parents rate their child's noncompliance (disobeying parent commands) and disruption to family daily functioning. Parents are also asked to list other child behavior problems and time missed from school. Additional events that children or parents deem important may be written on the front or back of the logbook.

Briefly instruct clients about how to complete the logbooks. You may wish to show a sample of a completed logbook to demonstrate what to do. In addition, ask children and parents to complete the logbooks in the evening after most of the day has passed. Before the clients leave, ask if they have questions, and address them at this point. Ask family members to contact you should questions arise about the procedure and to bring completed logbooks with them to the next session. The consultation session should take place within the next 5 to 7 days, or sooner in more dire situations.

Contacting School Officials

Following parental consent, contact various school officials for additional information. School officials who may be most helpful include teachers (including specialized ones such as physical education teachers), school psychologists, guidance counselors, principals, deans, school attendance officers, nurses, librarians, or other staff members. Maintain contact regularly during treatment. Important supplementary information might involve:

■ Course schedules, grades, written work, and required make-up work

Child's Daily Logbook

Your Name: _____

Please rate the following every day on a 0–10 scale where 0 = none, 2 = mild, 4 = moderate, 6 = marked, 8 = severe, and 10 = extreme (for younger children: 0–10 scale where 0 = none, 2–3 is a little, 5 is some, 7–8 is much, and 10 is very much).

Date	Anxiety	Depression	Distress
_____	_____	_____	_____
_____	_____	_____	_____
_____	_____	_____	_____
_____	_____	_____	_____
_____	_____	_____	_____
_____	_____	_____	_____
_____	_____	_____	_____
_____	_____	_____	_____

Please list any problems you have had at home or school since the last session:

_____

_____

_____

_____

_____

_____

_____

_____

_____

_____

Parent's Daily Logbook

Your child's name: _____

Please rate your child's behaviors every day on a 0–10 scale where 0 = none, 2 = mild, 4 = moderate, 6 = marked, 8 = severe, and 10 = extreme.

Date	Anxiety	Depression	Distress	Noncompliance	Disruption
____	_____	_____	_____	_____	_____
____	_____	_____	_____	_____	_____
____	_____	_____	_____	_____	_____
____	_____	_____	_____	_____	_____
____	_____	_____	_____	_____	_____
____	_____	_____	_____	_____	_____
____	_____	_____	_____	_____	_____
____	_____	_____	_____	_____	_____

Please list any specific problems your child has had at home or school since the last session:

_____

_____

_____

_____

Please list the amount of school time your child has missed since the last session:

_____

_____

_____

_____

- Goals and attitudes of school officials and peers regarding the child

- Procedures and timelines for reintegrating the child into school

- Potential obstacles to reintegrating the child into school

- Confirmation of past school refusal behavior

- General social or other behaviors of the child in school

- Outline of the school, such as locations of lockers, cafeteria, library, and other places

- Feedback as to the effectiveness of the treatment procedures

- Disciplinary procedures and procedures for contacting parents

- Applicable 504 or individualized education plans

- Rules about absenteeism, conduct, or leaving school areas

- Alternative school programs

- Advice previously or currently given to parents about handling the school refusal situation (e.g., home schooling, medication, forced school attendance)

Many parents and children experience considerable friction with school officials and may not want you to cooperate with them. However, cooperation from school officials is often crucial for resolving a child's school refusal behavior. For example, helpful school officials are essential for reintegrating a child to school and keeping her there. In cases of substantial parent–school official conflict, persuade the family to allow you to act as a mediator between them and school officials. *In any case, start developing a close working relationship with relevant school officials during the assessment phase.*

Contacting Medical Professionals

Following parental consent, contact medical professionals as appropriate for additional information. Ongoing consultations with a child's pediatrician are often warranted if a child has somatic complaints or other health concerns that affect school attendance. Such consultations may also help you decide if a child's physical symptoms are real and anxiety-based or exaggerated and part of the child's attention-seeking behaviors. Consultations with specialists such as gastroenterologists are sometimes necessary as well if a more severe or complicated medical picture applies to a particular child. *For any child with school refusal behavior, primary medical conditions should be ruled out before using the procedures in this guide.*

For certain cases of school refusal behavior, consult with child psychiatrists as well. These cases apply especially to children with severe levels of anxiety, children with comorbid conditions such as attention-deficit/hyperactivity disorder (ADHD), and children with highly complex clinical symptoms. In some cases, pharmacotherapy may facilitate the procedures in this guide by lowering a child's anxiety so she can engage in behavioral exposures or by enhancing a child's ability to concentrate on therapeutic procedures if she has ADHD.

A Sample Case of Assessment and Assigning Treatment

A brief sample case is described here of a 9-year-old boy with intermittent difficulties attending school for 3 months. Primary behaviors included crying, clinging, pleas for nonattendance, and running out of the classroom. These problems had worsened over time, and the child had not been in school for 4 weeks. His parents referred him for treatment and were afraid to force him to attend school. In the meantime, during the day, the boy played games with his mother, watched television, or rode his bicycle around the neighborhood.

A descriptive functional analysis was conducted using the SRAS-R and the procedures described above. Mean item scores across the child, mother, and father SRAS-R for each of the four functional conditions were 1.50, 2.00, 5.00, and 5.17, respectively. This indicated that the boy was refusing school for attention *and* tangible rewards (i.e., the third and fourth functional conditions).

This initial hypothesis was supported by experimental functional analysis. The child was willing to attend school if he knew his mother was sitting in the main office and if he could contact her whenever he wished. This was not the case if only the therapist was at school. In addition, the child displayed temper tantrums when not allowed to continue his daily fun activities. Prescriptive treatment was thus assigned. A combination of parent training in contingency management as well as contracting between the child and parents was recommended.

Chapter 3

Consultation Session and General Treatment Session Procedures

This chapter provides an overview of recommended procedures during the consultation session. Specifically, suggestions are provided for summarizing assessment results and making treatment recommendations to the family. General considerations for each treatment phase in this guide are also discussed.

The Consultation Session

Discussion of the Past Week

Begin the consultation session by speaking with the child and parent(s) separately, and speak with the child first. Remind each party about confidentiality and its limits if necessary and ask about the past few days. You may wish to obtain feedback from the child and parents about a number of variables because the school refusal situation could have changed, and often does change, dramatically. Specific feedback could be obtained, for example, about time missed from school, sudden changes in behavior, parental responses to a child's behavior, negative affectivity levels, school and home activities, and family interactions, among other variables.

If substantial changes have taken place in a child's school refusal behavior or a family's situation, then you may wish to repeat some assessment procedures (e.g., interviews, questionnaires, observations) discussed in chapter 2. In fact, as one party is re-interviewed separately, another party could complete a relevant version of the School Refusal Assessment Scale-Revised to see what changes, if any, occurred in the function of school refusal behavior. One common change is a child who now refuses school for multiple reasons or functions instead of just one previously. This sometimes results when parents allow a child to stay home from school and inadvertently provide much extra attention or tangible reward. If a substantial positive or negative change in the school refusal situation has occurred in past days, then prescriptive treatment may no longer be necessary or may need to be altered accordingly. If little change has taken place, then you may wish to progress to the next step.

Discussion of Daily Logbooks

A discussion of the daily logbooks with the family is important for two reasons. First, the logbooks provide an excellent assessment of a family's motivation for treatment. If the logbooks are forgotten, incomplete, or done haphazardly, this may reflect poorly on each party's interest or desire for behavior change. If this is the case, review the logbook procedures in case family members have questions about them. In addition, explore issues of motivation and compliance. An instructive and directive approach is very useful for clients in this population who may be wavering about their commitment to the assessment and treatment process. Finally, watch for and reconcile discrepancies between what family members record in their logbooks and what they say to you.

Second, a review of the logbooks is essential for assessing the variables listed in chapter 2 and for directing treatment. Specifically, trends in anxiety, depression, distress, noncompliance, and family disruption can be seen instantly. For example, children with school refusal behavior often show particularly severe anxiety ratings on Sunday and Monday nights as a new school week starts. This may indicate where treatment will have to be focused at some point.

You may also wish to closely examine sudden improvements in behavior for authenticity; a child may have falsified his ratings to end the therapy process right away ("See? I'm cured!") and maintain the status quo. Compare child ratings with parent ratings and actual school attendance. Sudden improvements in behavior may also indicate self-corrective school refusal behavior, a common occurrence in about a third of this population.

A sudden *worsening* of behavior should also be examined closely in case the timeline for treatment has to be advanced. For example, a family may be entering a crisis-like state that demands a more intense, immediate focus. In other cases, sudden rating changes come from a family member who is reacting apprehensively to therapy. This is particularly common to children whose anxiety level rises after thinking their parents are now taking firm action against their school refusal behavior. Finally, written comments on the logbooks should be explored in depth, as the events they describe are often quite important to the family member who took the time to write them down. Such comments often describe family fights, particularly troublesome school refusal behaviors, and personal feelings about the situation.

Discussion of Assessment Results

Following a discussion of the logbooks, describe the assessment results with the child and parent(s) separately. Specifically, the following areas should be covered, if applicable:

- Information from interviews and diagnostic information

- Information from questionnaires or formal tests, including scales and subscales indicating particular areas of concern

- Information from behavioral observations

- Information about the function of school refusal behavior

- Discrepancies in child and parent reports

- Teacher or relevant school official reports

- Other information received from the school, including academic status

- Other information obtained from other sources such as a medical doctor

- Other information deemed relevant by you, including information about crises, family members, individual perspectives, history, environment, interpersonal relationships, and current stressors and resources to cope with them

When describing assessment information to family members, first summarize different viewpoints (e.g., child, parent, teacher, school counselor, psychiatrist) you received regarding a child's school refusal behavior. Concentrate on, and synthesize, those aspects most helpful and accurate for understanding the case. Next, juxtapose and/or incorporate these aspects with interviews, questionnaires, observations, and other data you have collected. Subsequently, communicate your overall viewpoint of the school refusal problem by generally answering the three questions raised in chapter 2. Specifically, describe what you think are the primary school refusal behaviors, what you believe is maintaining school refusal behavior, and your thoughts about treatment goals, prognosis, and timeline.

Care should be taken not to insinuate blame during this process, but rather to emphasize the multifaceted nature of the school refusal problem. Parents will sometimes ask about the etiology of the school refusal behavior, possibly in an attempt to further finger a child for blame. However, extended discussions of etiology are often difficult and usually fruitless. If the etiology of the school refusal behavior is clear (e.g., bully at school) and highly relevant to treatment, this may be conveyed. If the etiology of the school refusal behavior is unclear, however, as it often is, and extended discussions of etiology would potentially impede treatment, then encourage parents to look beyond prior cause and toward the current maintaining variables of the behavior.

As you discuss these areas, get client feedback about disagreements they may have with you. Keep in mind that many clients have trouble discussing personal issues related to school refusal behavior and/or have trouble accepting the fact that some change in their own behavior may be needed to resolve the child's behavior problems. Also, because you will be discussing much information, ask clients if they have questions as you go along. Be appropriately flexible in the treatment plan if a client wants to dispute or add to information you present.

Providing a Rationale for Treatment

Following this discussion of assessment results, you may want to present a treatment rationale. This can be done more generally first and more specifically later. An example of a general treatment rationale for *chil-*

dren is presented here. The language, of course, must be adjusted to the cognitive developmental level of a child and to the specifics of your case. This rationale is specifically meant for children refusing school to avoid stimuli that provoke negative affectivity and for children refusing school to escape aversive social and/or evaluative situations:

As we've just discussed, you sometimes experience trouble going to school. Up to now, the course of action you've taken to reduce your negative feelings has been to avoid school or not go altogether. You have probably noticed that this has worked okay in the short run but that avoidance is really just worsening your problem in the long run. In addition, you have probably noticed that you think and feel about school in ways that you do not like. In fact, these thoughts and feelings most likely lead to a continued avoidance of school.

Basically, you have learned a certain way of responding to negative feelings in school-related situations. What I want to do here is teach you a different way of coping with your negative feelings. I want to give you some skills that will give you an alternative to avoiding school. Instead, you will practice facing your negative feelings and cope with difficult situations. At first, you may notice that the things I ask you to do will cause you to have even more negative feelings than before. In fact, I would be surprised if you felt the same as you did before. For you to make progress, though, you will have to experience these negative feelings and push yourself hard. The more you push yourself in therapy, the faster you will progress in treatment.

An example of a general treatment rationale for family members, especially *parents*, is also presented here. Again, language should be adjusted to the cognitive developmental level of each family member and to the specifics of your case. This rationale is specifically meant for parents whose child refuses school for attention and for families whose child refuses school for tangible rewards outside of school:

As we've just discussed, (child) experiences trouble going to school. Up to now, the course of action that the family has taken to reduce this problem has been marked by conflict, confusion about what to do, or ignoring or giving in to the situation. Each of you has probably noticed that ignoring or giving in has worked okay in the short run but that giving in is really just worsening the problem in the long run. In addition, each of you has probably noticed that the family gets along in ways that you do not like. In fact, these conflicts most likely lead to continued school refusal behavior.

Basically, your family has learned a certain way of responding to noncompliance and other problems in school-related situations. What I want to do here is teach your family a different way of coping with this situation. I want to give you some skills that will give you an alternative to arguing and confusion. (Mr. and Mrs. _____) will practice facing (child's) negative behaviors and coping with difficult situations. In addition, the family in general will practice certain problem-solving techniques. At first, each of you may notice that the things I ask you to do cause even more negative feelings than before. In fact, I would be surprised if each of you felt the same as you did before. For the family to make progress, though, everyone must work hard and work through the difficult situations. The more everyone pushes themselves in therapy, the faster the family will progress in treatment.

More specific treatment rationales may then be given and are presented here. If a child is refusing school to avoid stimuli that provoke negative affectivity, indicate that psychoeducation, somatic control exercises, gradual re-exposure to the school setting, and self-reinforcement will help to:

- Reduce unpleasant physical symptoms

- Give the child a way of coping with uncomfortable situations

- Ease re-entry into school

If a child is refusing school to escape aversive social and/or evaluative situations, indicate that psychoeducation, role-play, practice in real-life situations, and cognitive restructuring will help to:

- Build social skills that will solicit positive feedback from others

- Decrease social anxiety that interferes with going to school

- Change negative thinking patterns that hamper school attendance

If a child is refusing school for attention, indicate that parent training in contingency management will help to:

- Give parents skills to address noncompliance to their commands

- Shift parent attention to positive behaviors such as going to school

- Put parents more in charge of what is happening at home

If a child is refusing school to pursue tangible rewards, indicate that familial contingency contracting will help:

- Reduce family conflict by providing a method of problem-solving

- Increase rewards for going to school

- Decrease rewards for missing school

For cases where school refusal behavior is maintained by *two or more functions*, then *two or more treatments* and *additional treatment rationales* will need to be conveyed. Other treatment components may also be added as appropriate, and some are described in this guide. Also, family members should paraphrase your treatment rationale in their own words to confirm that they understood it. Of course, soliciting questions and consent about the upcoming treatment process is necessary as well.

Pretreatment Considerations

In addition to discussing the form, function, treatment, and treatment rationale for school refusal behavior, consider factors that could mediate treatment success. Treatment mediators are individual factors that influence treatment outcome, sometimes in a negative way. For example, level of motivation, as described above, is a crucial treatment mediator in this population. With respect to children, other important treatment mediators include:

- Temperament/personality (e.g., hostility, sensitivity, motivation or reactivity to change, introversion versus extroversion)

- Degree of self-esteem, self-efficacy, and self-discipline (e.g., willingness to delay gratification, persistence in treatment)

- Social status (e.g., popular, neglected, rejected) and degree of racial/ethnic dissonance from peers at school

- Cognitive and academic status (e.g., high versus low verbal ability, intelligence, grades)

- Physical status (e.g., overweight, tall, athletic)

- Comorbid problems or disorders such as attention-deficit/hyperactivity disorder, aggression, learning disorder, and running away from school

- Birth order and presence of siblings

- Presence of traumatic life events

- Attitude toward treatment and the therapist (e.g., willingness to talk)

- Willingness to sabotage treatment procedures between sessions (e.g., refusal to complete homework assignments, increasingly secretive school refusal behavior over time)

With respect to parents or family members, important treatment mediators include:

- Parental disciplinary style and relationship with the child (e.g., authoritative, authoritarian, permissive, disorganized)

- Single- versus dual-parent family

- Degree of marital or family conflict

- General family dynamics (e.g., enmeshed, conflictive, isolated, detached)

- Presence and degree of parental psychopathology (particularly anxiety, depression, and substance-related disorders)

- Financial and time resources

- Expectations and level of optimism versus pessimism regarding the treatment plan (including degree of commitment to the plan)

- Family's level of communication and problem-solving skill

- Cultural variables (e.g., different levels of acculturation, language differences, ethnic identity, mistrust of the therapist)

- Willingness to sabotage treatment procedures between sessions (e.g., deliberately maintaining the child's role of day babysitter at home)

Other factors that could mediate treatment for a child with school refusal behavior include:

- Degree of cooperation and compliance from school officials and other school variables

- Persistence of school officials to try to convince family members to implement a quicker treatment (e.g., forced school attendance, medication) or treatment other than the therapeutically prescribed one

- Cases referred by the family versus an external agency such as a court

- Restraints on your time and resources (e.g., inability to contact the family daily or meet with the family frequently)

- School victimization

The last item refers to children who feel they will be victimized in some way if they attend school. Many children, for example, are victims of theft, property damage, threat, and/or injury. Others are troubled by unpleasant teachers or unfair rules. In addition, the violence and shootings that sometimes take place in American schools concern many parents and children. Such incidents may induce or affect school refusal behavior in different ways. For example, a child may miss school because he is worried about genuine potential harm or a threatening situation there. In addition, a child may exaggerate claims of school victimization to manipulate parents into letting him stay home. Finally, a school's victimization rate may induce a parent to withdraw a child from school whether or not the child feels affected.

If school victimization or another pretreatment consideration is pertinent, you may need to suggest a change in the treatment plan. In cases of potential school victimization, for example, investigate whether a change of school is appropriate or if another intervention is warranted. In cases where school officials are unwilling to help reintegrate a child back to a classroom setting, then more responsibility for treatment may rest on a parent. In cases where a single parent cannot implement parent training procedures because of work schedules, contact others (e.g., friend, neighbor, ex-spouse) who may help. *Be flexible as different circumstances arise and remember that the procedures in this guide may change at any time depending on your case.* In addition, some clients sometimes adhere too rigidly to the parent workbook during treatment and need to be encouraged to be more flexible.

These are *only the most frequent and important* treatment mediators relevant to this population. Therefore, consider other factors more idiosyncratic to your case. If your case does have a significant treatment mediator, convey your concerns to the family (if relevant and appropriate), address it immediately, and/or change or expand the treatment procedures described here accordingly.

Other Considerations

Addressing Difficult Clients

As you know, clinical practice is fraught with clients who are difficult to address. This is no exception in the school refusal population, and may even be more problematic given the "crisis-like" atmosphere that is often present. We have found the most difficult problems, and ones you may expect to find, to be (1) lack of motivation to change the current situation (especially, of course, on the child's part), (2) refusal to interact with the therapist, and (3) failure to complete homework assignments and logbooks.

Obviously, you will have to address these problems on a case-by-case basis using your own clinical style. *However, we recommend strongly that you maintain frequent contact with family members during the week.* In more difficult school refusal cases, contact the family daily to enhance rapport, ascertain their willingness to participate, obtain ratings, and build optimism and motivation among each relevant family member. Simplifying the treatment regimen is sometimes necessary in these cases as well. In general, family members are more willing to resolve a school refusal situation if a strong bond exists with the therapist.

Scheduling Future Sessions

Give the family an estimated timeline for addressing a child's school refusal behavior. This guide is designed to cover eight sessions in a 4- to 8-week-period, and that timeline may be conveyed to the family as the *average* treatment length. However, some cases take less time and some cases take more time to resolve. Meet with a family twice a week if possible, but at *least* once per week. Of course, the length of treatment will depend on many factors, including the mediators listed above. Thoroughly discuss these factors with family members and change your estimate about expected treatment length as appropriate.

A discussion of the family's weekly schedule at this point is also a good idea so regular sessions can be planned. Keep in mind that many clients of this population will require sessions in the late afternoon or evening, especially as a child attends school more frequently later in treatment. Weekend sessions may also be considered, but we find it useful to see clients after a stressful school day. In this way, problems can be addressed more immediately.

At this point, discuss with your clients what to do in case of missed sessions or if other agencies (e.g., insurance company, parents' jobs) limit the time available for therapy. Because the successful treatment of school refusal behavior is often an intense process, missed sessions can be quite disruptive. *Try to maintain a regular schedule of sessions and/or have a client make up missed sessions as soon as possible.*

Caveats About Treatment Sessions and Your Time

Consider the strong possibility that some of your sessions will last longer than a typical 50-minute session. Although individual session material in this guide could be covered in 50 minutes, other issues could (and likely will) dominate and extend the session. These issues include, among others, family member concerns and questions about treatment, crises, treatment noncompliance, and extensions of the treatment program into related areas.

This population, more so than many others, demands increased flexibility and frequent contact on the part of therapists during and between sessions. Do not be surprised if your clients contact you at different times of the day, especially in the early morning hours as the family prepares for work and school. Calls from cellular telephones on the way to school are not unusual. Therefore, you may wish to explain your policy regarding contact with you under different conditions.

Finally, be prepared for the possibility of "parking lot" therapy. This occurs when a child refuses to enter your practice setting, thus requiring you to go to the family vehicle to encourage attendance. This scenario is pertinent to many cases of school refusal behavior. In this situation, allow the child to ventilate negative feelings and provide support. Gentle persuasion and information about what is to be discussed may be useful as well. Offering inducements to the child to enter the clinic, however, is not a good idea because the child's misbehavior is rewarded. If a child continues to refuse to enter the clinic, and is safe in the vehicle, then meet with parents alone. This sometimes induces a child to attend the therapy session out of boredom, worry that parents will provide a one-sided view of the situation, reduced anxiety, and/or a simple change of heart.

Work Between Sessions

Toward the end of the consultation session, remind the family that much work on their part will be needed between therapy sessions if the school refusal situation is to be resolved. Examples include completing logbooks, practicing treatment techniques, bringing the child to school, following through on instructions to change parenting behaviors, and adhering to written contracts developed in the sessions. *Emphasize to clients that chances for successful treatment are significantly related to the amount of effort they give between sessions.* This is a message that should be reiterated continuously throughout treatment. In addition, continue to develop your relationship with school officials.

Scheduling Treatment Session 1

In urgent cases, treatment session 1 should begin *immediately following* the consultation session and consent. In addition, treatment sessions 1 and 2 should be scheduled within the same week (e.g., on a Monday and Thursday) and within 1 week of the consultation session. In less urgent cases, especially those where a child is regularly attending school or where time is not a critical factor, treatment session 1 may be scheduled for a few days later. In any school refusal behavior case, however, treatment should start as soon as possible.

Review of the Past Week and Feedback

At the beginning of each treatment session, talk with family members about events since the previous session. In particular, assess for changes in a family's situation or a child's school refusal behavior as well as anything else you deem important. Be sure to use this time to solicit any concerns or questions family members may have about anything. In addition, see how the homework assignments from the previous session were completed. If problems occurred, then discuss them at this point. Encourage family members to emphasize a child's successes as much as his difficulties.

You may also want to give some feedback regarding the child's and/or parent's performance during the past few days. Listen carefully to family members and correct problems that may have occurred. Ask if anyone disagrees with the therapy procedures and work to remove obstacles as much as possible.

Discussion of Daily Logbooks

At the beginning of each session, review the child and parent daily logbooks. Pay special attention to sudden changes in ratings, patterns in the ratings, differences between child and parent ratings, written comments, or missing ratings. This information is very important and will help you track treatment progress and the family's motivation level and implement the best course of action regarding treatment. If a child or parents had problems with the logbooks, address these problems immediately.

General Points Regarding Specific Treatment Sessions

Treatment Session 1

At some point in session 1, encourage the family to adhere as much as possible to a regular school-day schedule. This includes early wakening, dressing and preparing for school as if going, and completing school assignments. If the child has been out of school for some time, he may have slipped from a normal routine to sleeping late, dressing later in the morning, and otherwise treating the school morning like a holiday or weekend day. Emphasize to the child and parent(s) that getting back into the habit of rising and preparing for school will facilitate treatment progress. Children need to be reminded that the goal of this program is to help them return to, and enjoy, school. Even though a return to school may not be scheduled for this week, ask the child to rise and get ready as if he were going to school.

Review with the child and parent(s) the typical routine for a morning when the child was going to school, and compare this with mornings when the child does not go to school. If the child has been allowed to stay at home, he may be sleeping late, lounging in pajamas, and freely accessing the kitchen and food. Bedtime may also have slipped to a time later in the evening. If necessary, suggest procedures outlined in the sections regarding children refusing school for attention (chapter 6) or tangible reward (chapter 7). This may involve teaching parents to reward behaviors consistent with getting ready for school or developing a contract so a child can earn privileges or other rewards for compliance to a set routine.

Treatment Session 2

In each treatment program, session 2 is often the most informative for several reasons. First, by this time, you should have a good sense of the family's motivation for treatment. For example, if a family comes to the second session and has completed the first homework assignments and the logbooks, then their motivation level and perhaps their prognosis are probably good. Second, trends in the child's school refusal behavior should be more evident now than before. Trends will be found in the logbooks and will help you decide how quickly or slowly to proceed in therapy. Finally, rapport with family members should be fairly well developed at this point. This might allow you to introduce upcoming treatment procedures more salient to school refusal behavior.

You may find at this point in therapy that, as family members become more familiar with prescriptive treatment procedures, new ideas to "improve" treatment become more prevalent on their part. Sometimes these new ideas are innovative and can be incorporated into the prescriptive treatment. For example, parents sometimes develop ingenious methods for tweaking, and indeed improving, the treatment procedures described here *for their particular child*. In other cases, however, incorporating these new ideas may not be a sound approach. For example, family members sometimes want to shield or protect a child from certain anxiety-provoking situations, and suggest behaviors a child can use to avoid these situations. However, avoidance will likely contradict the exposure-based procedures described in this guide. You will, of course, have to use clinical judgment in these situations and consider a client's right to choose treatment. However, you and family members should bear in mind that, to successfully treat many cases of school refusal behavior, new skills for solving problems are clearly necessary. Therefore, we do not recommend significant deviations from the procedures described here to develop these new skills.

Treatment Sessions 3 and 4

By sessions 3 and 4, the treatment process should be starting to mature as you become more comfortable with the family and their situation. In addition, the family's motivation for behavior change should be more evident and will, of course, determine the scope, pace, and direction of treatments described here. Also, a close working relationship between you and relevant school officials should continue to develop. Such a relationship will help ease a child's transition to the regular classroom setting.

Sessions 3 and 4 often represent the "heavy lifting" portion of therapy. During these sessions, a child's school attendance will start, increase, or be subject to additional consequences. As a result, do not be surprised if these sessions become lengthy: more than an hour may be necessary to listen to family members' concerns, implement treatment procedures, adjust them as necessary to fit your particular case, assign homework, and address related problems. During this period of treatment, continue to provide daily support and feedback to the family and encourage them to complete homework assignments. The risk of dropout is often highest during these sessions because family members are faced with hard choices and must increase their efforts to address school refusal behavior. Specifically, some family members start to balk at therapy procedures and/or stay interested more in blame than behavior change. Any action on your part to change this process will generally promote treatment success. Examples include providing support, allowing family members to ventilate negative feelings, and encouraging a redirected focus onto the treatment procedures.

Treatment Sessions 5 and 6

By sessions 5 and 6, prescriptive treatment should be quite intense and focused on school refusal behavior. Although secondary issues should be discussed if appropriate, substantial therapy time should be devoted to addressing a child's specific school refusal behaviors. Procedures described in sessions 5 and 6 should be used *only if* things are going fairly well to this point. If a child has started attending school with more regularity, then the procedures discussed in sessions 5 and 6 may be used. However, if a child or family is continuing to struggle with early treatment procedures, then spend more time covering these initial procedures. In many stubborn cases of school refusal behavior, "backtracking" to correct new or ongoing problems or relapses is necessary. Remember that the procedures outlined in this guide are meant to be flexible enough to fit your particular case. As mentioned earlier, some cases take more time and others take less time to resolve. Do not be too concerned if your therapy schedule does not exactly match the one described here.

Treatment Sessions 7 and 8

By sessions 7 and 8, a child's school refusal problems should be nearly resolved. As a result, sessions 7 and 8 may focus on tying up loose ends, completing full-time school attendance, branching out into other areas of concern, setting up long-term follow-up procedures, bracing for termination, and/or obtaining post-treatment information. If treatment needs to extend longer than the eight sessions outlined here, then structure additional sessions using the techniques and principles described in this guide. Extended treatment is especially pertinent to cases involving highly problematic school refusal behavior, ongoing slips or minor relapse, comorbid problems, or family dysfunction.

Treatment success in this population is sometimes defined as full-time school attendance for at least 2 weeks and/or a substantial (>75%) reduction in daily stress. Each case is different, of course, and so your definition of treatment success may change accordingly. In many cases, full-time school attendance for several weeks or even months is necessary before deciding that treatment was successful. In addition, even small amounts of remaining distress about school can trigger relapse in some cases. Therefore, a nearly complete eradication of a child's anxiety about school may also be necessary to define treatment success. However, in other cases, especially more chronic ones, even part-time school attendance in an alternative high school may define treatment success.

Stepping Down the Therapy Program

Latter sessions of therapy may be spaced apart to give a child time to test new skills and uncover less obvious anxieties about school. Homework assignments may be given as appropriate during this time and can mirror those from earlier sessions. Sessions can be planned for every other week or monthly through the end of the school year. This tapering of treatment sessions also allows you to end the therapeutic relationship in a structured and supportive way. Although you will work with a child to eventually terminate treatment, the child should end therapy systematically—that is, to say goodbye to the therapist and discuss plans for the future.

The End of Treatment

When should treatment end? Ultimately, this is a question best answered following a thorough discussion with your clients. Some parents and children prefer to end treatment as soon as a child is back in school, but we strongly discourage this approach. In many cases, residual problems and questions remain, or a child "tests" his parents by refusing school one day a couple of weeks later. An appropriate analogy to give to parents to consider is what happens when someone is prescribed an antibiotic medication. This medicine usually must be taken for 10 full days, long after symptoms dissipate. A person who stops the medication once the symptoms disappear risks relapse due to an incomplete course of treatment. Similarly, you and your clients need to fully wrap up work together before ending. This may involve tapering sessions over time and focusing on relapse prevention. Chapter 8 describes specific techniques used by therapists to ensure children stay on course and avoid slips or relapse.

In other cases, families are beset with problems that go beyond a child's school refusal behavior. Treatments regarding these other problems should therefore continue even if a child is back in school. Common examples of such problems in a school refusal population include general family conflict, anxiety, depression, lack of motivation, delinquent and oppositional behavior, learning disorder, and hyperactivity, among others. In complex cases such as these, extended treatment is often appropriate and desirable to ensure a child stays in school and to address these comorbid problems.

Reading This Guide

Chapters 4 through 7 discuss different treatments for school refusal behavior. If your case involves a child refusing school *only* to avoid school-related stimuli that provoke negative affectivity, then proceed to chapter 4. If your case involves a child refusing school *only* to escape aversive social and/or evaluative situations, then proceed to chapter 5. If your case involves a child refusing school *only* for attention, then proceed to chapter 6. If your case involves a child refusing school *only* to pursue tangible rewards, then proceed to chapter 7. If your case involves a child refusing school for *multiple reasons,* then proceed to those treatment chapters that are relevant.

Note that some material in this guide may apply to different reasons why children refuse school. Examples include sections on escorting a child to school and downplaying excessive reassurance-seeking. Therefore, read each section in this guide in case it is necessary and in case you find a particular point relevant to your case. Recommend this for family members as well, but remind them to discuss any new treatment technique with you before trying it on their own.

As you use this therapist guide with different clients, thoroughly reread each section (e.g., session 1) prior to each session. Familiarize yourself with the main aspects of each section and compile a list of the major points you want to cover in the session. Consider relevant family and other factors during this process. In this way, the therapeutic techniques can be applied more fully, efficiently, and effectively.

Chapter 4 — Children Refusing School to Avoid School-Related Stimuli That Provoke Negative Affectivity

(Corresponds to Chapter 4 of the parent workbook)

SESSION 1 *Starting Treatment*

Materials Needed

- Model of Anxiety
- Anxiety and Avoidance Hierarchy
- Feelings Thermometer
- Relaxation and Deep-Breathing Scripts
- Relaxation Log
- Blank audiotape

Session Outline

- Teach a child about anxiety.
- Work with a child to create an Anxiety and Avoidance Hierarchy.
- Teach a child relaxation training and deep diaphragmatic breathing.

  School refusal behavior is often motivated by a desire to avoid symptoms of dread, anxiety, panic, or depression associated with certain school-related stimuli. For children who avoid stimuli that provoke such negative affectivity, the main goal of treatment is to change avoidance behavior and build coping and active school attendance behaviors. Treatment for this condition will involve:

- Building an anxiety and avoidance hierarchy of stimuli

- Teaching somatic management skills to decrease negative emotional arousal

- Conducting systematic exposure to anxiety cues identified on a hierarchy in a step-by-step fashion

- Gradually reintegrating a child to school

- Having a child access self-reinforcement to cope with transient negative emotions

Treatment thus involves training a child to use self-control procedures. During this treatment program, you will teach a child to identify personally relevant objects and situations that provoke negative affectivity and to use specific somatic skills to prevent her from spiraling into a full-blown anxiety reaction. These somatic skills can also be used to prevent the start of an anxiety spiral. Gradually, the child will enter situations that are most anxiety-provoking while using these somatic management skills.

Special Topic 4.1: Medicating a Child With Severe Distress

Some children have such high levels of distress that pharmacotherapy may be an attractive option. *If you consider this option for a child's distress, consult with a child psychiatrist familiar with the literature on medications for child anxiety and depression.* Medications may be effective for some children with high levels of distress and are designed to help ease a child's physical feelings of distress.

Several caveats regarding medication should be noted. First, some children with distress do not benefit from medication. Children whose distress is mild or moderate, for example, may not benefit as much from medication as children whose distress is severe. The psychological techniques in this guide will be more helpful if your client's level of distress is mild or moderate, not severe. Second, side effects from medication may occur. Third, medication may help ease physical feelings of distress but may not ease the "thinking" or "doing" parts of distress. A child taking medication for distress about school may feel physically better, but she may still have thoughts about not wanting to attend school or may still try to avoid school.

The majority of your time will be spent with the child, but you should invite parents into the last portion of each session to access their input and review the session. Each session will detail specific homework assignments that involve parental support and active participation and that should become a family activity. Parents are invaluable resources for distracting or involving other children and managing a situation to provide uninterrupted family time to focus on homework assignments.

Psychoeducation

Initial treatment involves helping a child understand the nature and process of anxiety. As a child's understanding of anxiety progresses, you can help her observe her own anxiety reactions, identify where anxiety reactions occur, and use specific skills or tools to cope with negative emotions. The following is an example of how to explain the process of anxiety to a child. Simplify this for younger children or those with special needs. Utilize a flip chart or paper to illustrate and present the model to the child (Figure 4.1).

When you say that you're scared (anxious, upset), it feels like there's one big ball of bad stuff rolling over you, and there's nothing you can do to stop it. It's like a train is going to run you over! If we think of feeling anxious in that way, then we stay upset and feel like we can't handle the situation. But being upset (anxious) is really made up of three parts.

First is what you feel; all those feelings in your body that let you know you're scared. Things like your heart beating fast, shaking, your hands feeling sweaty, and butterflies in your stomach are all signals that you're scared. (Draw a circle and label it "What I feel.")

The second part to being scared is what you say to yourself. Usually, you say something like, Get me out of here, I'm afraid, I can't do this, I want to go home, or I need my Mom or someone to help me. (Draw a circle and label it "What I think.")

Finally, the third part to being scared is what you do when you're scared. This is usually something like leaving a place, or avoiding going to a place, or trying to be near someone who can help you feel better. (Draw a circle and label it "What I do.")

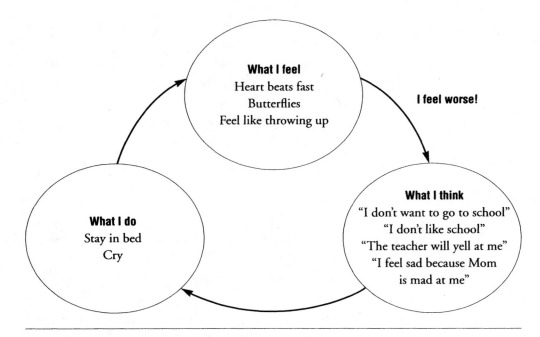

Figure 4.1
Anxiety Model

After presenting the model, ask the child for personally relevant responses to each of the three components of anxiety: What I feel, What I think, and What I do. With the child, begin to identify targets for change within each component. Cognitive-behavioral treatments rely heavily on the Socratic method, or questioning a client so she becomes an active participant in the therapy process. Questioning leads the client to uncover her own biases, beliefs, behavioral patterns, and coping resources. You will initially lead the questioning process, but as the questioning method becomes a learned response, the child will be able to engage independently in the process of deductive, rational thinking. The following is a sample dialogue of questioning a child. In the dialogue, C represents the child and T represents the therapist.

Case Vignette

T: Let's look at the three circles here on the board. This one is called "What I feel," meaning those feelings in my body. This one is called "What I think," and this one is "What I do." Think for a moment about the last time you were nervous going to school. Do you remember when that was?

C: Yes. I had to go to school last week, and didn't want to go.

T: Okay, think about that time. Was it in the morning, before school?

C: Yes. Mommy woke me up and told me to get dressed for school.

T: And what were you thinking about when Mom said to get dressed?

C: I don't know. I didn't want to go.

T: Okay, there's one thing you were thinking, "I don't want to go." We'll put that right here in this circle. (Therapist writes "I don't want to go" in the thinking circle). What happened next?

C: I stayed in bed. And then Mommy came and yelled at me.

T: So, right here (begins to write in the "Things I do" circle) we'd put "Stayed in bed." That's something that you did when you thought about not wanting to go to school. What happened next, after Mommy yelled at you?

C: I started to cry.

T: (Writes "Cry" in the behavior circle) What were you thinking about that made you cry?

C: I don't like school. I get scared that I'll get yelled at by the teacher.

T: (Writes "I don't like school" and "The teacher will yell at me" in the thinking circle) When you think about having to go to school, and worry that the teacher will yell at you, do get any funny feelings in your body?

C: I feel sick. Like I'm going to throw up.

T: So, the feeling you get is an upset stomach, maybe like having butterflies?

C: Yeah. And my heart beats really fast.

T: (Writes "Heart beats fast" and "Butterflies" in the feelings circle) This is a good start. See, we're looking now at what goes on inside you when you get afraid.

Next, describe for the child the way in which these three components interact to spiral into overwhelming feelings of anxiety:

T: Let's look at these circles. When you were in bed (points to the "What I do" circle), you were thinking that you didn't want to go to school because you don't like it, and the teacher might yell at you. Right?

C: Yeah.

T: Did it make you feel better to think about what could go wrong at school?

C: No.

T: Did your butterflies feel better when you cried?

C: No. I felt worse.

T: And what did you tell yourself then?

C: That Mommy was mad at me. And I was sad that she yelled at me.

T: (Writes "I feel sad because Mommy is mad at me" in the thinking circle) Look at this now. Each time something happens in one circle, something else happens in another circle. (Draws arrows from each circle, linking to the next circle in the chain) So, when you tell yourself the teacher will yell at you, your butterflies get worse. And so you don't get out of bed. Then Mom comes in and yells, and you think about that, and you get sad. See, our feelings have three parts to them, and they each work on one another.

Emphasize the role of the physical sensations of anxiety, how these sensations spiral to uncomfortable levels, and the resulting avoidance behavior that occurs. Introduce a child to the skills she will learn to address each component. Relaxation and deep breathing will be used to manage physical feelings of anxiety; step-by-step practices of entering anxious situations will be used to change avoidance and escape behaviors; self-reinforcement, thinking realistically, pride, and praise will be taught to change negative thoughts that accompany anxiety. Inform the child you will help her gradually return to school by taking bigger and bigger steps as time goes on. In addition, inform the child you will be nudging her to attend school more and more during treatment.

Building an Anxiety and Avoidance Hierarchy

The Anxiety and Avoidance Hierarchy (AAH) is a list of objects or situations most upsetting to a child that will be actively targeted during treatment. The information is organized into gradual steps so a child may begin with the easiest (or lowest) item and progress toward the most difficult (highest) hierarchy item. Most children progress through several hierarchies during treatment until all upsetting situations or activities are challenged. Figure 4.2 represents a sample AAH for a 7-year-old girl who refused to attend school due to separation concerns. A blank hierarchy is also included. You may photocopy it from the book or download multiple copies from the Treatments *ThatWork*™ Web site at www.oup.com/us/ttw.

Problem: School refusal due to anxiety about being away from home and from her parents

Situations or Places That Scare Me!	Anxiety Rating	Avoidance Rating
1. Staying in school all day without calling Mom and Dad	8	8
2. Staying in school all morning, and not calling Mom or Dad, or going to the nurse	8	8
3. Riding the school bus all by myself	7	8
4. Waiting for Mom, and she's late to pick me up	6	7
5. Staying with the babysitter, and Mom doesn't call home to check on us	5	5
6. Getting my school clothes ready the night before school	5	3
7. Having tutoring at the school, without Mom there	4	2
8. Going to school to get my homework, and visiting with my teacher	3	2
9. Going to lunch at school	3	2
10. Meeting with the tutor while Mom goes shopping	3	2

Figure 4.2

Sandy's Anxiety and Avoidance Hierarchy

Anxiety and Avoidance Hierarchy

Problem: _____

Situations or Places That Scare Me!	Anxiety Rating	Avoidance Rating
1.		
2.		
3.		
4.		
5.		
6.		
7.		
8.		
9.		
10.		

To create an AAH, review information gathered from the child and parents during assessment and note additional objects or situations currently avoided. Organize the information by writing each object or situation on a separate index card. Keep several blank cards for additional information you uncover during treatment. Present the index cards to the child and ask her to sort the situations into categories based on the Feelings Thermometer (Figure 4.3). The Feelings Thermometer will help a child identify and rate the degree of anxiety/general distress experienced in each situation. Ratings range from 0 (none) to 8 (very, very much). Based on the child's ratings, construct the first 10-item AAH using the 10 lowest-ranked items. A blank copy of the AAH form is available in the corresponding parent workbook and available for download from the Treatments *That Work™* Web site at www.oup.com/us/ttw. For the remainder of treatment, have the child rate her anxiety about these objects or situations at each session to provide you with feedback and an ongoing measure of behavior change. Ask parents to complete AAH ratings separately from the child, thereby providing valuable cross-informant information and a broader and more accurate view of a child's presentation and functioning. Begin all sessions with one AAH form for the child and one for each parent.

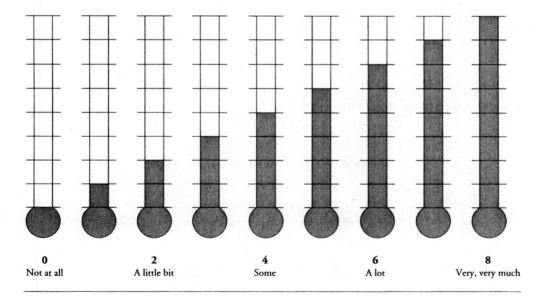

| 0 | 2 | 4 | 6 | 8 |
| Not at all | A little bit | Some | A lot | Very, very much |

Figure 4.3

Feelings Thermometer

Special Topic 4.2: Home Schooling

Children who do not want to go to school often ask their parents to enroll them in home schooling or homebound instruction. This refers to a situation where a child is taught at home by a parent, tutor, or some other adult who usually follows some school-based curriculum. Traditionally, home-based instruction was reserved for children with severe medical or other problems that did not allow them to attend regular school. In recent times, however, more parents have switched to home-based methods of education.

Home schooling does have certain benefits, such as good supervision of a child, increased parent–child contact, and better control over what a child learns. However, withdrawing a child from school tends to isolate her from social gatherings and peer groups where she can build social skills, learn to perform well before others, and develop friendships. In addition, the quality of a child's education at home versus school must be considered.

We do not generally recommend home schooling for addressing children distressed about school. If a child is trying to avoid such distress, then acquiescing to this behavior by enrolling her in home schooling only reinforces avoidance. A better method of addressing school refusal behavior in particular and avoidance in general is to practice the skills for managing distress in this chapter and in chapter 5. These skills include learning to relax, thinking more realistically, and gradually facing whatever situation causes distress. As children learn to manage their distress, school attendance should improve.

Relaxation Training and Breathing Retraining

The next treatment component is to teach a child relaxation training and deep diaphragmatic breathing using the scripts below. Ideally, this segment should be audiotaped for a child to use at home. If a tape recorder is not available, parents can use the Relaxation and Deep Breathing Scripts included in the parent workbook or they can download them from the Treatments *ThatWork*™ Web site at www.oup.com/us/ttw.

Relaxation training involves talking a child through a series of muscle tension and relaxation exercises, each designed to teach her to discriminate physical sensations of tension and calmness. Begin the relaxation process by asking a child to find a comfortable position in the chair or couch. Next, have her close her eyes or let her gaze settle and focus on one spot in the room. At each step of the process, focus the child on letting go of tension and feeling calm and relaxed. The child should isolate each muscle group one at a time, so give ongoing direction to her to tense only a particular muscle. Instruct a younger child to watch and emulate as you perform the step and use imagery to help her follow the exercises. Introduce deep breathing (into the stomach or diaphragm) to prolong relaxation and make it more complete.

The entire process of relaxation should last about 20 minutes. Parents may be called into the session for a discussion and summary at this point. To facilitate a child's learning of the treatment model and procedures, have the child tell the parents about the session. Add comments or guide the child to give a more complete summary of the session as needed. At this point, you may wish to discuss with parents how they can assist their child with the homework. For example, a parent could be encouraged to keep distractions to a minimum while the child practices the relaxation procedures.

Relaxation Script (modified from Ollendick & Cerny, 1981)

Have the child recline in a comfortable position and either close her eyes or focus the eyes on one spot on the wall or ceiling. Legs and arms should not be crossed; have the child take off her shoes and loosen any tight clothing such as belts.

I would like you to sit as comfortably as possible in your chair. During the next few minutes, I am going to give you some instructions about tensing and releasing different muscle groups. I want you to listen carefully and do what I ask you to do. Be sure not to anticipate what I say; just relax and concentrate on my voice. Any questions? (Answer questions as they occur) *Okay, put your feet on the floor, and put your arms on the arms of the chair.* (Child focuses or closes eyes as desired) *Try to relax as much as possible.*

Using this tension-release relaxation protocol, tensed muscles are held in place for approximately 5 seconds. The procedure is audiotaped.

Hands and Arms

Make a fist with your left hand. Squeeze it hard. Feel the tightness in your hand and arm as you squeeze. Now let your hand go and relax. See how much better your hand and arm feel when they are relaxed. Once again, make a fist with your left hand and squeeze hard. Good. Now relax and let your hand go. (Repeat the process for the right hand and arm)

Arms and Shoulders

Stretch your arms out in front of you. Raise them up high over your head. Way back. Feel the pull in your shoulders. Stretch higher. Now just let your arms drop back to your side. Okay, let's stretch again. Stretch your arms out in front of you. Raise them over your head. Pull them back, way back. Pull hard. Now let them drop quickly. Good. Notice how your shoulders feel more relaxed. This time let's have a great big stretch. Try to touch the ceiling. Stretch your arms out in front of you. Raise them way up over your head. Push them way, way back. Notice the tension and pull in your arms and shoulders. Hold tight, now. Great. Let them drop very quickly and feel how good it is to be relaxed. It feels good and warm and lazy.

Shoulders and Neck

Try to pull your shoulders up to your ears and push your head down into your shoulders. Hold in tight. Okay, now relax and feel the warmth. Again, pull your shoulders up to your ears and push your head down into your shoulders. Do it tightly. Okay, you can relax now. Bring your head out and let your shoulders relax. Notice how much better it feels to be relaxed than to be all tight. One more time now. Push your head down and your shoulders way up to your ears. Hold it. Feel the tenseness in your neck and shoulders. Okay. You can relax now and feel comfortable. You feel good.

Jaw

Put your teeth together real hard. Let your neck muscles help you. Now relax. Just let your jaw hang loose. Notice how good it feels just to let your jaw drop. Okay, bite down hard. That's good. Now relax again. Just let your jaw drop. It feels so good just to let go. Okay, one more time. Bite down. Hard as you can. Harder. Oh, you really are working hard. Good. Now relax. Try to relax your whole body. Let yourself get as loose as you can.

Face and Nose

Wrinkle up your nose. Make as many wrinkles in your nose as you can. Scrunch up your nose real hard. Good. Now relax your nose. Now wrinkle up your nose again. Wrinkle it up hard. Hold it just as tight as you can. Okay. You can relax your face. Notice that when you scrunch up your nose, your cheeks and your mouth and your forehead all help you and they get tight, too. So when you relax your nose, your whole face relaxes too, and that feels good. Now make lots of wrinkles on your forehead. Hold it tight, now. Okay, you can let go. Now you can just relax. Let your face go smooth. No wrinkles anywhere. Your face feels nice and smooth and relaxed.

Stomach

Now tighten up your stomach muscles real tight. Make your stomach real hard. Don't move. Hold it. You can relax now. Let your stomach go soft. Let it be as relaxed as you can. That feels so much better. Okay, again. Tighten your stomach real hard. Good. You can relax now. Settle down, get comfortable and relax. Notice the difference between a tight stomach and a relaxed one. That's how we want to feel. Nice and loose and relaxed. Okay. Once more. Tighten up. Tighten hard. Good. Now you can relax completely. You feel nice and relaxed.

This time, try to pull your stomach in. Try to squeeze it against your backbone. Try to be as skinny as you can. Now relax. You do not have to be skinny now. Just relax and feel your stomach being warm and loose. Okay, squeeze in your stomach again. Make it touch your backbone. Get it real small and tight. Get as skinny as you can. Hold tight now. You can relax now. Settle back and let your stomach come back out where it belongs. You can feel really good now. You've done fine.

Legs and Feet

Push your toes down on the floor real hard. You'll probably need your legs to help you push. Push down, spread your toes apart. Now relax your feet. Let your toes go loose and feel how nice that is. It feels good to be relaxed. Okay. Now push your toes down. Let your leg muscles help you put your feet down. Push your feet. Hard. Okay. Relax your feet, relax your legs, relax your toes. It feels so good to be relaxed. No tenseness anywhere. You kind of feel warm and tingly.

Conclusion

Stay as relaxed as you can. Let your whole body go limp and feel all your muscles relaxed. In a few minutes it will be the end of the relaxation exercise. Today is a good day. You've worked hard in here and it feels good to work hard. Okay, shake your arms. Now shake your legs. Move your head around. Open your eyes slowly (if they were closed). Very good. You've done a good job. You're going to be a super relaxer.

Breathing Retraining Script

Ask the child to imagine going on a hot-air balloon ride. As long as the hot-air balloon has fuel supplied by the child's breathing, destinations are unlimited. Ask the child to breathe in through her nose and out through her mouth with a SSSSSSSS sound. You may encourage this process through imagery, such as having a picture of a hot-air balloon nearby. If necessary, have the child count to herself slowly when breathing out. The following is an example:

Imagine going on a ride in a hot-air balloon. Your breathing will give the balloon its power. As long as you breathe deeply, the balloon can go anywhere. Breathe in through your nose like this (demonstrate). Breathe slowly and deeply. Try to breathe in a lot of air. Now breathe out slowly through your mouth, making a hissing sound like this (demonstrate). If you want, you can count to yourself when you breathe in and out.

Homework

✏️ Practice the relaxation and breathing procedure at home every day, twice a day if possible, between sessions. A relaxation log is provided in the parent workbook and multiple copies may be downloaded at the Treatments *ThatWork*™ Web site at www.oup.com/us/ttw. Following each practice, the child should note any difficulties she encountered, such as inability to concentrate or falling asleep during the practice. If a child is too young to write or may not be able to comply with this instruction independently, then a parent should question the child and record any difficulties on the relaxation log.

✏️ The child and parent should continue to complete the daily logbooks.

✏️ Encourage the child and parent to record any specific situations or experiences that arise during the week.

✏️ Encourage general adherence to a regular school-day schedule, even if only in the morning prior to school. This includes early wakening, dressing and preparing for school as if going, and completing school assignments.

SESSION 2 *Intensifying Treatment*

Session Outline

- ◼ Review homework from last session.

- ◼ Prepare the child for exposure.

- ◼ Conduct systematic desensitization using one of the easier items from the child's Anxiety and Avoidance Hierarchy from session 1.

- ◼ Conduct imaginal desensitization.

In session 2, begin to expose a child to school-related objects or situations that provoke her anxiety. Systematic desensitization is a therapeutic process of confronting anxieties in a step-by-step fashion through

---

Special Topic 4.3: When to Keep a Child Home From School

Parents often ask which somatic complaints should keep a child home from school. We recommend a child go to school except when there is:

- A temperature of 100 degrees or more

- Frequent vomiting

- Bleeding

- Lice

- Severe diarrhea

- Severe flu-like symptoms

- Another very severe medical condition such as intense pain

If a child has these problems, seek the advice of a pediatrician. In addition, a child with these problems should remain in bed during the school day or complete schoolwork at home. Do not allow a child to do many fun things during the school day, because this rewards her for missing school. If a child is absent from school for 2 or more days because of these problems, ask parents to contact the child's teacher(s) to arrange for homework that can be completed during the day.

Try to establish an attitude within the family that a child is expected to attend school unless some severe medical problem is present. Minor headaches, stomachaches, or nausea are not enough to keep a child home and might be managed by over-the-counter or prescription medication. If a child's symptoms become more severe during the school day, then she can visit the nurse's office. *Parents will have more success getting a child to go to school if they expect and encourage school attendance every day.* Only extreme circumstances, and not more minor ones such as a cold, should keep a child home from school, especially one with a history of school refusal behavior.

---

imagination (*imaginal* exposure) and real-life situations (in vivo exposure). The effectiveness of systematic desensitization has been well documented as a treatment for anxiety disorders in children and adults. Imaginal systematic desensitization will be followed by in vivo desensitization exercises. For the child and parent, these in vivo practices are called "*Show That I Can*" or *STIC* tasks. Parent support and participation in establishing and conducting these home-based STIC tasks is essential for treatment success.

Preparing a Child for Systematic Desensitization

Explain the term "systematic desensitization" to the child if she is an adolescent and can understand more complex concepts.

Case Vignette

T: Let me ask you something. Do you know how to ride a bike? Or swim? Or do you ski or ride horses? (Probe until you find some activity the child can perform with some skill)

C: Yes, I can ride a bicycle. I learned that when I was 5 or 6.

T: Okay, tell me about what you do when you want to go (biking, skiing, horseback riding).

C: Well, I get my bike out of the garage, and I ride it up the street or to my friend's house.

T: Okay, you have to get the bike out of the garage. What do you think about when you're riding your bike?

C: Nothing. I mean, I think about what me and my friend are going to do. Like maybe we'll play video games.

T: Are you riding your bike in the street or on the sidewalk?

C: Well, I have to ride on the sidewalk. But sometimes I have to cross the street, so I look both ways.

T: And what are you doing with your hands, feet, and eyes when you ride?

C: Nothing. I just pedal and hold the handlebars. And I have to look where I'm going.

T: Okay. So, what you're telling me is that you get on the bike, ride along the sidewalks and street, pedal along, and watch where you're going, and you do not think about those things. Instead, you think about what you're going to do with your friend. Right?

C: Yeah, I guess.

T: Sure, it's automatic that you ride now, and watch out for where you're going. You've learned how to do these things, haven't you? (Child nods) And you do not even think about how you're doing these things anymore. But do you remember when you first went out on the bike? Do you remember that it used to be scary?

Using Socratic questioning, question the child and prompt her to recall the first time riding a bike or doing some similar activity that requires skill. Then, ask her about physical feelings, thoughts, and behaviors that may occur in someone learning to ride for the first time. Ask the child as well about her personal reactions during her initial learning experiences. Focus the child on how initial steps to learning this skill were small, but with practice she developed skill and mastery. The main point to convey is that continued practice and over-learning has made the situation easy and automatic. Next, ask the child about what happened to her initial anxieties:

T: Why aren't you scared of falling off the bike now?

C: Because I don't fall anymore. And if I do, I may get scraped, but it gets better.

T: So, even if you do fall, you know you're going to be okay. Right?

C: Yeah, I've fallen. I just have to get on the bike again. That way I don't get scared again.

T: Right! That's exactly right! You have practiced riding your bike, and you started out in steps. Someone helped you, and you used training wheels. Then you took them off when you started feeling more comfortable and less nervous. Right? So you did this step by step and, as you developed more skill, you became less nervous. Now you do not even think about how you were once nervous.

Introduce the concept of taking steps, one at a time, and mastering each step until little or no anxiety is felt. The imaginal desensitization process can be presented to the child as "practicing thinking about troubling situations." Systematic desensitization involves training a child in progressive muscle relaxation procedures and then alternating the presentation of relaxing scenes with talking through a scene from the child's anxiety hierarchy. When the child indicates that her anxiety is at an uncomfortable level during an anxious scenario, you quickly switch back to the relaxing scene. The child is instructed to raise her hand when anxiety becomes uncomfortable.

Constructing the Anxiety Scenario

Begin with one of the easier steps from the child's AAH. This will be the first situation to confront imaginally. Ask the child about what she thinks will happen in the situation and develop a scenario about that situation based on what the child thinks and is anxious about. You may embellish the scenario to some degree. Often, parents are surprised at the graphic nature and intensity of their child's anxieties. However, note that these are the child's anxieties and, left to her imagination, can continue to develop unchecked. Hence, you must guide a child in thinking about these anxieties, mix in relaxing scenes so the thoughts themselves are no longer frightening, and discuss what is realistic for any given situation. The goal of desensitization is to gradually get a child to listen to an entire anxiety scenario "as if watching a movie" and realize that the scene is not that scary itself. Another goal is to have the child recognize that almost any scenario can be coped with in a positive, proactive way. A sample scenario, using situation 8 from Sandy's AAH (Figure 4.2), follows:

It's after 2 o'clock, and you and your mother are driving to school to see your teacher. You have to go in and get your own homework. You haven't been in school for 3 weeks and haven't really seen any of the other kids or the teacher. The last time you were there you felt real funny in your stomach, and you felt like throwing up. As you get closer to school, you start to feel a bit dizzy and start to sweat a bit. You look up at Mom and want her to turn the car around, but she says you have to get the work. Mom has to stay in the car, because there's no place to park, so you have to go in alone. Mom drives up to the front door of the school. Some kids are there, and some teachers, but not anyone you know. You open the car door and feel really dizzy now, and your stomach feels like you're on a roller coaster. You start to walk up to the door, and you feel really shaky and sweaty. These are the feelings that you get sometimes that scare you. What if you get sick? You look back, and Mom is moving the car and is now pulling out of the school driveway. You walk in through the door and feel so dizzy that you have to hold on to the wall to stay standing. Some kids walk by and laugh. You're really feeling scared now, and it's getting harder to breathe. What if you faint, and no one comes to get you and help you? What if Mom just stays in the car? You start walking down the long hall to the classroom, and when you get there, several kids are in line to see the teacher, so you have to wait. It's really hot in the classroom, and you feel like you might throw up. You're so dizzy now and can taste real sour stuff coming up in your throat. You feel dizzy and faint and wish that the teacher would look at you and help you, but she's talking to someone else. You can feel it coming now: it's at the top of your throat. You yell out for help, and when you do, you get sick all over the place. The teacher and all the kids are looking at you now, with wide eyes. You feel really sick and really embarrassed. If only your mother had come in with you!

Tracking Anxiety During Desensitization

Throughout systematic desensitization, ask a child to rate her anxiety levels using the Feelings Thermometer or other measurement scale. Record the child's ratings. This way, you can illustrate, using charts or graphs, what happened to the child's anxiety during desensitization. These charts or graphs will show how a child gradually mastered her anxiety over the course of treatment.

Some children are able to track their own anxiety levels. Recording their own ratings gives children instant information about how they handled certain situations. The ratings can illustrate how they coped with panic symptoms, separation concerns, fears of specific objects or situations, or any other situation where anxiety ratings can be taken and recorded. You may suggest that parents keep their child's ratings in a log or notebook to remind her of progress made during therapy.

Conducting the Imaginal Desensitization

Audiotape the following desensitization procedure for later processing and for home use. Desensitization begins by instructing the child to raise her hand whenever anxiety becomes uncomfortable (i.e., a level of 3+ on the Feelings Thermometer). Give the child a copy of the thermometer to keep on her lap. You will first conduct a relaxation procedure with the child. During initial sessions, you may wish to present a full relaxation procedure. With repeated practice, you may change the relaxation induction to (1) include breathing retraining, (2) focus on being relaxed in general, and/or (3) focus on releasing tension in specific parts of the body. Instruct the child to listen to you and follow your voice. Ask the child to listen and imagine the scene in her mind as if it is actually happening.

Explain that the child will relax first and you will then talk her through a challenging scene. When anxiety becomes uncomfortable (i.e., 3+), the child should raise a hand to signal this to you and point to the level of discomfort on the thermometer. Ask the child to switch to thinking about something pleasant, such as being on a beach, in the park, or some place relaxing and pleasing for her. Once anxiety declines to a level of 0 or 1, present the troubling scene again. This switching back and forth should continue until the child can tolerate listening to the scene completely without indicating uncomfortable levels of anxiety.

As the child progresses through each scene, ask her to wait to raise a hand until anxiety reaches a level of 4 or 5. This allows her to develop increased tolerance and eventually habituate to sensations and feelings of anxiety. As tolerance increases, these feelings will lose their ability to signal the child to escape or avoid and will allow her to try new situations while tolerating normal levels of arousal. If necessary, divide the anxiety scenario into smaller steps or less volatile scenes. The desensitization process should always end with a relaxation scene.

Processing the Imaginal Desensitization

Invite a parent into the session to discuss the child's progress. To facilitate understanding of desensitization, play a portion of the audiotape for the parent. Encourage the child to explain and demonstrate the pro-

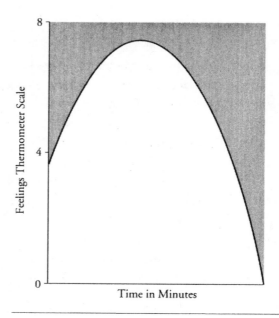

Figure 4.4
Inverted-U Curve

cess to the parent. Ask the child about what happened to her anxiety during the practice. The typical response is that anxiety dropped during the session and the child's tolerance increased with repeated presentations. Illustrate habituation of anxiety during desensitization by drawing an inverted-U curve of the child's anxiety ratings (Figure 4.4).

If the child did not habituate (i.e., anxiety did not drop), then praise her for any effort or degree of participation and process what may have been particularly difficult. Divide the scenario into smaller steps or less volatile scenes. Be sure to praise and encourage a child for making any step, regardless of how small. By praising a child for her efforts, you will also be modeling this behavior for parents. Typically, desensitization begins slowly and the pace increases with time. This may occur in one session or across two or more sessions if necessary.

As noted, the child and parent should be presented with a graphic illustration of the habituation curve. This visual medium provides additional feedback to the child about her specific reaction to a feared stimulus. Note that ratings may be made on a more traditional 0-to-100 scale

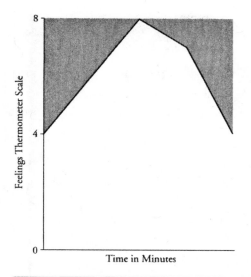
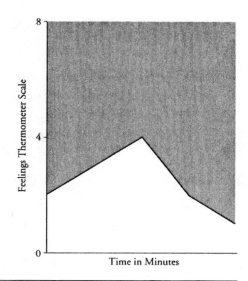

Figure 4.5

Sandy's Anxiety Ratings

(SUDS) or may parallel the 0-to-8 scale on the Feelings Thermometer. As an example, compare in the diagram above Sandy's anxiety about riding the school bus in her first imaginal desensitization session with her anxiety in a later in vivo desensitization practice (Figure 4.5).

Illustrations allow a child to receive concrete information about her initial concerns about riding the bus. In this case, for example, initial anxiety ratings during imaginal practice began near 3 and quickly reached their worst level of 8. However, Sandy can clearly see from her later chart that her anxiety during in vivo situations now starts on a lower level, peaks at a lower level, and dissipates much faster than before. You can help children learn that what they imagine is often worse than what will actually occur, and that they can handle the situation despite anxiety.

Habituation Curves

Examples follow of various habituation curves and some cautionary notes for their interpretation. First, in the "inverted-U" curve shown in Figure 4.4, beware that some children will give lower anxiety ratings over time to please the therapist or escape the exposure. Check for this by ex-

Special Topic 4.4: A Child Who Will Not Ride the School Bus

Many children distressed about school do miss school, but others simply have problems riding the school bus. If your client has problems riding the school bus, she may be worried about becoming sick or getting closer to school. In other cases, though, children cannot say why they get distressed on the school bus.

If your client has this problem, then ask her to take just a short trip on the school bus. This may involve simply standing at the school bus stop, getting on the bus, and then stepping off before a parent drives her to school. Or, the child may get on the school bus and ride it to a later stop, which may be just a minute or so away. As the child does this, she should practice the methods for lowering distress detailed in this chapter. In addition, ask parents to rate a child's level of distress during each step.

As the child masters these early steps, gradually increase the length of time she rides the bus. This may involve riding for a longer period of time or arriving at more stops, for example (perhaps add one stop every few days or so). Praise the child for doing each step successfully. Try to get to the point where a child can ride the bus all the way to school with a parent driving behind the bus.

At this point, work backward. When the child is 5 minutes away from school, for example, the parent should drive away and let her finish alone (you can tell the child in advance about this). Once she can handle this, then gradually increase the amount of time she rides without the parent following behind. Be sure that you and parents praise the child for being able to ride the bus alone.

amining a child's thoughts and behaviors in extended exposures. Second, the "peaks and valleys" curve indicates uneven but continued habituation (Figure 4.6). In this situation, therapists should check for automatic thoughts. This curve may represent a child focusing on negative outcomes at various times. A focus on the child's cognitive restructuring skills may be in order (see chapter 5).

Third, the "steady climb" curve indicates that anxiety is increasing and habituation is not occurring (Figure 4.7). This may indicate that a hierarchy item is too challenging or complex for a child. Divide the item into smaller steps or consider that the child is not yet ready for exposure. If this is the case, then continue to work on somatic management and/or

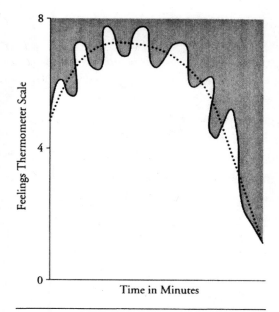

Figure 4.6

Peaks and Valleys Curve

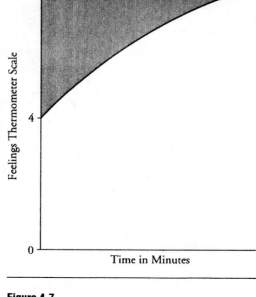

Figure 4.7

Steady Climb Curve

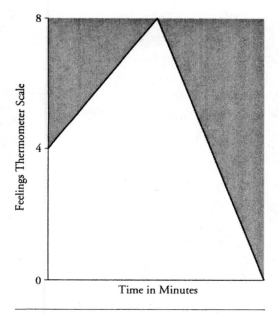

Figure 4.8

Bottoms Out Curve

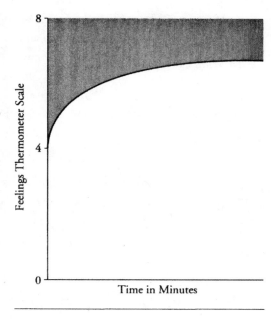

Figure 4.9

Steady-State Curve

begin cognitive restructuring if applicable. Fourth, the "bottoms out" curve indicates a suspiciously fast decline in anxiety (Figure 4.8). In this situation, a child may be trying to escape the exposure. In later sessions, this curve may indicate an appropriately faster habituation, but the level of anticipatory anxiety is still high. In this case, continue somatic management and/or begin cognitive restructuring if applicable. Finally, the "steady state" curve indicates that anxiety remains at a high level and a child is neither habituating nor getting worse (Figure 4.9). This may indicate that a hierarchy item is too complex or the child is focusing on anxiety instead of the situation. In the latter situation, check for automatic thoughts (see chapter 5).

Homework

Homework assignments after session 2 may require more assistance from parents and may include the following:

✎ The child should continue to practice the relaxation procedure using the audiotape or relaxation scripts just before bedtime each night.

✎ At least once daily, the child should listen to the desensitization tape and go through an imaginal procedure (STIC task). The parent can assist by asking for anxiety ratings or by keeping other children from interrupting the procedure. Encourage a parent to talk with the child after each practice. You can model this process, which should involve focusing the child on how anxiety dissipated during desensitization. Also, instruct parents to praise and encourage a child for attempting and/or completing each practice.

✎ Provide the child and parent with structure for each day. Beginning with the next school day after this session, the parent should wake the child about 90 to 120 minutes before school is scheduled to start and implement the normal school-day routine. The child should only complete schoolwork and read school-related books when home during the day.

✎ Instruct the child and parent to continue to maintain the daily logbooks, noting any specific issues or situations that may arise during the week.

Session Outline

■ Review child's progress with systematic desensitization from previous session and address any problems encountered.

■ Introduce the child to in vivo desensitization by working initially on her easiest item from the Anxiety and Avoidance Hierarchy.

Sessions 3 and 4 will continue to focus on systematic desensitization, with an introduction to *in vivo desensitization.* In vivo desensitization involves having a child gradually enter an anxiety-provoking situation and use relaxation techniques to manage anxiety. Parents are expected to arrange a time and place for in vivo desensitization and help a child engage the situation. Parental involvement is, of course, determined by your consideration of the child's age, developmental level, and severity of diagnosis or problem.

Continuing the Systematic Desensitization

Review the child's progress listening to the home-based desensitization tapes (STIC tasks) and process any problems encountered during the week. If the child reports noncompliance with the STIC task, ask her about difficulties completing the task. Some children avoid doing homework to avoid rising feelings of anxiety. If this is so, divide the scenario into smaller and more manageable steps. Plan strategies with the child to increase compliance. You may wish to incorporate coping scenes known as emotive imagery during the desensitization. If a child is having a particularly difficult time listening to a scene and is unable to habituate to anxiety, then present images of the child and a favorite athlete or superhero confronting and coping with the situation. An example of this type of desensitization follows:

You are waiting for your mother to pick you up after school, but she is late! As you stand out front, the other kids are all being picked up, and the teachers have gone back into the school or driven home. It is really getting late, and you are worried that something may have happened to Mom. What if something bad happens to you? You notice that the sky is getting dark, and big thunderclouds are coming. It starts to thunder, and flashes of lightning are happening. You try to go back into the school, but now the door is locked! Where is Mom? You are really scared now and feel like crying. You think something terrible must have happened to Mom, and now you could get caught in the lightning. But wait! You start to think, "What would (name of child's famous role model) *do in this situation?" There must have been times when he had to wait for his parents, and probably he was alone and outside too. Would he cry if he were here? What would he tell you to do? Picture* (name of child's famous role model) *standing next to you. He says, "Okay, you're afraid that something bad happened to Mom, but why else could she be late?" You answer, "Well, maybe she's in traffic, and there are a lot of cars. Or, maybe she had to run an errand and it's taking a bit longer than she thought." (Name of famous role model) tells you, "Yeah! Good thought! She could just be running late. Now, what should you do about the weather here?" Now picture yourself telling* (name of famous role model) *"Well, I suppose I could stand under the awning, and wait by the door. That way I can see Mom when she comes, and I'll be out of the storm." "Great job," says* (name of famous role model). *"Take some deep breaths, and wait by the door for her. She'll be here soon." (Name of famous role model) gives you a high-five, and you feel so proud! Now, picture yourself going to the door, standing under the awning, and waiting calmly for Mom.*

Some children avoid doing STIC tasks because they anticipate that getting better means getting back into school more quickly. If so, focus a child on goals of the program and examine whether additional factors (e.g., attention-seeking, tangible rewards for staying home) need to be addressed more directly in treatment.

Treatment progresses sequentially with the continued development of scenarios for each AAH item. A specific hierarchy item is considered complete when a child can listen to an entire scene completely and report minimal anxiety ratings without switching to a neutral, relaxing scene.

Introducing the Child to the In Vivo Desensitization

In vivo desensitization involves entering and confronting real-life situations or activities. Begin by prompting a child to think about the difference between imaginal confrontation of an anxiety-provoking situation and actually entering the situation. A sample dialogue for how you may present this to a child follows:

Case Vignette

T: Let's think about something. Remember when we talked about how you learned to ride a bicycle?

C: Yes, from practice.

T: Right. And you've been doing a great job here, practicing here and at home imagining doing these things that make you upset.

C: Yes, I "Show That I Can" all the time. I do my practice every day!

T: Yep. That's great! Let's think about something. Suppose that you didn't know how to ride a bicycle. Suppose it was back to that time before you learned how to do that. Can you remember that?

C: Yes, I remember.

T: Okay. Now, suppose that I show you a movie about how to ride a bicycle. And you watch the movie again and again. But, you just watch the movie; you never really get to try a bicycle. Do you think it would be easy to just get on a bike and ride?

C: No, I have to practice on a bike. I'd be all wobbly and could fall down if I don't practice.

T: Right! So, watching the movie may help you to know what it looks like to ride, and it may show you some things to think about while you ride. But you really have to try a bicycle again and again to practice and learn how to ride.

C: Right. You have to get on the bicycle to learn how to ride it.

T: Well, the same thing goes here. We've been imagining going into these situations that scare you, and you've been doing a great job of learning that you do not have to be scared. But we need to help you really go into these situations and practice really being there. Do you understand what I mean?

C: So, I have to ride the school bus?

T: Well, eventually, yes. But first, we'll only practice for real the situations we've done in here and on tape. And we'll work up to the bus and those other things that are really scary for you. We'll do this step by step, just like we do in your imagination. We'll first do it in your imagination, and then we'll do it for real. Taking it easy, going one step at a time, and we'll get Mom and Dad to help out here and there.

Conducting the First In Vivo Desensitization

Initiate in vivo desensitization by having the child role-play one of the easier items from the AAH. This role-play, made as close to reality as possible, will involve the child acting out and confronting an anxiety-provoking situation. For example, if a child is anxious about being alone either at school or home, construct a situation where she waits in a therapy room by herself for a period of time. Initially, set up the situation to be minimally anxiety-provoking and encourage the child to use relaxation and deep-breathing skills to manage anxiety. As the child develops tolerance of the situation, slowly make the situation more challenging and encourage her to refrain from safety behaviors to make herself feel better. Following are examples of trials in graduated in vivo desensitization for a child afraid to be left waiting alone:

1. Sitting alone in the therapy room for 3 and then 5 minutes, knowing that the therapist is in the hall.

2. Sitting alone in the therapy room for 5 and then 10 minutes, knowing that the therapist may not be in the hall.

3. Sitting alone in the therapy room for 10 minutes, with the lights dimmed, and knowing that the therapist is not in the hall.

4. Sitting alone in the therapy room, not knowing how long it will be, with lights dimmed, the therapist not in the hall, and Mom or Dad told not to be in the waiting room.

Desensitization trials begin with assistance from the therapist and with relatively easier situations, and demands increase with each successive trial. The child's expectations also are addressed, as she first knows what to expect in the situation (e.g., trial 1, knowing the therapist is in the hall) but is later exposed to unknowns (e.g., trial 4, not knowing how long it will be). This process is designed to build a child's ability to cope with ambiguous, challenging, and often uncontrollable situations. Anxiety often results from feeling unable to control a situation or predict what could happen in any situation, along with concern that something very negative will occur. These desensitization procedures are focused on teaching a child that even when a person does not have total control in a situation, she can still cope effectively and the worst scenario is not likely to occur. The child learns to tolerate normal levels of arousal while gathering information about her coping resources and skills.

Review each session's progress with the child and parent. Encourage the child to tell her parent about the in vivo desensitization. Offer corrective information or detail during the child's summary. Shape the child's ability to accurately communicate the process and progress of these treatment sessions. In addition, review with the child and parent progress in managing the daily routine. Provide instructions on what steps to take next in adjusting to the school routine. For example, you may suggest that the next STIC task involve a trip to the school library or meeting after school hours with a teacher to collect homework. These tasks combine the in vivo desensitization process with the STIC tasks. Discuss potential problems with adherence to the school schedule, and make recommendations as needed.

Setting the Pace of, and Assistance With, the In Vivo Exposures

There are several ways to conduct in vivo practices to manipulate the pace of the exposure. A slower pace is ideal for younger children, those with special needs, and those with exceptionally high levels of anxiety.

Special Topic 4.5: Sunday Evening Blues

When children finally go back to school, some are still a bit distressed on Sunday evenings before the start of the school week. If your client is distressed in the evenings before school, particularly on Sunday evening, address her concerns. Be supportive but make clear she is expected to attend school the next day. Ask the child to practice the breathing and relaxation methods described in this chapter. In addition, if a child is focused on the entire school week, then encourage her to focus on attending school just one day at a time.

Some parents plan many activities on Sunday night to distract children from thinking about school. Children will still think about school, however, so we recommend that parents plan a fun family get-together on Sunday afternoon and allow a child to rest comfortably Sunday evening. Planning something small but special on Monday evening is also a good idea so a child has something to look forward to. Examples include getting to stay up 20 minutes later as a reward for going to school on time that morning, enjoying a favorite dessert, or playing a game with a parent.

You and parents should talk to the child during the week and praise even minor things such as entering the school building, crying less, and being brave. In addition, point out to the child how going to school helps Mom and Dad. Children should know that you and parents appreciate her efforts, and it is hoped that this praise will make the morning seem less dreadful.

Moving slower allows a child to fully habituate to anxiety and build trust that she will not be forced into anything overwhelming.

In assisted exposure, you or the parent performs the exposure with the child. This allows a child to receive support from a trusted individual and observe a model who manages the situation. These procedures are especially helpful in early sessions, when confronting an anxious situation for the first time, or when more challenging exposures are developed. Educate parents, however, about the difference between *modeling*, where one shows a child how to manage the situation, and *rescuing*, where one takes over and does the situation for the child. A child's anxiety may interact with parents' natural tendencies to comfort their children and lead to rescuing. Therefore, instruct parents to allow their child to experience normal rises in anxiety. Modeling and assisted exposure keep the focus on the child, with the goal of having her confront anxious situations alone.

Several steps make up this process. First, model for the child how to deal with the situation as the child observes. This gives the child a chance to observe how you process and manage a difficult situation. Second, help the child manage the situation together as a team (i.e., with the therapist and/or parents as coaches). Third, have the child manage the situation on her own as words of encouragement are given by a "coach." Prompt the child to use the somatic control exercises during this procedure. Fourth, have the child engage in the situation on her own while verbalizing self-reinforcement for performing the in vivo exposure.

Massed exposure or flooding involves having a child confront a stressor at a high intensity. Rather than gradually progressing up the AAH, the therapist chooses a higher item and begins there. Relaxation procedures are typically downplayed, so the advantage of flooding is less time. The child simply enters the anxiety-provoking situation and endures it until anxiety naturally dissipates. Flooding is not often used with young children, when anxiety is extreme, at the beginning of therapy, for children with chronic school refusal behavior, or for children with social and/or evaluative anxieties. Deciding to use more rapid exposure or flooding depends on a child's progress to this point and whether she understands the reason for this process.

Homework

Homework assignments after sessions 3 and 4 may include the following:

✎ Continue to practice relaxation at bedtime using audiotape or relaxation scripts from the parent workbook.

✎ At least once daily, the child should listen to and conduct a tape (imaginal) desensitization procedure.

✎ An additional STIC task will be assigned, which will involve a minimum of 3 different days practicing an in vivo desensitization. You, the child, and parent should agree on which task to assign. The in vivo desensitization may involve any of the following: practice at home, such

Special Topic 4.6: Gradually Increasing School Attendance

In many cases of school refusal behavior, exposure to the school setting has to occur on a gradual basis. This is most pertinent, of course, to children missing most of the school day. This graded exposure may be done in one or more of several ways, each of which is covered here. Before proceeding with a part-time attendance schedule, however, *meet with relevant school officials* to plot a course acceptable to you and them. Key school officials include a child's guidance counselor, school psychologist, or principal. Find out whom you need to visit to implement a part-time schedule. In addition, explain to this person why you are doing so: to gradually get a child more accustomed to school while easing physical feelings of distress. Monitor attendance daily. Part-time attendance schedules can involve one of several strategies.

Morning

Younger children usually respond best to a part-time schedule that involves some morning classroom time before they are allowed to come home. If you decide on this option, then tell the child she is expected to go to school and a parent (or someone) will pick her up at 10 A.M. Praise appropriate morning preparation and attendance. When the child is home the rest of the day, require her to complete schoolwork collected from her teacher(s). If a child completed all of her schoolwork or none was sent home, then ask her to complete academic tasks such as reading books, practicing multiplication tables, or tackling educational games on the computer.

Do not let a child do fun things during regular school hours. If a child did go to school as planned (even if for only an hour) *and* completed academic tasks during the day, then she can be allowed to play or do other fun things *after* school hours. If a child did not attend school as planned or did not complete academic tasks during the day, then she should be grounded and not allowed fun activities that day. Instead, parents should require the child to work around the house, send her to bed early, and convey that better behavior is expected the next day (for more detailed information about rewards and punishments, see chapter 6).

Track the child's level of distress each day (see chapter 2). Once her level of distress is low when attending school for an hour, another hour can be added. We recommend that the distress level at each step be reduced by at least half. So, if a child's distress rating averages about a 6 every day, then wait until the distress level is 3 or less before pro-ceeding to the next step. If a child still seems quite distressed after some period of time, such as more than one school week, then she may be in school too long. You may wish to reduce her required time in school by 30 minutes, *but still require the child to attend school.*

If a child's distress level becomes low rather quickly, which sometimes happens, then proceed to the next step. The next step can be adding another hour to the school day. The rest of the day should then go as discussed above. Once a child has mastered this step, add an hour at a time until she can attend school for the entire day. Monitor her level of distress and talk to her and her teacher(s) to be sure distress has been truly lowered.

If a child misses the scheduled hour of school, parents should keep trying during the school day to get that hour of attendance. If necessary, parents should sit with the child at school or in the car at school and encourage her every 15 minutes to enter the school building. Be sure the child practices the methods described in this chapter for lowering physical feelings of distress. *An important rule is no backsliding!* If a child has shown she can attend school for at least 2 hours, for example, then this is the *minimum* amount of school she should attend.

Afternoon

Other children prefer to attend school in the afternoon and gradually add more time to school by working backwards. For example, a child may be expected to go to school at 2 P.M. and be allowed to come home as school normally ends (e.g., 3:10 P.M.). In this case, the same gradual process of adding school applies. Once a child can attend school from 2 to 3:10 P.M. with little distress, for example, then an hour can be added (so, 1:00 to 3:10 P.M.). This is continued until full-time school attendance is reached. During the day up to formal school attendance, the child should be completing schoolwork or other academic tasks.

The downside of using this schedule is that a child may refuse to go to school at 2 P.M. and little time is left to salvage some school attendance. Therefore, consider this option very carefully and perhaps as a last resort. This option is probably best for a child whose

continued

parents are confident she will follow through with instructions to go to school in the afternoon.

Lunch

Another part-time school attendance option is to start at lunchtime and work from the middle of the day outward. In this case, require a child to eat lunch with her classmates, which is often an enjoyable and less distressing time for youngsters. The advantage of this approach is that a child is exposed to at least part of the school day and will likely interact with peers who will encourage her to go to class. If you choose this option, then the child is first expected to attend lunch only. She can complete schoolwork or other academic tasks during the morning and afternoon at home.

Once the child can eat lunch at school with ease, gradually increase classroom time just before and just after lunch. A good place to start is 30 minutes before lunch and 30 minutes after lunch. If a child has lunch from 12:00 to 12:45 P.M., require that she be in class from 11:30 A.M. to noon and from 12:45 to 1:15 P.M. As the child is better able to handle this schedule, gradually increase the amount of time in class until full-time attendance is reached.

Favorite Time of Day

Some kids say they would be willing to go to school if they only had to go to science class. So, we tell them: go to science class! *Attending school for at least one class or for at least part of the school day is much better than no attendance at all.* If a child is in this category, then require her to attend a class she likes best. Once the child attends this class regularly with little distress, her second-favorite class can be added. Once the child attends these two classes regularly with little distress, her third-favorite class can be added, and so forth. *Remember: no backsliding!* Once a child has shown she can attend a certain number of classes, this is the *minimum* amount of time she should be in school each day.

Parents may ask whether switching a child's classes is a good idea. If the switch involves just a class or two, this is usually not a problem. If a child wants her entire schedule changed, however, she may be delaying the process of going back to school. Work with a child's guidance counselor to "tweak" the child's schedule if necessary, but make clear to the child she is expected to attend school full-time eventually and no matter what the schedule.

Attending School, but Outside the Classroom

Other children say being in school is not a problem, but being in the classroom is a problem. In this case, arrange with school officials so that she attends school in a supervised setting outside the classroom. A child may, for example, spend the day in the school library doing schoolwork or helping a librarian restock shelves. Or, she may sit in the main, nurse's, or counselor's office all day. Each of these scenarios is much better than sitting home all day.

As a child becomes more used to the school building and becomes more relaxed and less distressed, gradually increase the amount of time she spends in the classroom. This may involve small steps such as an hour at a time or larger steps such as a whole morning or afternoon (whatever the child can handle). If a child resists going to class, arrange to have a couple of her classmates (or the entire class) visit the child and encourage her to come to class. The classmates can, for example, say what fun things they are doing or that they miss the child. Be sure to secure the cooperation of school officials before embarking on this procedure.

as practicing staying alone in a room or the house for varying periods of time; allowing the parent to leave the house and staying with a sitter for varying periods of time; visiting the school bus stop in the morning; visiting the school or some room at the school; or similar situations. Be sure the parent agrees to find time to assist the child with these in vivo practices.

✎ Encourage adherence to a regular school-day schedule, including early wakening, dressing and preparing for school, and completing school assignments. Bear in mind that parents may inadvertently reinforce a child for not going to school. For example, a parent may find it easier to take a child to the store or on errands; however, these types of outings reinforce a child's avoidance of school, increase dependence on the parent, and convey that it is acceptable to be home. Arranging for a sitter or, in the case of responsible older children, leaving the child alone for specified periods is preferred to taking her on such excursions.

Session Outline

- Review the week's progress and examine any difficulties encountered during in vivo desensitization.

- Conduct in vivo exposures involving increased school attendance.

Sessions 5 and 6 involve helping a child move more swiftly and aggressively through the AAH. You may want to schedule two or three sessions per week to facilitate progress or arrange therapy sessions at school or in places outside the office to conduct assisted in vivo practices. Begin to place greater responsibility on the child for identifying challenging situations. Over time, the child will learn to construct and conduct her own exposures and reframe anxiety-provoking situations as positive opportunities to address challenges. The main goal of this phase of treatment is to train a child to recognize when negative emotions occur and immediately set up an exposure and take coping action rather than avoid or escape. The therapist is the expert and the one who assumes responsibility during treatment to transfer his or her knowledge of coping with negative emotions to the parents and child by modeling for and training a parent to conduct in vivo desensitization at home, and helping the child practice anxiety management skills. Through systematic homework assignments, the parent likewise becomes an active and crucial part of the transfer process by fostering a child's sense of control and mastery of negative emotions.

Review of Assigned In Vivo Desensitization and STIC Tasks

Review the week's progress and examine difficulties encountered during in vivo desensitization practices. Examples of assigned tasks include visiting the school and/or teacher, staying alone for increasingly longer periods, and approaching and remaining in other situations. Emphasize the importance of using relaxation and deep-breathing techniques to remain calm during difficult situations and stay in a situation rather than avoiding or escaping. In addition, review the child's progress adhering to a school schedule and her initial attempts at attending classes or school functions.

Stepping Up the STIC Tasks: Eliminating Safety Signals

As treatment continues, increasingly more challenging situations are presented to the child for in vivo desensitization within and between sessions. One focus of the child's desensitization practices should be to enter difficult situations without help or use of "safety signals." A *safety signal* is any object or person one relies on to feel better or less anxious in a situation. Although a safety signal may lessen a child's anxiety in the short term, the long-term use of safety signals maintains anxiety and prevents a child from learning she can manage the situation.

Those with anxiety disorders often rely on safety signals when confronting anxiety-provoking situations. These individuals, for example, carry water bottles, medication, or cellular telephones in the mistaken belief they "need" these things to prevent panic attacks or access help. Similarly, the presence of a safe person (e.g., friend) is often interpreted as someone who can "save" the individual from untoward consequences of a panic attack. Of course, a panic attack only produces discomfort that will pass even if a person does nothing.

Anxious children will likewise develop safety behaviors and safety signals. For example, an anxious child may become more "clingy" or in need of attention and reassurance. Although parents want to comfort their child, frequently doing so may prevent her from learning to manage normal levels of discomfort. Children with anxiety disorders who refuse to attend school due to these negative emotions can often be "bribed" into entering these situations with assistance. For example, some children will ride the school bus only if a certain sibling or friend accompanies them. If the "safety" child is absent, the anxious child resists riding the bus. Similarly, adolescents with panic attacks may require elaborate safety measures such as carrying a cellular telephone in case they need to call for help. Adolescents with panic attacks find it difficult to be away from home or their primary caretaker for fear that no one else will understand or be able to help them if an attack occurs.

Increasing the complexity and challenge of the STIC tasks is important to uncover, and then dispose of, as many of these unnecessary and unhelpful safety signals as possible. Table 4.1 lists some common safety sig-

Table 4.1. Negative Emotions and Behaviors and Accompanying Safety Signals

Negative emotions or behaviors	Safety signals
Worry: "What if" thinking; reassurance-seeking; anxiety in new or changing situations; perfectionism.	Repeated questioning; needing to know every detail and plan; carrying everything in the book bag (anxiety about leaving something behind); rewriting and erasing to get a paper "perfect."
Panic: Fear of the sudden rush of certain body sensations, such as a racing heart, sweating, dizziness, shortness of breath, or shaking.	Having someone always close by "just in case" (e.g., friend, parent); carrying certain objects to feel better (e.g., water, medicine, cellular telephones or beepers); checking the heartbeat or pulse; dropping out of sports or gym activities.
Anxiety about specific objects or situations: Anxiety about fire drills, riding the bus, insects or animals, thunderstorms, a ringing bell, small places like classrooms, doctors, needles, or the dark.	Watching a weather report and anticipating a storm; sleeping with the lights on or needing someone to sleep with the child; earplugs.
Separation anxieties: Anxiety that something terrible will happen when separated from home or loved ones, and then two people will never see each other again.	"Shadowing" or clinging to Mom or Dad; always being in sight of Mom or Dad; never being alone; needing much reassurance if a separation is going to occur.
Sadness, the "blues," or depression: Being down more days than not; feeling hopeless or that things will never work out; feelings of worthlessness or guilt; loss of interest in usual activities; irritability; crying; thoughts of death or harming self.	Clinging; not wanting to be alone; having someone else (parent, friend) solve or handle one's problems due to beliefs that "I can't ever get things right" or "I don't deserve this."

nals for children who refuse school. Help a child construct in vivo practices to confront and challenge these negative emotions. As each practice progresses, accompanying safety signals will be systematically taken away to give the child the opportunity to learn for herself how to manage the situation alone.

In Vivo Practices

Increasing the challenge of the STIC tasks, along with decreasing the use of safety signals, will give a child much-needed experience with managing difficult situations. Begin with an imaginal desensitization so the child is prepared for the in vivo practice situation. The imaginal desensitization will involve describing the child confronting a stressful or anxiety-provoking situation and *not* engaging in a safety behavior. If the child is progressing fairly rapidly, then move quickly to in vivo desensitization. Following are examples of in vivo desensitization plans for three of the most common forms of negative distress in a school refusal population.

Example 1: The Clinging Child—"Don't Leave Me Alone!"

Problem Focus

School refusal due to anxiety about something terrible happening to Mom or Dad, or being kidnapped or killed, or getting lost and not being able to find the way home

Safety Behaviors and Signals

Needing to call home every hour during the school day; needing Mom and Dad to call home every hour when they go out without the children; having Mom or Dad always arrive early to pick up child from school; having Mom or Dad drive down the same streets to prevent getting lost

In Vivo Desensitization Plans

Practice going for increasingly longer periods of time without talking to Mom or Dad, and gradually work up to not knowing their whereabouts. Telephone calls initially can be stretched to every 90 minutes, then to twice in the morning and once in the afternoon, then to once only in the morning, and then to no calls at all. A similar schedule would apply when the parents go out without the children: call home every 90 minutes, then every 2 hours, then once during any 4-hour period, and then not at all.

In vivo practice for anxiety about not being picked up on time would involve having the parent arrive 5 minutes late and giving a plausible excuse (e.g., stuck in traffic), then 10 minutes late with an excuse, then 10 minutes late without an excuse, and then 20 minutes late (working up to 45 minutes). To increase the challenge in this situation, employ "confederates," or assistants who are unknown to the child, who will walk by or ask for directions. Concurrently with this type of exposure, instruct the child about what to do to stay safe if a parent is running late: wait inside the school building and inform the office staff where you are; stay outside and inform a teacher or an adult who is well known that you are waiting for your parents; do not approach strangers; if a stranger approaches you, walk quickly toward a group of kids, an adult who you know, or someone in authority such as a police officer or crossing guard. The goal of this type of exposure is to enhance a child's tolerance for normal inconveniences and to develop the necessary skills to manage and remain safe in an ambiguous situation.

To desensitize anxiety about getting lost, blindfold a child (using a mask or scarf) and, without talking, take the child on a walk around the office building or outside area. Lead the child by the hand, but refrain from conversation. The child's inability to see the surroundings will arouse anxiety and worry. By increasing the practice time, the child will again learn to tolerate an ambiguous situation. Next, ask parents to simulate getting lost by driving on unfamiliar roads and occasionally mumbling, "Oh boy, where are we?" Instruct parents not to give any reassurance to the child and stay "lost" for increasing periods. Tell the parent to verbalize a plan for finding the correct street while remaining calm and in control: "Okay, let's see where we are. Breathe slowly, relax. This is Hylan

Boulevard, and I know that it runs into New Dorp Lane at some point. Take it easy, stay calm and relaxed. I'll keep driving in this direction for another mile. Okay! There's New Dorp Lane! I knew I could find it if I just remained calm!"

Example 2: Pushing the Panic Button—"I Feel Sick and I Need Help!"

Problem Focus

Panic attacks occur in various situations or places, and may cause nausea, dizziness, shortness of breath, heart palpitations, sweating, shaking, numbing or tingling sensations, and feelings of unreality. These attacks seem to come "from out of the blue" and may have happened to the child in school, on the bus, in public places such as malls and movie theaters, and/or in crowds.

Safety Behaviors and Signals

Carrying a paper bag in case of hyperventilation, a bottle of water to keep the throat "open," and a cellular telephone to call for help; needing to have Mom available by telephone at all times; parents rearranging their work schedules to drive the child to and from school to avoid the bus that "triggers my panic attacks"; attending school only for half days because panic is more likely to occur in the afternoon; staying home to rest in bed each afternoon to stave off panic; being given an open pass by the teacher to go to the school nurse at any time during class if any panic symptoms are felt (on average, spending at least 1 hour each morning with the nurse), and then lying on a cot.

In Vivo Desensitization Plans

For those with panic attacks, interoceptive exposure exercises help desensitize a child to the physical sensations of panic. Interoceptive conditioning is the process of learning to be afraid of physical sensations. In-

Table 4.2. Interoceptive Exposure Exercises for Target Sensations

Spinning in a chair	Dizziness, lightheadedness
Running in place or up stairs	Shortness of breath, racing/pounding heart
Breathing through a straw	Shortness of breath, chest tightness
Staring at a light and then reading	Visual disturbances, unreality
Shaking head from side to side	Lightheadedness
Tensing all muscles, and holding them very tight	Muscle tension, tingling sensations
Hyperventilation	Shortness of breath, pounding heart, lightheadedness, tingling sensations
Putting your head down below the knees, and then "popping" up very quickly	Lightheadedness, dizziness, unreality

dividuals who experience panic begin to feel a change in their physical state and become vigilant about the change and scared of its implications. They thus typically avoid running up stairs, aerobic activity, drinking caffeinated beverages, or other situations or activities that may cause physical changes. One key to overcoming panic is to learn to tolerate normal physical arousal and changes without becoming frightened and distressed. Interoceptive exposure involves the systematic provocation of these sensations over repeated trials to reduce anxiety. Construct a hierarchy of sensations that scare a child and begin exposure with the least-anxiety-provoking sensation, then gradually progress to exercises designed to elicit the sensation at higher and higher intensities. Typical exercises and their targets are listed in Table 4.2.

The goal of having a child engage in these exercises is to teach her that these sensations are temporary, predictable, and controllable. Most importantly, the child learns that changes in physical states are normal and harmless. Forewarn parents that a child will be somewhat uncomfortable, but only temporarily. The sensations of a panic attack are harmless and will eventually dissipate even if the child does nothing. Most importantly, the child will learn that normal functioning does not have to be altered because she experiences panic attacks.

Encourage the child to enter situations she avoids. Instruct the child to gradually leave safety signals (e.g., paper bags, cellular telephones, water bottles) at home. Slowly increase school attendance and limit visits to the nurse. These steps involve cooperation with the teacher and school nurse, so be prepared to communicate how they may coach the child to comply with the desensitization. Similarly, practice at home will involve spending less time in bed and an increasing amount of time engaging in physical activities (e.g., bike riding) that arouse physical sensations. Instruct the child to use deep breathing whenever anxiety is aroused and to remain in the situation despite experiencing panic-like sensations.

For further detail regarding this technique, read *Mastery of Your Anxiety and Panic, Therapist Guide, 4th Edition,* available from Oxford University Press.

Example 3: The Worrier—"What If, What If, What If?"

Problem Focus

Excessive worry about new situations, changes in routine, or doing things perfectly or to an unrealistic standard; difficulty with concentration and resting and sleeping well; complaints of muscle tension or aches; and repeatedly asking the same question, in the same manner

Safety Behaviors and Signals

Constantly seeking reassurance from parents, teachers, and peers; teacher reporting that the child is "always at my desk"; child needing to know what the family's plan is for every day of the week and having difficulty if plans are changed or unexpected events occur

In Vivo Desensitization Plans

Teach the child to experience less-than-perfect or less-than-desired circumstances and accept consequences without asking for reassurance. For example, ask a child who is an extreme perfectionist and puts undue pressure on herself to purposely make mistakes on homework papers or in sporting activities (e.g., strike out in baseball). Similarly, ask a child overly preoccupied with looking perfect to wear something wrinkled, have messy hair, and not use the mirror to check on her appearance (see also chapter 5). Do not provide reassurance to the child. Instruct parents to refrain from responding to her when she repeatedly asks, "Do you think this is okay?" Help parents set limits on reassurance-seeking (see parent workbook and chapter 6). When the in vivo desensitization involves making mistakes on schoolwork, ask the teacher to expect a change in the child's work and to prepare some worksheets that will not enter into the child's official grade. Teach the child that even if mistakes occur, there are usually no long-term consequences, and most mistakes can be remedied.

For a child overly concerned with details of plans and activities, teach her to confront unknown and changing experiences. Have the parent schedule an outing that involves several planned stops (e.g., first to the mall, then to Grandma's house, then to the library). Typically, children who worry excessively will want to know all details of each stop, such as how long they will be there, what will happen, and who else may be involved. Instruct parents to change the order of the plans (e.g., go to Grandma's first) and the length of time the child expects to be in each place (e.g., leaving ahead of schedule or staying longer in one place). As the child begins to adjust, have parents advance desensitization by confronting established expectations (e.g., Grandma is not at home, the library is closed) and canceling an individual element of the plan. Lastly, tell parents to cancel an entire scheduled outing at the last minute without giving notice to the child.

Homework

Homework assignments after sessions 5 and 6 may include the following:

- ✎ Practice the relaxation tape at bedtime and complete daily logbooks.
- ✎ STIC tasks will involve various in vivo desensitization plans, in addition to imaginal desensitization as needed.

✎ Attendance in school will be increased over the course of these sessions, with the goal of having the child attend most of the day, every day.

SESSIONS 7 & 8   *Completing Treatment and Preparing for Termination*

The main focus of this latter part of treatment is to have a child spend increasingly longer periods of time in school, with the eventual goal of full-time attendance. Initially, you may wish to accompany the child to school or arrange your scheduled appointments in a private office of the school building during the day (e.g., a non-academic class period such as study hall). These assisted exposures may prompt a child to progress more rapidly to full-time attendance. Once the child has returned to school, however, therapy appointments should be avoided during school hours. Appointments may continue at school after school hours if appropriate. At this point, have the child take most of the responsibility for treatment and apply what was learned in real-life situations. Continue to implement techniques from previous sessions to help the child achieve this goal.

Chapter 5

Children Refusing School to Escape Aversive Social and/or Evaluative Situations

Materials Needed

- Model of Anxiety

- Thought Bubble

- Anxiety and Avoidance Hierarchy

- Feelings Thermometer

Session Outline

- Teach the child about social anxiety.

- Work with child to create an Anxiety and Avoidance Hierarchy.

- Help child develop a plan to identify and change negative thoughts using the STOP method.

- Help child identify automatic thoughts.

  Many people can recall when being in a social situation, being the focus of attention, or being tested or evaluated was accompanied by butterflies, shaking, or some other indication of anxiety. For most people, these initial feelings of anxiety disappear quickly and their ability to perform in the social or evaluative situation is not impaired. Many people can also recall times during their school years when being called on in class to give an oral report, being teased by others, or taking a test would also trigger physical sensations of anxiety. For some children, anxiety in social and evaluative situations is so distressing that they cannot tolerate these situations. Instead, avoidance behavior takes over. Treatment for children who refuse school to escape aversive social and/or evaluative situations will involve:

- Teaching a child to identify what he tells himself in anxiety-provoking situations

- Learning a method to change negative thoughts to coping, helpful statements

- Developing graduated exposure to anxiety-provoking social or evaluative situations in session with the therapist

- Gradually increasing school attendance

- Practicing coping skills in real-life social and evaluative situations

Treatment for children with social and/or evaluative anxiety requires you to work with the child for most of the session. Parents are invited into the last part of the session to add input, review material, and plan homework. If a child has been avoiding social situations such as attending parties, initiating or joining conversations, or talking on the telephone, give parents specific instructions about ways to help the child enter those situations. Similarly, if a child has difficulty with evaluative or performance situations, he will learn to engage those situations in a graduated and structured manner.

Psychoeducation

Treatment begins with an explanation of the nature and process of social and evaluative anxiety. Explain this process in a manner that young children or children with special needs will understand. Anxiety is divided into three components: physical (*What I feel*), cognitive (*What I think*), and behavioral (*What I do*). The following is an example of explaining to a child how the interaction of these components maintains social anxiety:

Do you remember what it was like the first time you tried to ride a bicycle? Think back to how you felt getting on the bike for the first time. Were you able to just jump on it and ride away, or did you feel shaky and think you might fall? Remember how it was to have someone hold onto the seat, to help you be steady? What did you think would happen if they let go of the seat and left you to go on your own? Well, with practice, again and again, you learned to feel comfortable and ride that bike straight and steady. Do you think about how scared you were, whenever you jump on a bike now? Of course not! Because you got used to riding the bike, now you do not even notice if you feel a little shaky at first.

Now, what do you think would have happened if, that first time you were on a bike, feeling all shaky, you got off the bike and never got back on it again? What if you told yourself, "This is too scary! I may fall, and then I could get hurt." Do you think you would've wanted to jump back onto that bike again? No way! If you tell yourself that something is scary, and that you can't do something, then it really feels scary and it keeps you from wanting to try again. This is the same thing that happens to some people when they have to give an oral report, or play an instrument in front of other people, or take a test in school, or even when they try to start conversations. Because they tell themselves it's a scary situation, and that they can feel shaky or butterflies or such, then they do not want to do those things anymore. And, the more they avoid those things, the worse it can get. This is because they feel more afraid than they really would be in that situation.

To illustrate the physical, cognitive, and behavioral components of anxiety, draw three circles, each depicting one component. Ask the child to identify his own physical feelings, thoughts, and behaviors when confronted with a social anxiety situation (completed circles in Figure 5.1 from the above dialogue).

You may wish to use cartoons or pictures from magazines that depict children in various situations such as standing near a group of children or talking with an adult. Using a Thought Bubble (Figure 5.2), for example, ask the child to describe what the child in the picture may be feeling, thinking, and doing. This procedure allows you to understand what provokes a child's anxiety and how the child interprets various situations. Connect the three circles with arrows and, using other arrows or your own drawings, illustrate for the child the process of escalating anxiety as

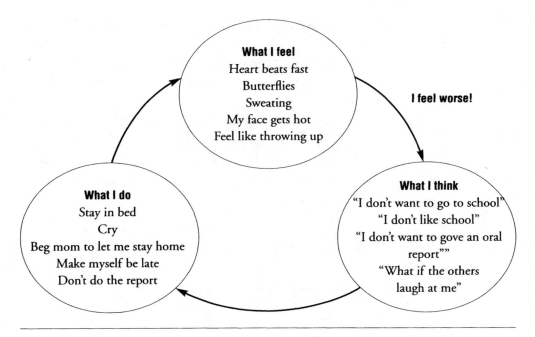

Figure 5.1
Anxiety Model

well as the opposite process of calming or de-escalation. Convey the notion of an interaction among the three anxiety components.

Building an Anxiety and Avoidance Hierarchy

The Anxiety and Avoidance Hierarchy (AAH) is a list of situations or activities most upsetting to a child and that will be actively targeted during treatment (see chapter 4). For these children, aversive social and/or evaluative situations will be emphasized. Most children progress through several hierarchies over treatment until all upsetting situations are challenged. Figure 5.3 presents an AAH for a 12-year-old boy who refused to attend school due to anxiety about social and evaluative situations. Steps on the AAH are gradual, so Mark will begin with the easiest (or lowest) item and progress to the most difficult (highest) hierarchy item. To help address cognitive and behavioral components of a child's anxiety, have him rate anxiety and avoidance of these situations at each session. Independent ratings from parent(s) are also helpful for gathering information about a child's behavioral strengths and limits.

Figure 5.2
Thought Bubble

To create an AAH, review information gathered from a child and parent(s) during assessment and note additional situations you may have learned. Organize the information by writing each situation on a separate index card. Keep several blank cards for additional information you uncover during treatment. Present the index cards to the child and ask him to sort the situations into categories based on the Feelings Thermometer (see chapter 4, Figure 4.3). Ratings on the Feelings Thermometer range from 0 (none) to 8 (very, very much). Based on the child's ratings, construct the first 10-item AAH using the 10 lowest-ranked items. A blank AAH form can be found in the previous chapter, as well as in the corresponding parent workbook. It is also available for download from the Treatments *ThatWork*™ Web site at www.oup.com/us/ttw. For the remainder of treatment, have the child rate his anxiety and avoidance of these situations at each session to give you feedback and an ongoing measure of behavior change. Ask parents to complete separate ratings for the AAH, thereby providing valuable cross-informant information and a broader and more accurate view of a child's functioning. Begin all sessions with one AAH form for the child and one for each parent.

Special Topic 5.1: Panic Attacks

Some parents say a child has "panic attacks" because he feels distressed or anxious for as long as 3 to 4 hours. But being generally distressed *does not necessarily mean* one is having a panic attack. Instead, a panic attack involves *a short period of time,* often 10 to 15 minutes, in which a person suddenly and for little reason experiences many physical feelings and becomes terrified. These physical feelings usually include increased heart rate (feeling of heart "pounding"), sweating, shaking, hot flashes, shortness of breath, nausea, dizziness, chest pain, trouble swallowing, and numbness or tingling sensations.

With these physical feelings often come thoughts or worries about dying, losing control, or going crazy. Panic attacks usually start very suddenly and often without warning, but end just as quickly. Panic attacks themselves are *harmless,* but people with panic attacks often worry that the physical feelings are dangerous. In addition, many people with panic attacks eventually avoid different social, evaluative, and public situations because they are afraid of having a panic attack and being humiliated as a result.

If your client is generally distressed about school, he is not likely having a panic attack. Social worry or distress that lasts for a while is different and is the focus of this chapter. Also, panic attacks are quite unusual in children younger than age 13 years. However, some teenagers do have panic attacks. If you feel your client is having specific and severe panic attacks related to school, then note the interoceptive procedures discussed in chapter 4.

Identifying Negative Thoughts

Anxiety about social and evaluative situations is largely the result of negative thoughts or "self-talk." When anticipating a social or evaluative situation, an anxious child is likely to focus on what could go wrong, how bad he may look, or the belief that others will laugh or think badly of him. During these situations, children may focus on negative thoughts instead of how things are really progressing. As a result, anxiety increases and can overwhelm a child. You will help the child develop a plan to identify and change these negative thoughts.

For young children, the acronym S-T-O-P (Silverman & Kurtines, 1996) may be used to help identify and change negative thoughts:

Problem: School refusal due to anxiety about social or evaluative situations

Situations or Places That Scare Me!	Anxiety Rating	Avoidance Rating
1. Starting a conversation with two kids I don't know well	8	8
2. Going to the lunch room, and sitting with some kids I don't know too well	8	7
3. Volunteering to read out loud or write on the blackboard	7	7
4. Calling up someone from class and asking about the homework	7	7
5. Raising my hand to answer a question	6	7
6. Giving an oral report	6	6
7. Answering and talking on the telephone when it rings at home	5	4
8. Asking the teacher for help or to explain something	4	4
9. Ordering my own food in the cafeteria or a restaurant	4	4
10. Starting a conversation with someone I know	3	3

Figure 5.3

Mark's Anxiety and Avoidance Hierarchy

S: Are you feeling **Scared?**

T: What are you **Thinking?**

O: **Other Helpful Thoughts?**

P: **Praise** yourself for using these steps and **Plan** for the next time

Depending on a child's age and developmental level, you may rehearse these steps sequentially with the child and focus on using the steps in different social or evaluative situations that may trigger anxious thoughts. However, the child does not have to learn the steps in detail. In fact, younger children and those with limited cognitive abilities respond well to a picture of a **STOP** sign, which can be used as a signal to "stop and think" when confronting an anxious situation (Figure 5.4).

Older children and adolescents can be taught to identify automatic thoughts (ATs). ATs are negative, unhelpful, anxious thoughts that seem

Figure 5.4
Stop Sign

to happen automatically and focus us on what is dangerous or alarming about a situation. Beck and colleagues (1979) identified a number of automatic thoughts or cognitive distortions in people with depression. These cognitive errors also pervade the thoughts of anxious people and can make a truly benign situation seem very upsetting. Examples of common ATs are:

All-or-None Thinking: It must be perfect. I can't do this at all.

Catastrophizing: This is the worst thing that can happen to me.

Overgeneralization: I never do anything right.

Negative labeling: I'm such an idiot. I'm so stupid.

Can'ts or Shoulds: I can't ever get this right. I can't do this. I should have done better.

Mind Reading: She thinks I'm stupid. I know they don't like me.

Fortune-Telling: I'm going to fail this test. Nobody is going to talk to me.

Canceling the positive: (This usually occurs when someone gives a compliment) I should have done better. This wasn't my best work.

In session 1, your main focus is to help a child identify his thoughts in situations that trigger anxiety. Step 1 will be to teach a child to recognize cues or "triggers" for his anxiety (focus is on the "S" step). You may wish to have younger children draw pictures of things that cause anxiety. Ask older children to maintain a logbook or list of situations that cause anxiety and a list of thoughts that occur when they encounter an anxiety-provoking situation. These lists can be used to help a child identify how he anticipates and predicts negative events.

The Coaching Team

We recommend you present to the parents and child the concept of working as a team, such as a football, basketball, or baseball team. In this analogy, place the child as the "key player" (e.g., quarterback, point guard, pitcher), the therapist as the "head coach," and the parents as "sideline coaches." This provides a framework for restructuring a family's interactions regarding anxiety-provoking situations, and for integrating procedures and lessons learned in therapy into the child's everyday life. Initially ask the child to name his favorite sport and use that sport to illustrate the coaching process. Provide the parents and child with an explanation similar to the following:

Let's think about how (quarterback and most recent Super Bowl-winning team) work together. After all, they're a Super Bowl-winning team, right? When (quarterback) first got to the pros, he was really new at being a pro quarterback. He had to learn the plays and practice them over and over. So, at first, his coach would call him over to the sidelines and tell him which plays to run. Have you ever noticed how the quarterback of a football game runs to the sidelines to talk with the coach? As time went on, (quarterback) became better at calling the plays. The coach let him call more plays, and after each game they talked about what worked best, and what (quarterback) could do differently in the next game. Well, at this point, (quarterback) now calls the plays himself. He doesn't really go to the coach anymore, unless there's something really tricky going on, like fourth down with only inches to go!

This is very much like how we are working together. At first, I, the head coach, will call all the plays. As the head coach, I'll help you figure out the STOP plan for changing and challenging your negative thoughts. I'll work closely with you, figuring out what practices will be best to help you learn to tackle your anxiety. The sideline coaches are Mom and Dad. They're going to help you at home. This is what happens in football practice. The other coaches help at practice a lot. So, Mom and Dad will help make sure there's time to do your therapy homework assignments. They will also help coach you on using your STOP steps. Your parents will remind you to use the STOP steps, and can even help you question your negative thoughts. As you get better at using your STOP steps, I'm going to let you call more of your own plays! You will start to figure out what practices would be best, and how to challenge your anxiety.

So, the whole team will assist you at first, but as you get to really understand the plays, then you can start to call them on your own.

This analogy helps illustrate for parents the process of helping a child learn the anxiety management skills and exposure plans and set up the initial exposures. However, with time and practice, the child will assume greater responsibility for his own therapy. A primary reason for using a coaching analogy with families is to help change family interactions that have developed since the onset of school refusal behavior. Typically, parents and children with school refusal develop patterns of struggling, arguing, and fighting in response to a child's misbehavior. Because some parents "have tried everything" to get a child to attend school, they may feel frustrated and hopeless about what will work. In fact, each time a new episode of whining, begging, crying, or stalling occurs, a parent's level of frustration begins at a higher level than before and a child's behaviors intensify quickly. This results in negative interactions and crying and fighting.

The sports team analogy is intended to help put a parent–child relationship on neutral ground while gradually building a healthy and productive style of problem-solving and positive interactions. The coach should assist (not coerce) and offer encouragement to follow a plan of action. Instruct parents to offer praise and other forms of positive attention (smiles, hugs) when a child is successful. However, if the child is unsuccessful, ask parents to remain neutral and not judge the child's behavior or intentions. Try role-playing to teach parents how to manage typical interactions that occur in the family. If necessary, help family members coach a child's behavior by introducing contingency management and communication skills training techniques (see chapters 6 and 7).

Homework

✎ The child should maintain a log of situations that cause anxiety. Parents can maintain a separate log to provide you with more information about the child's reactions.

✎ Have the child and parent continue to complete the daily logbooks. Request that they note specific situations or experiences that arise during the week.

✎ Encourage general adherence to a regular school-day schedule, even if only in the morning prior to school. This includes early wakening, dressing and preparing for school as if going, and completing school assignments.

SESSION 2 *Intensifying Treatment*

Session Outline

■ Review the past week and help the child identify anxiety triggers and negative thoughts.

■ Begin behavioral exposures.

This session will begin with a continued focus on a child's self-talk. Specifically, this will involve teaching a child to identify and dispute negative, unhelpful thoughts. Through the use of behavioral exposures, you will prompt the child's anxiety reactions and his use of coping self-talk skills. In a behavioral exposure, the therapist and child role-play an anxiety-producing situation (e.g., starting a conversation with someone in the cafeteria). The purpose of this role-play is to prompt a child to experience anxiety and identify negative thoughts that perpetuate anxiety. You can then help the child dispute these thoughts. Behavioral exposure will allow a child to practice gradually entering situations that cause anxiety, gain experience, and eventually master these situations. Real-life (in vivo) practice entering these situations occurs between sessions, often with parental assistance. These real-life practices are called "Show That I Can" or STIC tasks.

Consider the level of parental involvement in treatment. The degree of parental involvement will depend on the age and developmental level of the child and the individual characteristics of the situation. Younger children may benefit from more parental involvement and assistance than adolescents. Parents of younger children can coach a child in using the cognitive restructuring procedures and can assist by establishing in vivo practices for the child. For example, if a young child has difficulty speaking with adults, a parent may arrange to have several adult friends available to practice conversations with the child. The parent can likewise take the child to a restaurant or store, and have the child interact with workers in making change or placing a food order.

Adolescents (ages 13 years and older) can take more responsibility for arranging and conducting their own in vivo practices, but this decision varies according to the adolescent's developmental level and the clinical

---

Special Topic 5.2: Extracurricular Activities

Extracurricular activities refer to school-related clubs, groups, teams, and other peer gatherings where kids share a common interest and can make new friends. Extracurricular activities can actually have a strong impact on school attendance. Many youths have trouble attending school because they feel isolated, lonely, and "on the outside looking in." They may be in a racial minority, new to a school, or shy in general. As a result, they sometimes do not feel motivated to attend class. If this applies to your client, then one way to change this is to get him more involved in extracurricular activities so he can develop friends who might share his classes.

Obtain a list of available extracurricular activities from the child's guidance counselor or knowledgeable school official. Discuss with the child which activities interest him the most. Some activities will be more liked than others, and the child can try those first. We recommend that the child try at least three activities for a month. In this way, if one or two do not work out, another is still available. Also, encourage the child to make friends with peers in these groups. Encourage him to call these other kids on the telephone, make plans to see a movie, or invite them for dinner.

severity of the diagnosis. Parents can help set up the logistics of an exposure (e.g., driving the adolescent to the mall or a friend's home), but the burden of actually conducting the exposure is on the adolescent.

Challenging and Changing Negative Thoughts

Review the past week and focus on identifying triggers of the child's anxiety as well as corresponding negative thoughts and images. Using a chalkboard or flip chart, help the child identify his specific pattern of arousal and negative thoughts. The Socratic questioning method is preferred to encourage a child to think through the situation and identify his own reactions. The following is an example of dialogue that may accompany this exercise with a younger child.

Case Vignette

T: So, one of the things that happened last week was that you walked out to the playground, and a bunch of kids were already playing a game. This made you nervous?

C: Yeah, I was upset.

T: Okay, so the "trigger" was seeing a group of kids playing a game. Let's write that up here on the board, and call it the trigger (Figure 5.5). Okay, so think about what was going on right before you saw the kids. You were walking out of the school, headed toward the playground. What were you thinking?

C: I don't know. I wanted to go out and play.

T: Okay, so you wanted to go play. Did you think about what game you wanted to play, or who you might play with?

C: Yeah, I thought I'd play tag with my friend Bethany. I was looking for her.

T: Okay, and how were you feeling right then, before you got out onto the playground?

C: I wanted to play, and was glad that it was recess. I felt happy.

T: Then you saw the kids playing together. What did you notice then?

C: Bethany was out there with a bunch of kids. I got nervous.

T: All right, that's the "S" in STOP. Let's put that on the board. When you say that you saw Bethany with a bunch of kids, that's when you first noticed you were scared. Now, what were you thinking?

C: I don't ever really play with those kids. Bethany may not want to play with me. What if they don't want to play with me? (The therapist writes these thoughts on the board under "T.")

T: Okay, let's look at these thoughts that you are having. One at a time we'll look at each. Start with "I don't ever play with those kids." Do you remember back before you used to play with Bethany? Before you knew her?

C: Yes, in first grade.

T: Were you afraid to go and play with her, when you first saw her?

C: A little. But we started playing together. And it was okay.

T: So once you started playing together, you were less and less scared?

C: Yeah, I wasn't scared of her anymore. We became friends then.

T: Right! There's always a time when we haven't done something, but once we do it, it gets easier. So, what other things can you say to yourself instead of "I never play with those kids"?

C: Well, I haven't played with them before, but I could get to play with them and know them. (The therapist writes these thoughts on the board under "O.")

T: Great! That's a really helpful thought, and gives you a good plan for what to do.

Question the child about each negative thought and urge him to think about his experience with similar situations. This process will teach the child to examine evidence for these thoughts and dispute the thoughts with rational, realistic thinking. The following questions are called "dispute handles" and are commonly used to refute anxious thoughts:

Trigger	Scared?	Thoughts?	Other helpful thoughts?	Praise!
Recess	Seeing Bethany playing with a bunch of kids	I don't ever play with them. Bethany may not want to play with me. What if they don't want to play with me?	I haven't played with them before, but I could try and get to know them!	This is a good plan for me!

Figure 5.5
STOP Example

Am I 100% sure that this will happen?

Can I really know what that person thinks of me?

What's the worst thing that can really happen?

Have I ever been in a situation like this before, and was it really that bad?

How many times has this terrible thing actually happened?

So what if I don't get a perfect grade on this test?

Am I the only person that has ever had to deal with this situation?

Help the child process several troublesome situations using the STOP procedure. This will help the child practice challenging and changing negative thoughts. Once the child has worked through various STOP examples, proceed to the next section of the session, behavioral exposure.

Tracking Anxiety During Behavioral Exposure

Before each behavioral exposure, ask the child for an anxiety rating. This is the child's best estimate of how nervous or anxious he feels. You can have the child use a Feelings Thermometer or other measurement scale to anchor his rating. Take anxiety ratings every minute during the exposure. Most exposures last 10 to 15 minutes, although you have the flexibility to stop or prolong the exposure based on a child's reactions. Record the child's ratings throughout treatment. Also, prior to the exposure, ask the child to define several very specific goals for the exposure. These goals should be concrete, observable, and attainable behaviors or actions that the child will work toward performing. For example, in an exposure focused on starting and maintaining a conversation, a child may have the following goals: I will introduce myself and say hello, I will ask two questions, and I will look up and make good eye contact during the conversation.

Keep track of whether a child meets these goals during the exposure. After the exposure, discuss with the child how he feels and whether he thinks the goals were met. Using graphics on a flip chart or board, present the child's anxiety ratings and evaluate each goal. Process the exposure with the child, focusing on his behavior, whether anxiety interfered with performance, and whether the child was able to use the STOP procedures to change negative thoughts. Discuss strategies for building on successes and overcoming trouble encountered during the exposure. The main lesson in this process is that practice helps and that anxiety will naturally go away as a child learns to focus on the situation instead of his feelings.

Some children are able to track their own anxiety levels. Recording their own ratings gives children instant information about how they handled a certain situation. The ratings can illustrate how they coped with any situation where anxiety ratings can be taken and recorded. You may ask a child to maintain his ratings in a log or notebook to remind him of progress made during therapy.

Initial Behavioral Exposures

Help the child choose a relatively easy situation on his AAH. Through the use of role-playing or behavioral exposure, create the situation in the session and allow the child to practice using the STOP procedures. Behavioral exposures provoke anxiety. This allows the child to practice using anxiety management skills while approaching and engaging in situations that he normally avoids. Instead of responding to normal levels of anxiety by trying to escape or avoid, the child will learn to tolerate normal rises in anxiety and allow these feelings to go away naturally while remaining in the situation. Behavioral exposures allow a child to gain mastery and control over his anxiety reactions. The parent workbook includes a detailed explanation of the process and purpose of behavioral exposures.

Processing Exposures

Ratings are kept throughout the exposure to track a child's progress. Throughout treatment, give the child feedback about what happened to his anxiety during the exposures. Illustrate the process of mastering anxiety and negative feelings by drawing a graph of the child's anxiety ratings. This graphically presented feedback allows you to process the exposure with the child, focus his behavior, and decide whether anxiety was interfering in performance and whether the child was able to use the STOP procedures to change negative thoughts. You can then discuss strategies for improving on these successes and overcoming tough spots or any trouble encountered during the exposure. The main lesson in this process is that practice helps, and that anxiety will just naturally go away as a child learns to focus on the situation and not his feelings. Following each exposure, present the child and parent with the graphic illustration of the habituation curve (see next section). Anxiety ratings may be made on the Feelings Thermometer or some other measurement scale.

Some children are able to track their own anxiety levels on a rating sheet. Exposure charts give children instant information about how they handled a certain situation and can be used to illustrate coping with any social and/or evaluative situation where anxiety ratings can be taken and recorded. Encourage the child and parent to maintain these charts in a logbook to later remind the child of his progress.

An Exposure Record Form is provided here, as well as in the parent workbook. You may photocopy this form or download multiple copies from the Treatments *ThatWork*™ Web site at www.oup.com/us/ttw.

Exposure Record Form

Child's Name: _____ Date: _____

Description of hierarchy item or situation: _____

_____

_____

Exposure number: _____ Persons involved: _____

_____

Goals for this exposure: **Tracking of Goals**

1. _____   _____

2. _____   _____

3. _____   _____

4. _____   _____

Exposure Record   **Rating**   **Comments**

1 minute   _____   _____

2 minutes   _____   _____

3 minutes   _____   _____

4 minutes   _____   _____

5 minutes   _____   _____

6 minutes   _____   _____

7 minutes   _____   _____

8 minutes   _____   _____

9 minutes   _____   _____

10 minutes   _____   _____

The following graphs provide examples of common habituation curves. Use extreme caution when interpreting these curves. The "Inverted-U" curve (Figure 5.6) illustrates the expected curve and typical slope of habituation. However, some children will give lower anxiety ratings over time to please the therapist or escape the exposure. Check for this by examining a child's thoughts and behaviors in extended exposures. Figure 5.7 illustrates the "Peaks and Valleys" curve that is consistent with uneven but continued habituation. This curve may represent focusing on negative outcomes at various times. Examine the child for automatic thoughts and possibly focus on cognitive restructuring skills.

The "Steady Climb" curve in Figure 5.8 indicates that anxiety is increasing and habituation is not occurring. The exposure session may be too challenging or complex for the child. Divide the exposure into smaller steps or re-evaluate a child's readiness to confront the situation. Continue to work on cognitive restructuring and/or begin somatic management (see chapter 4) if applicable. The "Bottoms Out" curve (Figure

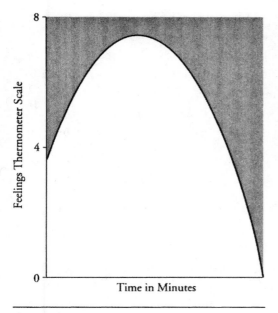

Figure 5.6
Inverted-U Curve

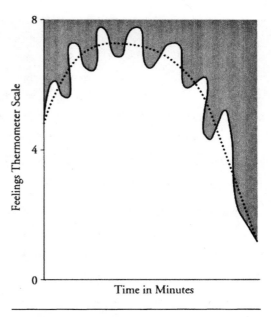

Figure 5.7
Peaks and Valleys Curve

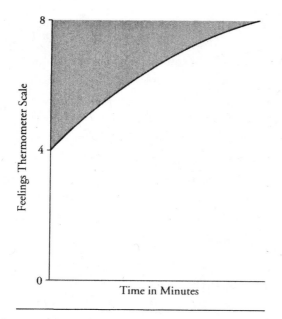

Figure 5.8

Steady Climb Curve

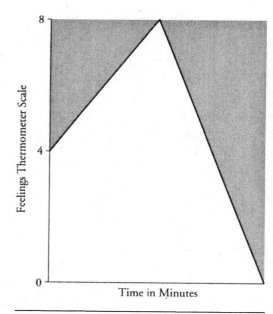

Figure 5.9

Bottoms Out Curve

5.9) indicates a suspiciously fast decline in anxiety. The child may be attempting to avoid or escape the exposure. In later sessions, this curve may indicate an appropriately faster habituation, but the level of anticipatory anxiety is still high. Continue cognitive restructuring and/or begin somatic management (see chapter 4). Finally, the "Steady State" curve in Figure 5.10 specifies continued high levels of anxiety. The child is neither habituating nor getting worse. The AAH item may be too complex, causing the child to focus on anxiety instead of the situation. Check for automatic thoughts and engage in cognitive restructuring as necessary.

Setting the Pace of, and Assistance With, Exposures

You may conduct role-play and in vivo practices in several ways to manipulate the pace of the exposure. A slower pace is ideal for younger children, those with special needs, and those with exceptionally high levels of anxiety. Moving slower allows a child to fully habituate to anxiety and build trust that he will not be forced into something overwhelming.

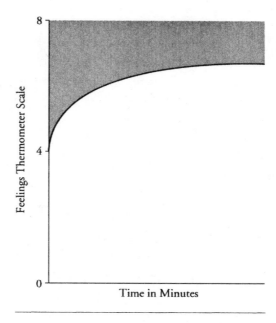

Figure 5.10
Steady-State Curve

In assisted exposure, you or the parent perform the exposure with the child. This allows a child to receive support from a trusted individual and observe a model who manages the situation. These procedures are especially helpful in early sessions, when confronting an anxious situation for the first time, or when more challenging exposures are developed. Educate parents, however, about the difference between *modeling*, where one shows a child how to manage the situation, and *rescuing*, where one takes over and does the situation for the child. A child's anxiety may interact with parents' natural tendencies to comfort their children and lead to rescuing. Therefore, instruct parents to allow their child to experience normal rises in anxiety. Modeling and assisted exposure keep the focus on the child, with the goal of having him confront anxious situations alone.

Several steps make up this process. First, model for the child how to address the situation as the child observes. During this step, say aloud the STOP steps. This gives the child a chance to observe how you process and manage a difficult situation. Second, help the child manage the situation together as a team (i.e., with the therapist and/or parents). Third, have the child manage the situation on his own as words of encouragement are given by the "coach." Prompt the child to use the STOP steps or somatic control exercises during this procedure. Fourth, have the child engage in the situation on his own while verbalizing self-reinforcement for performing the in vivo exposure.

Homework

✎ Continue to maintain the daily logbooks and have the parent help the younger child write down his thoughts during anxiety-provoking situations. Encourage the parents of younger children to follow the STOP model to identify and change the child's negative thoughts. Adolescents (generally ages 13 years and older) should be encouraged to do this homework on their own, with minimal parental involvement. Encourage parents and children to reduce arguments due to anxiety-related concerns.

✎ Assign the child an in vivo exposure (STIC task) of the situation that was role-played during this session. Ask the child to do this situation at least three times prior to the next session. For example, if his difficulty involves calling a classmate on the telephone, the assignment will be to call a classmate(s) three times during the week. The child should also be asked to record an anxiety rating immediately prior to, and immediately after, this exercise. Encourage parents to talk with the child after each practice, much like the therapist would during a session, and focus the child on what actually occurred during the practice and what happened to the anxiety. Model the use of praise and encouragement for attempting and/or completing each practice.

✎ Beginning with the next school day after this session, have parents wake the child about 90 to 120 minutes before school is scheduled to start and implement the normal school-day routine. The child should do schoolwork and read academic-related books when at home during the day.

Session Outline

- Review child's progress with exposures from previous session and address any problems encountered.

- Introduce more challenging items from the child's AAH and begin exposures.

  Sessions 3 and 4 will begin with a review of the child's STIC tasks and a discussion of any difficulties conducting and following through with the homework. Role-play difficulties encountered by the child since the last session, including troubles that may have occurred during the STIC exposures. The main focus of these sessions will be to guide a child to confront more challenging social situations. This task is accomplished by creating exposure situations that are increasingly more difficult for the child. You will need to be creative in developing challenging scenarios where the outcome is less than desirable, and where the child will have to cope with rising levels of anxiety.

Review of the Week

Review with the child any progress or problems in conducting the previously assigned STIC tasks. In particular, be vigilant for avoidance, escape, or otherwise inappropriate management of these situations. If the child did not complete the assigned tasks, ask him to use the STOP procedure to examine which "thinking traps" may have interfered with conducting the STIC task.

Case Vignette

T: Okay, so last time we assigned you the STIC task to call up a classmate. Let's see, you were going to call Janie, and then MaryBeth. And then, you were going to call one of them back again later in the week. Well, how did it go?

C: Well, I didn't get to call them. We were too busy with other things going on. I had to do a lot for my dad, and watch my little sister all the time.

T: Hmmm. That's too bad. Did you watch any fun shows on television?

C: Oh yeah, after my sister went to bed I got to watch stuff. She has on those little kid videos, until she goes to bed at 8 o'clock. Then I get to watch television.

T: Yeah. You know, 8 o'clock isn't so late to call up these classmates of yours. I get the feeling that something else kept you from calling. Can you think back, and tell me what was going through your mind when you really could have used the telephone?

C: I don't know. I just felt so stupid. I haven't talked to them at all since I was in school.

T: Okay, so you felt stupid because you haven't spoken to them in several weeks. What did you think would happen if, after not seeing any of them since you were in school, you suddenly call them up?

C: I won't know what to say! What if they think I've really been sick, or dying? Maybe they'll think I'm a loser because I've been afraid to go to school. They must know that.

T: I know it's hard for you to do this, because you worry about what other people think about you. Let's try to make a pact. Instead of not doing the STIC task, let's try to really talk about what you're afraid will happen, and we'll practice again and again how things can go and what you can do to deal with these situations. We really need to examine your thoughts, and look at how realistic they are. Okay? Let's take each thought and work through what you are saying to yourself.

To help a child process his avoidance of the task, use dispute handles to challenge negative thoughts. If the child completed the STIC assignments, examine difficulties, successes, or other issues, with the goal of reinforcing compliance with the homework. Focus the child on what it felt like to actually complete the STIC task, what actually happened, and how the child coped with the situation.

As treatment progresses, continue to focus the child on practicing entering anxiety-provoking situations. Use new and more challenging items from items on the child's AAH. For example, on Mark's AAH (see Figure 5.3), item 6 is "Giving an oral report in front of the class." Using the Socratic questioning method, Mark's therapist will uncover various negative thoughts pertaining to this situation:

What if I stutter?

What if someone starts laughing at me?

I may not know what to say.

Suppose I can't read a word?

Suppose I mispronounce a word? I'll look stupid.

Mark's therapist should construct behavior exposures that provoke Mark's anxiety. Through repeated exposures, Mark will learn that situations are usually less than perfect, and that is normal. Mark's therapist should emphasize that anyone may stutter, shake, mispronounce a word, or lose his place during an oral report. The following are examples of behavior exposures a therapist could construct to challenge Mark's negative thoughts and give him experience in coping.

What if I Stutter? What if Someone Starts Laughing at Me?

Mark will be asked to give an oral report in front of the therapist and possibly some assistants. During the report, he will be prompted by the therapist to stutter on purpose several times. Each time, an assistant will laugh, look away, roll his eyes, lean over and talk to another person, or otherwise be distracting. Mark's goal for this situation will be to continue to give his report regardless of the audience's reactions. Following the exposure, the therapist should help Mark process his experience in the following ways:

■ Encouraging Mark to focus on how anxious he felt and how he actually performed. Mark should be instructed to report physical sensations that occurred, automatic thoughts he experienced, and anxiety ratings. These indicators of anxiety can be compared to Mark's actual performance. Did he meet his main goal in spite of his anxiety? Did he meet some goals (no matter how few)? Illustrate to children that no matter how bad they may feel, their performance may not be impaired.

- Directing Mark toward an objective assessment of the exposure. Mark should realize that although the audience was less than totally attentive and his performance was less than perfect, it does not matter. What impact would this performance really have on his class grade or relationships with the teacher or peers? When processing an exposure, encourage a child to think about how he would act toward someone else in the class who had "messed up" during a presentation. Does he still like this other child? Would he still play with or work with this other child? Does he think badly of this other person because he stuttered?

- Asking Mark about other possibilities that could account for the audience behavior (e.g., when someone laughs, leaves the room, falls asleep, or looks away). The goal is to require a child to consider alternative reasons for the audience's behavior that have little or nothing to do with performance. For example, maybe the person was laughing at something he read, or was tired and just couldn't stay awake. Perhaps the person had to use the bathroom, or had an excuse to leave the room for some reason. Finally, maybe the person wasn't being nice.

I May Not Know What to Say. Suppose I Can't Read a Word? Suppose I Mispronounce a Word?

During another practice, Mark will be given a report to read that contains difficult words (probably technical or scientific words). The goal of this exposure is to have Mark actually be unable to pronounce some words. The audience is instructed to initially pay attention and listen to the talk. However, with repeated exposures, the audience will again act disinterested, snicker, or otherwise display disruptive behaviors. The therapist will help Mark cope and master this less-than-ideal situation

Special Topic 5.3: Perfectionism

Some children have trouble going to school because they are afraid of making mistakes. These kids may be perfectionistic: this means they want everything to be perfect and worry about the consequences of doing something wrong or handing in an assignment or worksheet that might have an error. Other perfectionists cannot complete written work because they constantly check and recheck their paper. As a result, some kids become very distressed and may even fail classes because nothing is being handed in. Many also refuse to go to school.

If your client is perfectionistic, then concentrate on his cognitions. Be sure the child understands that the consequences of handing in a paper with some misspellings or a test with some errors are not dire—that is, a child will not fail class or be yelled at or judged harshly if some mistakes are made. *In addition, be sure parents are not aggravating a child's perfectionism.* Many perfectionistic children have perfectionistic parents who place much pressure on their child to do well. Parents should convey that mistakes are normal and that they will not be angry if minor mistakes are made.

Children with perfectionism should also be encouraged to deliberately hand in work that has mistakes (see other examples in chapter 4). As they do so, they should practice relaxation, think realistically, and see that the consequences of making mistakes are not that bad. In addition, stress that work needs to be handed in on time and that the child must attend school even if minor mistakes are made.

through repeated questioning, use of dispute handles, and taking the perspective of others (see next section).

Processing the More Challenging Exposures

Spend considerable time with a child examining thoughts and behaviors that occurred during behavioral exposures. Many children quickly understand that it is normal to make mistakes or to be embarrassed or uncomfortable, or for other individuals to be rude. These children recognize that discomfort is momentary and that, in spite of being anxious or slightly embarrassed, they will be fine. However, some children push for situations to turn out perfectly, and it is much more difficult for them to tolerate being anything less than perfect. They are anxious about embarrassment, rejection, or humiliation, and their overriding thought is, *"No one will like me or want to be around me."*

To process the exposure, take a child through the scenario step by step. Thoroughly analyze his thoughts, anxiety ratings, and actual performance behaviors. Refer to the following example, an exposure involving a young girl initiating and carrying on a conversation with a peer. The child reports feeling anxious because, *"I may not know what to say. She may not like me. What if I say something stupid?"* During the course of the exposure, the child meets all of her goals: she introduces herself, asks three questions, maintains eye contact, and smiles. However, her anxiety ratings remain above 6 on a 0-to-8 scale, indicating continued high anxiety. Following the exposure, the therapist may process the situation as follows.

Case Vignette

T: Okay, Stacy, look at your goals. Seems that you met every one. In fact, instead of asking three questions, you actually asked five. What do you think about that?

C: Well, I guess I did okay on that, but I just didn't feel good.

T: What were you thinking about while you were doing this practice?

C: I just kept thinking I was messing up. I thought I looked stupid.

T: Take a look at these goals. How did you mess up? What did you do that was so bad?

C: I don't know. I thought I wasn't talking enough.

T: But you actually asked more questions than you had hoped. And I counted that you answered all five of the questions that were asked of you.

C: I did? I didn't realize that.

T: The point is that even though you felt nervous, you were doing fine. You were asking and answering questions, and having a real conversation. Can you see that?

C: I kept telling myself I wasn't doing well.

T: Aha! So, even though you were doing everything you wanted to, you kept those negative thoughts coming. Do you realize what kind of negative thought that is?

C: Canceling out the positive. Even though I was doing okay, I was telling myself I was doing bad.

T: That's it. You've got to let yourself focus on what you're doing, and feel better about that. Let's try it again.

For children who are particularly critical of themselves, a perspective taking (or "role reversal") practice may prove helpful. Here, the therapist probes for what the child is most anxious about in a social situation. A typical example is a child who fears eating in front of others because he is afraid of being watched and laughed at if food spills, or of being asked a question while having food in his mouth. Begin by asking the child if he has ever noticed any other child in this situation.

Case Vignette

T: So, you're concerned that if you spill your drink on your shirt, the other kids will laugh and make fun of you.

C: Yeah, I'll look stupid.

T: And if you look stupid, then what will happen?

C: Kids may start to tease me, and I'll feel terrible. Then I will not want to go to school anymore.

T: Let me ask you something. Have you ever seen anyone else spill a drink?

C: I don't know. I guess so.

T: Now really think hard. Who was the last kid you saw spill something?

C: I don't remember.

T: Okay, let's try this. Have you ever seen another kid in school throw up?

C: Yes. Yuck.

T: Okay, so throwing up is really yucky, worse than spilling a drink, right?

C: Yes.

T: Okay, so who was the kid that threw up?

C: The last one was Maggie. She threw up in the hallway.

T: Okay, anyone else that you remember throwing up?

C: Michael did it once. In second grade.

T: Okay. Do you ever play with Maggie or Michael?

C: Yes.

T: Why do you play with them?

C: Because they're nice. They're my friends.

T: But these two THREW UP! Yuck! Don't you think they're gross now?

C: No, they're my friends. They're nice. So what if they threw up? It happens to a lot of kids.

T: Yeah, I guess it does. But why do you still like them? What they did is worse than spilling stuff.

C: Well, just because they were sick and threw up is no big deal. They couldn't help it. They're still really nice and fun.

T: So, if you went to the cafeteria, and spilled some milk, wouldn't you STILL be fun? And still be nice? Wouldn't it be just like if some other kid did something, no big deal?

C: What?

T: You seem to be really hard on yourself, but you're okay with your friends making mistakes, or getting sick, or throwing up or spilling things. If you still like other kids who do those things, don't you think they would still like you if you spilled something?

C: Oh, yeah. You're right. I guess that's right.

Construct an exposure that involves the child interacting with participants who have spills on their shirts, and ask the child to carry on conversations while the participants spill more drinks or food. Encourage the child to spill on himself to gain the experience of making mistakes in front of others. The essential point of these exposures is to illustrate that personal discomfort is temporary and that most people's reactions are also temporary.

Cognitive restructuring involves processing an exposure until the core anxiety is uncovered and disputed. By constructing increasingly more challenging exposures, you will be able to elicit these core anxieties and allow a child to challenge them directly. This gives the child evidence of coping and mastering a situation. Beware of incomplete cognitive restructuring where underlying thoughts are left unrecognized. Do not necessarily accept a child's word at face value that "everything is okay; this doesn't bother me anymore." In such cases, further probing and conducting a behavioral exposure may reveal anxiety and suggest that a child is trying to look good for the therapist. A complete analysis of the child's thoughts, and testing these thoughts through increasingly challenging exposures, is recommended.

Homework

✎ Continue to maintain the daily logbooks. The child should continue using the STOP procedures or cognitive restructuring to challenge and change negative thoughts that occur in anxiety-provoking situations.

✎ STIC tasks will continue to involve conducting real-life practices with more challenging situations from the child's AAH. Give parents specific instructions about coaching the child in conducting and processing these assignments.

✎ Continue to adhere to a normal school-day schedule. As part of the assigned STIC tasks for this week, the child should spend more time at school. This may involve moving tutoring or study time to school, sending the child in to meet with the teacher on various days, and setting up some structured interactions with peers. Parents must make time to help the child get to school for these exercises. This may mean parents sharing responsibilities so that stress on one person's schedule and responsibilities are minimized. If the child is in a single-parent family, brainstorm ways that the parent can access support from family or friends to assist with this part of treatment. *Read Special Topic 4.6 in Chapter 4 to become acquainted with different methods of gradually reintegrating a child to school.* These methods include having a child go to school (1) in the morning for a set period of time and then gradually working forward by adding more time, (2) at 2 P.M. until the time school normally ends and then gradually working backward by adding more time, (3) only for lunch and then gradually adding more school time before and after lunch, (4) only for a favorite class or time of day and then gradually adding more classes or school time, (5) in a school room other than the classroom, such as the school library, and then gradually adding more classroom time.

SESSIONS 5 & 6   *Advanced Maturing of Treatment*

Session Outline

■ Review the child's weekly STIC tasks.

Sessions 5 and 6 will involve helping a child progress through the main portion of his AAH. A major focus of these exposures will be to elicit a child's negative self-talk and help him challenge and change these thoughts. In these sessions, the child will continue to practice changing thoughts to focus on coping. Therapy involves role-playing and modeling the process of cognitive restructuring (changing thoughts). Parents can be involved in sessions to observe you and gain experience coaching their child to use these cognitive strategies. The degree of parental involvement is a clinical decision based on many factors that include the severity of a child's school refusal problem, age and developmental level, special needs such as memory or attention problems, and motivation level.

Realistic Thinking

Begin each session with a review of the child's weekly STIC tasks. This gives you the opportunity to evaluate a child's ability to identify and challenge negative thoughts. As the child's skill in using cognitive restructuring improves, he will develop greater tolerance for approaching and staying in challenging social and/or evaluative situations.

The popular press and pop psychology movement once promoted the concept of "positive thinking" as a way to overcome negative and distressing emotions. Positive thinking entails repeating thoughts to oneself such as "I can do this," "I'm smart," and "I'm a good person" to neutralize negative thoughts. Research and clinical experience explain why some people never get better by using positive thinking. Positive thinking has been shown to interfere with focusing on and accomplishing a task. In fact, children who are test anxious actually do just as bad or worse when given positive statements such as "I'm smart, I can do this." Positive thoughts do not provide any real information or coping solutions for the child to rely on and use in a given situation. During a test, for example, a child can become so focused on trying to convince himself that "I am smart" that concentration on the task is disrupted. As the child recognizes that the task is not getting completed, his levels of frustration and physical tension increase. This sets into motion the cycle of disruptive physical sensations, thoughts, and behaviors, each reinforcing the other and making the situation worse. In this case, "I am smart" leads to sensations such as muscle tension or headache, disruption in completing the task, and the resultant, "Oh no, I can't do this after all!" that further perpetuates a child's tension, negative thoughts, and poor performance.

In contrast to positive thinking, research demonstrates that *healthy thinking* is the predominant style of thought used by well-adjusted individuals. Healthy thinking is characterized by realistically examining a situation and resources available to manage the situation. Healthy thinking is reality-based, focused on problem-solving and task management, and characterized by adaptive thoughts. By this point in treatment, you have helped the child use the STOP program or similar cognitive restructuring techniques to uncover irrational or negative beliefs (the "S" and "T" steps). The child has practiced changing these negative thoughts to more realistic and adaptive coping statements (the "O" step that involves the use of dispute handles). Role-plays and behavioral exposures give a child opportunities to test his thoughts and gather evidence that he can cope with anxious situations. Continued exposure to challenging situations will give the child evidence to refute and change negative thinking.

Examples of Social/Evaluative Exposures and Restructuring

Children and adolescents with social anxiety may be anxious about a wide range of situations involving other people, taking tests, oral presentations, or sports or musical performances. If a child's social anxiety is focused on one type of social situation, it is considered non-generalized (e.g., individuals who experience extreme anxiety only when giving a talk in front of others). Most children and adolescents, however, are anxious about many social situations. This is called generalized social anxiety. Social anxiety naturally increases as children enter adolescence. However, for children more prone to experiencing generalized social anxiety, adolescence may be an even more difficult and distressing stage of life. The goal of this phase of treatment is to conduct more challenging exposures and encourage a child to readily use his cognitive restructuring skills. Preparation for each exposure is the same: the child defines several concrete goals, identifies his negative or automatic thoughts, and provides a rational alternative thought for each, using dispute handles. The following are examples of exposures and cognitive restructuring procedures for various social anxieties.

Example 1: Tackling Test Anxiety

Exposures conducted for test anxiety will involve administering tests and quizzes to the child. This exposure requires sample tests representing the child's actual schoolwork. Tests may be requested from the teacher or tutor, or parents can help develop tests based on the child's current schoolwork. The exposure will involve manipulating several parameters a child is likely to encounter, such as being timed, having multiple-choice or essay questions, taking oral quizzes, and/or being surprised with a "pop" quiz. A typical post-exposure processing follows.

Case Vignette

T: Okay, so what happened during this test?

C: I got only 8 out of 10. I knew I'd bomb that test.

T: You do well in math; tell me the percentage that you got on this quiz.

C: Eighty. I only got an 80.

T: What is the worst thing that could happen with an 80 on a test?

C: I could fail the subject, and then I'd fail in my other subjects too.

T: Let's take one thing at a time. Tell me, is 80 percent a failure?

C: No, but it's only a B.

T: Wow, what kind of thought is that: "It's only a B"?

C: (Looks at list of thought labels) Oh, I just disqualified a positive. Okay, I did better than a C.

T: So, rephrase that thought. What's really going on with a B?

C: Okay, I got a B, and that's a passing grade.

T: Okay, and tell me, have you ever failed a test before?

C: No, but I did get a C once.

T: And?

C: A C is still passing.

T: Okay, so have you ever failed a subject before, because you got a C or a B?

C: No.

T: So, how likely is it you would fail the test and then fail the subject?

C: Well, it could happen.

T: Do you study for your tests?

C: Yes.

T: What else do you do to prepare for your tests?

C: I do my homework.

T: Okay, so tell me realistically, how likely is it you would fail the test and then fail the subject?

C: Okay, it's really not likely I'd fail the test.

T: Why? What is the evidence saying you wouldn't fail? Put it all together.

C: It's not likely I'd fail, because I do study and I do all my homework.

T: Give me a percentage for how likely it is from 0 to 100 percent.

C: Well, it's really only maybe a 5% chance.

T: What's really the worst thing that could happen?

C: I could get a B in the class, but that's not failing.

Administer repeated test simulations to the child, each followed by the cognitive restructuring steps outlined in STOP. Examine the evidence for the child's anxieties and look realistically at potential outcomes and their consequences. Some children are anxious about tests because of learning disorders or because they experience less-than-preferred academic outcomes. The focus of this treatment is on managing anxiety that can develop due to a history of poor performance. For children with learning problems, coordinate treatment with a tutor or special education teacher to ensure appropriate anxiety management and the benefit of necessary academic services.

Note that parents' expectations about their child's school performance may exacerbate a child's test anxiety. Some parents may believe, for example, that anxiety prevents their child from making straight As and that occasional Bs will prevent him from entering a good college. Carefully examine parents' beliefs and attitudes about their child's school performance and evaluate whether intervention and education is necessary to help parents accept their child's abilities and performance.

Example 2: Standing Up to Shyness

Some shy or quiet children who worry about what other people think of them may be at risk for developing clinical levels of social and/or evaluative anxiety. Shyness is generally accepted in our culture as a normal variant of personality. However, for the child who shrinks away from making friends, is unable to speak up for his own needs, or is otherwise unable to warm up to people, shyness is so extreme that it is considered problematic. In addition, shy or quiet children are often overlooked as teachers struggle to address more disruptive behavior. Children with extreme shyness often suffer with overwhelming anxiety before others recognize the need to help them. The focus of a shy child's exposures will not be to remake that child's personality. Instead, by addressing social anxiety in treatment, the child will be more relaxed in social situations. The child will be able to make decisions about what he wants to do based on his preferences instead of anxiety about rejection, embarrassment, or incompetence.

Exposures for shy children and adolescents will involve interactions with different people in different situations: starting conversations in the cafeteria, calling a classmate for missed homework, asking a question in class, joining a group of kids already playing together, asking someone to stop doing something annoying, or saying "no" when desired. The following is an example of a therapist helping a child question for his anxiety about other people's thoughts of him.

Case Vignette

T: What is the hardest thing about school for you?

C: I guess the other kids.

T: What is it about the other kids that bothers you?

C: I don't know. I don't think they really like me.

T: Why do you think that? What happens with the other kids?

C: No one really talks to me. I have no friends, and I don't have anyone to sit with in the cafeteria or at recess.

T: Have you ever tried to talk to the other kids?

C: Yes.

T: When was the last time you tried?

C: I don't know . . . it was a while ago. Maybe last year.

T: Well, then it sounds like you've given up trying to talk to others.

C: It's no use. I'm afraid of them not liking me. I know they already don't like me.

T: Wait, let's look at what's really going on. You may have tried last year, but this year you haven't at all, have you?

C: No.

T: What are some of the reasons why the other kids do not talk to you?

C: Because they don't like me, I told you that. They all know each other and they're all friends.

T: First, tell me what kind of a thought is "Because they don't like me"?

C: It's mind reading, or maybe fortune-telling. I know, I'm predicting that they don't like me, but I really can't know what they think.

T: That's right! What evidence do you have, besides the fact no one has tried to talk to you recently, that they do not like you?

C: Well, none, really.

T: So, what other reasons may there be for the kids not talking to you?

C: I don't know, I guess because I don't try to talk to them.

T: Maybe. Where do you usually hang out during lunch or recess?

C: I just stay in the classroom, or go to the library.

T: So, is it fair to say you do not even go near the other kids?

C: Yeah.

T: So, what evidence is there they do not like you?

C: None.

T: And what else may be going on?

C: Well, maybe because I don't hang around the other kids, and don't go talk to them, that's why they don't talk to me. But it's so hard! What if I don't know what to say?

T: Okay, right. One thing at a time. Remember, slow down that tape of automatic thoughts in your mind, and dispute one thought at a time. Maybe the other kids do not talk to you because you're not hanging around the cafeteria or recess area. Maybe they do not have a chance to talk with you.

C: Yeah, I can see that.

T: Okay, and because you haven't done this in a while, it'll be hard. Trying to talk with someone is hard if you're out of practice. But, you also said, "What if I don't know what to say?"

C: Yeah, then there will be some stupid silence, and I'll look like a jerk.

T: Oh, but if the other kid doesn't talk, will he look stupid?

C: What? No . . .

T: So, why would you look stupid if you were quiet for a moment? Let me ask you something. How may people does it take to have a conversation?

C: I guess at least two.

T: Yes. So, in a conversation with two people, and you being one of them, how much of the conversation are you responsible for?

C: Um, just half of it.

T: That's right. You're only responsible for 50 percent of the conversation. The other person is also responsible. So, if there's silence, it's not just because of you, but also because of the other person. Right?

C: Yeah, that's right.

T: So, what can you do to prepare yourself to start a conversation with someone?

C: Well, I guess I'm only responsible for half of the conversation. And, if I haven't talked with this person, it may be hard at first. I guess I have to try it, and make myself hang around where the other kids are.

T: Good going.

Shy children need repeated experience with conversations and being around other people. Therapy will focus on increasing a child's ability to physically place himself closer to peers, as well as improving conversational and social skills. A child's dysfunctional attitudes and beliefs will be challenged continuously as he gathers new information about social situations and about being the focus of attention.

Special Topic 5.4: Being Teased

Many kids have trouble going to school because they are teased by other kids. Teasing can be especially hurtful if directed toward sensitive areas such as weight or skin complexion. In addition, teasing can be harmful if it is part of bullying or serious threats. In more serious situations, consult with school officials to seek resolution of the problem.

Mild teasing is common among children, but your client may be especially sensitive to it and not want to attend school as a result. We recommend that children not respond to teasers. Although some children can deflect teasing by teasing back or by laughing it off, other kids are very bothered by teasing, and so we encourage them to simply ignore the insults that are made. Do not have a child respond to provocation. Most teasers are looking for some reaction, so if they do not get a reaction they usually just move somewhere else. If your client is being teased, have him practice breathing exercises (see chapter 4) and continue doing what he was doing before. If the teasing gets worse, ask him to walk away or seek the comfort of friends. In addition, conduct teasing exposures with you as the teaser to help the child devise statements and strategies for coping with teasing.

If this does not work, then ask your client to speak to an adult who can help at school. Although children sometimes do not like talking to adults at school about other kids, school should be a safe and comfortable place to learn. School officials are generally sensitive to these concerns, so encourage your client to speak to them as a last resort or when he feels physically threatened or when his personal space is being violated. In addition, frequently discuss this situation with the child.

Example 3: Overcoming Gym Jitters

A child with social anxiety may be especially anxious about performance-based activities and may develop an inappropriate strategy of avoidance to manage the problem. Parents may report that a child complains of stomachaches or illness on gym days or a guitar that suddenly snaps all its strings right before the annual recital. Children who refuse to attend school due to performance-based anxiety will try to avoid these situations at all costs. Or, they may endure the situation with great distress and then drop out of the activity or class at the first opportunity. The following dialogue illustrates the main concerns of a child who refused to attend school due to performance anxiety.

Case Vignette

C: Going to gym was the main problem. I just couldn't stand it when everyone laughed at me. I can't do sports. I'm always picked last for everything. It stinks.

T: Tell me more about gym class. I want to know who's in your class and the activities you have to do.

C: All the guys from my homeroom are there. They're all jocks, every one of them. We started out doing basketball. What a joke. I never played before. Then we had to play football. I was so bad in basketball that no one picked me for football. The coach had to put me on a team.

T: Let's break this down. All the guys in your gym class were jocks? That means that every single one of them played on a team sport at your school?

C: No, not everyone. Most of them.

T: How many kids are in that class, and how many are on teams?

C: All right, so there's 20 guys in the class, and maybe 6 play on the school teams. But that's a lot.

T: Okay, and of those 14 guys who were not on the teams, they were all total jocks too. Is that what you're telling me?

C: No. My friend Brian wasn't too good at anything either, but everyone likes him. He got picked before I did for the teams.

T: So, Joey, tell me this, when you go to gym, what do you do? When you first get to gym class, what are you likely to do?

C: I have to change. And I hate to change in front of those guys. So I go into the bathroom to change.

T: What are the other guys doing?

C: They're hanging out and fooling around with each other, waiting for the coach. They all get along. It's hard to go back in there.

T: Tell me about changing in front of the other guys. What bothers you about that?

C: Well, it's hard to say. I don't want to be laughed at. I don't lift weights or anything. They tease the skinny guys and the guys who are fat, and I don't want to be teased for being a runt.

T: It's not fun getting teased, if it's intended to hurt you. Teasing can also be just for fun and joking around, like among friends. Is it really hurtful, or just joking?

C: I don't know. Maybe a little of both. The guys who get teased seem to handle it okay. I just don't want to blush and make it worse.

T: Okay, so here's a few things to think about. You worry about looking different than others, because you do not lift weights. And you worry about blushing if you're teased. Ask yourself, how many of those 14 guys lift weights, look perfect, and do not blush at times when they are teased?

C: Well, okay, not everyone's a jock. They aren't perfect either.

T: What makes the difference between those guys and you?

C: They let it happen. They go in and change in front of the jocks, and get called names.

T: And then what happens?

C: I don't know; not much, I guess.

T: Do these guys get left out of the games? Are they great athletes, despite their size and shapes?

C: No. It's over pretty quickly. They don't really seem to be bothered. And they play everything, even the ones who aren't so good at sports.

T: Okay, so these guys stay with the situation. You're going into the bathroom, so you separate yourself from the beginning. When you come out changed, then what do you do? Do you go and hang around the guys?

C: No. I usually read a book until the coach tells me I have to do something. I try not to talk to anyone.

T: Oh. Hmmm. Why do you do that?

C: So no one will talk to me. So maybe they'll forget about me and I won't have to play the sport.

T: Then, is it possible that the other guys pick you last because you're sitting on the side, reading or trying to not be noticed?

C: Yeah, it's possible.

T: And, is it possible that if you tried to hang around a little more, that the other guys might start picking you sooner?

C: Sure, anything is possible.

T: Let me ask you this. You do not like all sports, right?

C: No, I like to play tennis. I just don't like basketball and football.

T: Oh. Do you get to play tennis in gym class?

C: Yeah, but not until the spring, and only for 3 weeks.

T: Oh. And are these jocks good at tennis, too?

C: No, especially the bigger guys.

T: So, is it fair to say not everyone can be good at everything?

C: Yeah.

T: And when those big jocks mess up on the tennis court, does anyone tease them?

C: Yeah, their friends laugh about it.

T: Okay. So, let's sum this up. Not everyone has a great body, but other kids still change together. And not everyone is good at everything, and even the jocks get teased. And if you sit by yourself with reading, you may be overlooked by the others, but not excluded on purpose. Right?

In this example, the therapist uncovered faulty beliefs and helped the child examine what he could do. Joey did play tennis, but he disqualified this fact and focused on his misery in the moment. Joey compared himself to the jocks and not all the other kids, thus making himself feel all the more different and awkward. In vivo exposures for Joey would involve leaving his book (a safety signal) behind and going up to the boys he is familiar with during gym class. Children in this situation may also benefit from basic social skills training in making and keeping eye contact, starting and joining conversations, and being assertive.

Special Topic 5.5: Gym Class

One of the toughest classes for many older children and adolescents to attend is gym or physical education class. Many kids do not like physical education because they have to change clothes or shower before others, perform athletically before others, and risk being teased, ridiculed, embarrassed, or picked last for a team. As a result, some kids skip gym class or do not participate very much during the class.

If this applies to your client, work with him using the methods described in this chapter. Be sure the child is relaxed and help change negative thoughts he may have when at gym class. If the child is not participating much in gym class, try to work on ways that he can talk to others and get more involved with the sports that are being conducted. If the child is teased or ridiculed or always picked last for a team, talk to the physical education teacher to see how this might be resolved. Perhaps the child can occasionally be chosen to pick a team, or a lottery system could be established where teams are chosen randomly. If the child is embarrassed about how he performs at a sport, ask parents to practice the sport with him.

A particularly tough problem involves not wanting to undress or shower in the locker room. Do not allow a child to avoid this or to get dressed in a private location. Instead, ask him to be as prepared as possible with his gear. This means bringing all necessary clothes and getting changed for class as efficiently as possible. In addition, encourage the child to speak to others in the locker room and during gym class so his focus is on making eye contact and starting and joining conversations, and not on worry about being watched or judged.

Involving Other People in the Child's Therapy

The successful treatment of social and performance anxiety often depends on the involvement of other people in the child's therapy. This involvement may be direct or indirect. Some therapy programs actively recruit non-anxious children to help children with shyness or social phobia practice the skills learned in therapy. These procedures are called peer pairing and are based on the finding that shy children are neglected by their peers because they become somewhat invisible to others. Children recruited to assist with a child's therapy do not need to know personal information about a child's diagnostic status, but only that a child may need help feeling less shy and getting to know other kids.

Parents can also arrange for less formal interactions with peers and other individuals. Suggest that parents arrange play dates, outings, and similar social events to facilitate their child's contact with others. These semi-structured activities provide the child an opportunity to practice social skills. These activities can also be arranged for classroom situations. For example, if a child is shy or quiet, people may expect less interaction with him. The child's teacher may need to be contacted to assist with school-based exposures. The teacher may call on the child or otherwise give him experience in performing in front of others. Similarly, parents and others should no longer speak for the shy child, such as ordering in a restaurant or paying at a store. All family members also need to be educated about the child's goal of interacting with others more comfortably and independently. Involving other people and various social situations will be the focus of the child's STIC tasks throughout the remainder of treatment.

Homework

Homework assignments after sessions 5 and 6 may include the following:

✎ STIC tasks are likely to be assigned for school-related situations. The child should be attending at least part of the school day after sessions 5 and 6. These STIC tasks will increasingly involve the child interacting with both children and adults. Parents should appropriately help a child follow through with these exposures.

✎ Continue to complete the daily logbooks.

SESSIONS 7 & 8   *Completing Treatment and Preparing for Termination*

The main focus of this latter part of treatment is to have a child spend increasingly longer periods of time in school, with the eventual goal of full-time attendance. Initially, you may wish to accompany a child to school or arrange your scheduled appointments in a private office of the school building during the day (e.g., a non-academic class period such as study hall). These assisted exposures may prompt a child to progress more rapidly to full-time attendance. Once a child has returned to school, however, therapy appointments should be avoided during school hours. Appointments may continue at school after school hours if appropriate. At this point, ensure the child takes most of the responsibility for treatment and applies what was learned in real-life situations. Continue to implement techniques from previous sessions to help the child achieve this goal.

Chapter 6   *Children Refusing School for Attention*

Starting Treatment

Materials Needed

- Parent Commands Worksheet

Session Outline

- Have parents describe and list their commands.

- Have parents describe their school-day morning routine.

- Help parents establish punishments for school refusal behavior.

  In this chapter, treatment procedures are described for a child refusing school for attention. Common behaviors in this functional group include noncompliance (i.e., refusing parent and teacher commands), overall disruptive behavior to stay out of school, clinging, refusal to move, tantrums, running away, constant telephoning, and guilt-inducing behaviors. The major focus of treatment is the parents (or parent in a single-parent family). The major goal of treatment is to shift parental attention away from school refusal behaviors and toward appropriate school attendance behaviors. This will involve:

- Restructuring parent commands

- Establishing fixed daily routines

- Implementing punishments for school nonattendance

- Implementing rewards for school attendance

This treatment plan therefore involves key elements of a contingency management approach. In discussing this treatment approach for children refusing school for attention, these four components will continue to be revisited.

In this treatment plan, almost all of your time will be spent with parents. However, the child should come to the treatment sessions and be told what will happen. The child will have the opportunity to ask questions about the treatment plan and think about the punishments and rewards that will occur. Keeping a child informed of the therapy situation also allows you to remind the child that her behavior will determine whether punishments or rewards will be given. If she decides to attend school without difficulty, then positive things will happen, such as time spent with parent(s). If she decides to refuse school, then negative things will happen, such as grounding.

You may invite the child to give feedback about what she thinks of the treatment plan. In some cases, you may make minor changes (e.g., eating cereal in the morning instead of pancakes) based on valid reasons the child gives (e.g., preference and saving time). In most cases, however, do not allow a child to "negotiate" procedures that have been set (e.g., rising at 7 A.M. instead of 6:45 A.M.). Often a controlling, attention-seeking child who sets the family agenda is the very problem parents had in the first place. One goal of therapy is to modify a child's controlling, attention-seeking behavior and put parents more in charge of what is happening at home.

You may wish to tell other children in the family about the treatment plan to get their support and assure them they will not be forgotten during treatment. Siblings sometimes misbehave for attention when they realize one child is getting extra attention for bad behavior. Watch for and address this as soon as possible. One solution is to implement the techniques for all children in the family (e.g., establish a routine for everyone). Be sure to probe for new child problems during treatment.

Restructuring Parent Commands

The first step is to restructure parent commands. In many families with an attention-seeking child, the child successfully negotiates what she wants and often draws the parents into a long discussion. A goal of therapy is to shorten these conversations into a simple parent command, a simple child response, and a simple parent response.

Begin by asking each parent to list 10 typical commands he or she gave to her child in the past few days. Be sure parents state the command exactly as worded to the child. These commands should include situations such as chores, interactions with siblings, finding things, or stopping disruptive behavior, to name a few. Next, ask parents to list 10 typical commands given to their child about school attendance. Probe for extenuating circumstances or other reasons why and how certain commands were given.

Check the lists to see if they are roughly similar or dissimilar in nature. If they are dissimilar, ask parents why this is the case. Knowing whether discrepancies exist will help you decide the scope of treatment. If parent commands are effective in many situations but not for school attendance, then treatment may be narrow in scope. However, if parent commands are ineffective in many situations, including mornings before school, then treatment may need to be broader in scope to include these other areas.

Check the lists for key errors parents sometimes make when giving commands to their child. Such errors often include commands given in the form of questions, commands that are vague or incomplete, commands that are interrupted or carried out by someone else, commands that are too difficult for the child, or commands given in the form of lectures. Look for patterns of errors parents may be making and provide constructive feedback.

Establishing Regular Routines

In addition to commands, ask parents to give you a detailed description of a typical school-day morning in their house. Ask them to be very specific about this routine, perhaps even describing it in 10-minute increments. If family members have no set morning routine, they should mention this as well as any general routine they follow. If their routine differs depending on the day of the week, have them describe routines for each day. If parents expect changes in their routine over the next 3 to 4 weeks (e.g., due to vacations, holidays, changes in work schedules, school breaks), have them mention these as well.

As parents describe their routine, pay special attention to the times the children rise from bed, wash and get dressed, eat, brush their teeth, do extra activities such as watch television, prepare for school, and leave the house to go to school. If these times or activities differ from child to child, obtain a description for each but especially for the child with school refusal behavior. In addition, find out about the parents' typical morning routine as well as differences in routines between the two of them. The latter is especially important in cases where a child takes advantage of one parent's absence to force the other parent to keep her home from school.

Probe as well for how parents respond to their child's behavior in the morning. Again, pay special attention to behaviors directed toward the child refusing to attend school. Focus on behaviors such as ignoring, calming the child, yelling, physical interactions, or lecturing, among others. Encourage your clients to be open about what is happening. Many parents are embarrassed that their lives revolve around a controlling 7-year-old, but information about their interactions with their child will be important for treatment. Examples of pertinent questions may include the following: When your child throws a tantrum or clings to the banister to refuse school, what exactly do you do? How long does this interaction take place? Do you eventually "give in" to your child because of other important matters? What does your child do with you during the day? What do you say to each other and what is the emotional atmosphere like?

Try to establish a pattern of how each parent responds to the child's behavior and provide feedback if possible. Remember that a central strategy of treatment is to reward school attendance and punish school refusal behaviors. Therefore, encourage parents to practice downplaying or ignoring school refusal behaviors (e.g., excessive physical complaints, clinging, tantrums) as much as possible and attend to appropriate behaviors (e.g., getting out of bed, eating breakfast on time). Because many parents have gotten used to attending to a child only when she shows "bad" behavior, they must start practicing a shift in attention toward positive behavior.

Implementing Punishments for School Refusal Behavior

Ask parents to list punishments they have used recently to discipline their child or to make it known that a certain behavior was unacceptable. Have them rate each punishment for its effectiveness and identify those still used. Examples include lectures, spankings, grounding, restriction of privileges, loss of valued items, and fines, among others. See if these punishments differ from child to child. Also, parents may have used very few punishments in the past or may wait until their child's behavior is severe before giving punishment. In addition, some parents do not believe in punishment. These practices can affect treatment and you should know about each of them as soon as possible.

Discover as well if punishments used by the parents differ from child to child. For example, some parents punish the child with school refusal behavior much more than their other children. If this is the case, have them describe in detail what they do. In addition, ask whether each punishment was effective and whether parents still use it. Identify the uses of each punishment over the past few days and how the child responded.

In addition, ask parents how they used these punishments in the past few weeks or months. For example, have they tried time-out? If so, what procedures did they use? How long did they try it? Did both parents implement time-out? Did the child know the house rules before being placed in time-out? Have the parents tried grounding? If so, did the child leave the house anyway, tear up the bedroom, or say, "I don't care"? All past punishments must be explored in depth. In exploring these past examples, assess parents' attitudes about how effective they think future punishments will be in changing their child's behavior. If possible, propose new rules and punishments and get feedback from parents.

Ask parents to list rewards they have used recently to encourage appropriate behavior. As with punishments, have parents rate each for its effectiveness or desirability to the child. Discover whether they still use the rewards. Examples include verbal praise, attention, extra play or reading time (with or without the parents), food, toys, money, or an easing of responsibilities. Also ask whether these rewards differ from child to child.

As with punishments, explore how parents used rewards in the past few weeks or months. For example, did they set up a system of rewards for the child for a few days but found it ineffective? Also, assess parents' attitudes about how effective they think future positive consequences will be in changing their child's behavior. If possible, propose new rewards

---

Special Topic 6.1: Parents Skipping Work to Be Home With a Child

When young children refuse school for attention, parents often wonder if they should miss work to attend school with their child. Many children with this functional condition say they would attend school if only a parent could go with them and stay for the morning, lunch, or most of the school day. Some parents also "volunteer" as room helpers so they can justify being in their child's classroom and to make the morning routine easier.

We do not recommend that parents skip work or make extra efforts to be at school with their child. Doing so only reinforces a child's dependence or attention-seeking behavior and will make it that much harder later to get a child to attend school independently. Parents should clarify with children what boundaries will occur at school. For example, a mother may tell the child she is willing to walk her only to the school playground or main lobby. A school official should then escort the child to class.

If a parent has been skipping work to spend class time with a child, then establish a schedule to gradually withdraw the parent from the classroom. If a parent is in class for 2 hours, for example, she should try to leave after 1 hour and 45 minutes. As the child can handle this, the parent should continue to leave 15 minutes earlier every few days or so. Gradually work backward until the parent can deposit a child at the school playground or main lobby and have her escorted to class. If the child shows disruptive behavior, then parents should implement home-based punishments.

and get feedback from parents. Finally, check the family's time and financial resources to make sure all possible consequences, negative and positive, are realistic.

Homework

- ✎ Keep a list of commands given to each child between this session and the next. Write the command in the exact wording used.

- ✎ Keep a daily record of the family's morning routine between this session and the next. List all activities and times.

- ✎ Think about changes in the morning routine that may help a child go to school.

- ✎ Think about other punishments and rewards used in the past and possible new ones that could be used in the future.

- ✎ Encourage general adherence to a regular school-day schedule, even if only in the morning prior to school. This includes early wakening, dressing and preparing for school as if going, and completing school assignments.

- ✎ Continue to complete the daily logbooks. Note specific situations or experiences that arise during the week.

SESSION 2 *Intensifying Treatment*

Session Outline

- ■ Begin restructuring parent commands.

- ■ Help parents create a realistic, flexible school-day morning schedule.

- ■ Help parents create punishments for school refusal behavior.

  This section describes how to intensify treatment procedures for a child refusing school for attention. As in session 1, the major focus will be the parents and the major goal of treatment will be to shift parental attention away from school refusal behaviors and toward school attendance. Again, this will involve restructuring parent commands, establishing fixed daily routines, implementing punishments for school nonattendance, and implementing rewards for school attendance.

Restructuring Parent Commands

Begin the session by reviewing the list of commands given by parents to their children over the past few days. Pay particular attention to those commands given to the child refusing school. As in session 1, check these commands for key errors such as question-like commands, vagueness, criticism, interrupted commands, incomplete commands, commands eventually carried out or ignored by the parent, commands with too many steps, and commands given in the form of lectures. Look for patterns of errors parents may be making.

In this session, start to restructure parent commands. Begin by closely examining each command on the list and provide subtle feedback and gain more specific information. In the following example, T represents the therapist, F represents the child's father, and M represents the child's mother.

Case Vignette

T: I see one command you gave yesterday was, "Clean your room." Can you tell me about that?

F: Yeah, I told him he should clean his room. He didn't get around to it, of course.

T: When you told him to clean his room, what was he doing at the time?

F: Watching television. He always seems to find something to do when we ask him to do something.

T: I see another command was more urgent and about school.

M: Yes, I asked him this morning to stop hanging on to me.

T: Okay, what does "hanging on" mean?

M: He was all over me, whining and complaining about having to go to school. He didn't want to go and was bugging me to let him stay home.

T: Okay, you say that he was "all over" you. What exactly does that mean?

M: Well, it's hard to describe. He comes over to me, sometimes grabs my leg or lies at my feet when I'm trying to do something, like make the kids' lunches.

At this point, change some of the statements parents make to the child. Specifically, check the list of parent commands and point out different ways commands could be more effective. For example:

■ Have parents say exactly when a command is to be carried out. In the example dialogue above, no timelines were set for starting the task. Have parents give a 5-minute limit for starting chores such as cleaning one's room or washing dishes. If the command needs to be carried out more immediately, as was the case with the mother's command, then the parents should give a 10-second limit. Help clients identify which commands need to be obeyed within the 10-second limit. This will include many of the commands given when parents try to get their child to school.

■ Have parents say exactly what is required of their child, and keep it simple. The command "Clean your room," for example, has many different possible meanings. Does this include dusting, vacuuming, making the bed, and straightening the dresser? Does it mean more than that? Instead of this vague command, encourage parents to say something more specific such as, "Pick up your clothes from the bedroom floor and hang them up on hangers in the closet. Start within 5 minutes." Instead of "Stop hanging on to me," a parent could say "Take your hands off me. You have 10 seconds."

■ Make sure parents give commands the child is physically capable of doing. For example, if a 5-year-old cannot hang up clothes in the closet, parents should not ask it of her. The child should also be able to understand all parts of the command. Have parents engage in simple one-step commands first. Encourage them to ask their child to repeat the command if necessary to be sure she understands it.

- As parents give a command, they should ensure that nothing competes with their child's attention (e.g., watching television, talking with friends). Although some children are quite crafty at "not hearing" or "forgetting" a command, parents should prevent any possibility of this. In particular, parents should make direct eye contact with their child when giving commands.

- Parents should make a command a command and not an option or question. In the above example, the father indicated the child "should" clean his room. In addition, the mother "asked" her son to "stop hanging on to me." These words suggest the child has a choice about compliance. Parents must eliminate this choice by giving short, direct commands in sentence form.

- Parents should eliminate criticism. In the above example, the father added a sarcastic comment about his child's compliance. Sarcasm is often noted by children, who may in turn think no reinforcement is available even when they do comply (e.g., "It's about time you took out the garbage"). Parents should change their commands to eliminate sarcasm or negative statements. Parents should also stay as neutral as possible in their tone when giving a command. This neutrality will be especially important later when addressing an attention-seeking child.

- Parents should reduce extra speech during a command (e.g., lectures) and be sure a child is not rewarded by having someone else carry out the command (e.g., do the dishes) for her.

- Parents should engage in a task *with the child* after giving a command (e.g., pick up toys in a room with the child; prepare for work as the child prepares for school).

- Parents should always provide some reward for obeying a command (compliance) and some punishment for failing to obey a command (noncompliance).

Go through each command on the parents' list and change them as necessary. As much as possible, ask parents to change commands themselves so they can learn to build effective commands on their own. Focus especially on commands given in the morning for school attendance. In addition, if excessive reassurance-seeking is a problem, consider the possibility of starting procedures to address this behavior (see material for sessions 5 and 6).

Establishing Regular Routines

Review with parents their description of a typical school-day morning in their house. As before, pay special attention to times children rise from bed, wash and get dressed, eat, brush teeth, do extra activities such as watch television, prepare for school, and leave the house to go to school. In addition, review with parents what their typical routine is during the morning, including behaviors directed toward their children.

Give feedback about changes necessary to regulate this morning routine and improve parents' responses to their children. For example, establish regular times for a child's activities in the morning. Be sure to give family members enough time to complete all morning tasks. Consider that you may be recommending a much stricter routine than what family members are used to. Parents should have a child rise from bed about 90 to 120 minutes before school starts. This should be done even if a child is not currently attending school. The child should be allowed only 10 minutes of time between waking and rising from bed.

In addition, start to set times for the remaining morning activities. The schedule should be flexible enough to allow parents to respond to child noncompliance but also strict enough to promote a smooth transition to school. The schedule in Table 6.1 may be used as a guide.

Implementing Punishments for School Refusal Behavior

Review the list of punishments used by parents in the past to discipline their children. Specifically, review how parents used these punishments, the effectiveness of each, and which punishments are still used. Finally, review parents' attitudes about these punishments and new rules or punishments they wish to raise.

Table 6.1. Sample Morning Schedule

Time	Action
6:50 A.M.	Wake the child (child required to be out of bed by 7:00 A.M.).
7:00–7:20 A.M.	Child goes to the bathroom and washes as necessary.
7:20–7:40 A.M.	Child dresses and accessorizes as necessary.
7:40–8:00 A.M.	Child eats breakfast and discusses her day with parent(s).
8:00–8:20 A.M.	Child makes final preparations for school (e.g., books, jacket).
8:20–8:35 A.M.	Child goes to school with parent(s) or rides the bus.
8:40 A.M.	Child enters school and classroom.

Choose five specific school refusal behaviors to target. These can be chosen from information gathered during formal assessment and should be ranked from most problematic to least problematic. For example:

1. Refusal to move (most problematic)

2. Aggression/hitting her sister or parent

3. Crying

4. Excessive reassurance-seeking (asking the same question more than twice in 1 hour)

5. Screaming (least problematic)

Next, ask parents to choose a specific punishment for the two lowest-severity behaviors (e.g., screaming and excessive reassurance-seeking). The punishment should be something practical that can be given in the morning and after school. The latter is important so that a child knows school refusal behavior is serious and will be addressed at all times of the day, not just the morning. Examples for an attention-seeking child include ignoring, time-out, working through misbehavior without extra attention, and going to bed early. In some cases, however, stronger or more tangible punishments are needed.

Focus on lower-level behaviors and punishments so parents can practice what to do with less effort and experience some success with the process.

However, if you or the parents feel comfortable addressing more of a child's misbehaviors at this time, then do so. Punishments should also be set for noncompliance to commands (e.g., failure to comply with a command to get out of bed or get dressed within a specified time limit).

Discuss all possible scenarios that could occur in the next few mornings and form a plan with the parents to address each one. Try as much as possible to include both parents in the plan. Although this may take some time, making sure parents know how to respond to any behavior is an essential component of this treatment protocol and for eventually getting a child to school.

In many cases, the child will escalate her behavior to get parents to acquiesce. This is an "extinction burst," or an upsurge of misbehavior over and above the previously highest level of misbehavior. An extinction burst can seriously damage the therapy process. Therefore, warn parents of this possibility and encourage them to diligently follow through on commands and punishments. Warn them that if their child successfully forces them to give up now, then she may misbehave even more later when parents try to reassert themselves. As such, parents must try as hard as possible to follow through on commands and punishments. Make sure the parents clearly understand what they need to do in any given situation during the morning. In addition, contact parents daily during this period to give them support and feedback on their behavior.

During this early point in treatment, expect that parents will likely contact you in the early morning as problems and questions arise. In some cases, parents will contact you by cellular telephone as they are driving their child to school. Be prepared for several "impromptu" therapy sessions when working with this population. In addition, expect a child to become more hostile toward you as these procedures are implemented or that she will negotiate with you or the parents to maintain the status quo.

Implementing Rewards for School Attendance

Review with parents their list of rewards used in the past to encourage good behavior. As before, review the effectiveness and desirability of each. Review the parents' attitudes about these rewards and how parents used them in the past. Discuss new rewards raised by parents.

In conjunction with the punishments, choose a reward for two "good" behaviors (e.g., no screaming or excessive morning reassurance-seeking). Because this treatment is geared toward a child refusing school for attention, make the reward attention-based. For example, if a child refrains from screaming and excessive reassurance-seeking, then parents should give substantial verbal praise in the morning and schedule a time at night when the child and parents can do something together (e.g., read, play a game). In some cases, however, stronger or more tangible rewards are needed.

Instruct the child about the expected routine, appropriate behaviors, and punishments and rewards. The child should be reminded that her behavior will determine whether punishments or rewards will be given. Make these statements to the child at the end of the session. However, ask parents to repeat these statements to the child to reinforce their role in taking charge and carrying out these procedures. These statements may be repeated to the child at home as well.

Homework

✎ Maintain the list of commands given to each child. Work on changing commands in accordance with what was discussed in session 2. Parents should meet each night to discuss changes to be made for the next day.

✎ Beginning with the next school day after this session, wake the child about 90 to 120 minutes before school starts and implement the normal school-day routine. Adhere to this routine as closely as possible. The child should do schoolwork and read school-related books if she stays home.

✎ Implement punishments for the presence of the two lowest-severity school refusal behaviors.

✎ Implement rewards for the absence of the two lowest-severity school refusal behaviors.

✎ Contact the therapist should problems arise. Remember that, in this population, clients are often quite eager to use this option. Also, be prepared for potential calls from several people such as a child, parents, school officials, or other professionals.

✎ Continue to complete the daily logbooks. Note specific situations or experiences that arise during the week.

SESSIONS 3 & 4 *Maturing of Treatment*

Session Outline

- Restructure parent commands with a special focus on those given to a child with school refusal behavior, and in the morning before school.

- Emphasize to parents the importance of ignoring inappropriate behaviors.

- Review the morning routine established with the family and discuss changes that were made or deviations from it.

- If necessary, discuss the issue of forced school attendance with parents.

- Discuss with parents past or present information relevant to the design and use of punishments for school refusal behavior.

- Discuss daytime procedures.

- Assign homework.

  At this point in treatment, parent training should focus specifically on the morning and evening routines and a child's school refusal behaviors. In addition, focus on how to address a child during the day if she remains home following tantrums or other misbehaviors. You may have a case where it is desirable to change how a parent responds to many different child behaviors. However, focusing parent training now on a specific problem like school refusal (1) takes advantage of new motivation on a parent's part to change, (2) nudges parents to use treatment procedures on an immediate problem, and (3) provides parents with evidence the procedures have an effect. Early success with school refusal behavior may also increase the parents' motivation to extend these treatment procedures to other behavior problems in the future.

In many ways, sessions 3 and 4 may be quite similar, with the latter an extension of the former. This section covers the maturing of treatment by revisiting components from sessions 1 and 2. However, a more in-depth focus is made on ignoring inappropriate behaviors, implementing forced school attendance, and using daytime consequences.

Restructuring Parent Commands

As before, review the list of commands given by parents to their children. Use the Parent Commands Worksheet in Table 6.2 as necessary. Check for key errors parents may be making and give constructive feedback. In particular, note patterns of errors parents keep making. For example, some commands may continue to be given in the form of questions or be too vague. Encourage parents to respond to this feedback. In addition, ask about nonverbal gestures and disagreements between parents that hurt the effectiveness of their commands. For example, some par-

---

Table 6.2. Parent Commands Worksheet

1. Have the parents say exactly when the command is to be carried out. Have the parents give a 5-minute limit for less immediate tasks (e.g., cleaning his or her room or washing the dishes). If the command needs to be carried out more immediately (e.g., put on your jacket now), then parents should give a 10-second limit.
2. Have the parents say exactly what is required of their child and keep it simple.
3. Make sure the parents give commands that the child is physically capable of doing. Have parents stick with simple one-step commands first. Encourage them to ask their child to repeat the command if necessary to be sure he or she understood it.
4. As the parents give a command, they should ensure that nothing competes with their child's attention (e.g., watching television, talking with friends). Parents should make direct eye contact with their child when giving commands.
5. Parents should make a command a command and not an option or question. Parents must eliminate choice-oriented statements by giving short, direct commands in sentence form.
6. Parents should work to eliminate sarcasm and criticism. Parents should also stay as neutral as possible in their tone when giving a command.
7. Parents should cut down on extra speech during a command (e.g., lectures) and be sure the child is not rewarded by having someone else carry out the command (e.g., do the dishes) for him or her.
8. Parents should try to engage in a task with the child after giving a command.
9. Parents should always provide some reward for obeying a command (compliance) and some punishment for failing to obey a command (noncompliance).

ents give commands without firmness of tone or eye contact, and other parents undercut their spouse by inadvertently or deliberately acquiescing to a child. As much as possible, address these problems immediately.

As before, restructure parent commands with a special focus on those given (1) to the child with school refusal behavior and (2) in the morning before school. Review every command and note important things *not* being said (e.g., specific commands to go to school; verbal praise for compliance). Review the mornings of the previous few days and note what was successful and unsuccessful. The following is an example.

Case Vignette

T: It seems you had two good days and two bad days since the last session. Can you tell me what the major difference was between these two sets of days?

M: On Monday and Wednesday, John (child's father) and I seemed really to be in "sync." We were working together to get the kids up and going to school, and we backed each other up as we talked about last time. (To husband:) Don't you think so?

F: Yeah, I do. I guess it broke down a bit on the other days.

T: Let's talk about that. What exactly "broke down"?

F: There was a lot more resistance to going to school on both those days, and he (child) had a lot of tantrums. We started yelling and nothing much got accomplished. I had to go to work, and I guess he wore her (mother) down.

Explore reasons why the treatment procedures "broke down." In this type of situation, the most likely reasons for breakdown include parent disagreements, one parent leaving the situation, and escalation of child misbehavior. When these things happen, unclear commands are more likely to be given (e.g., *Will you please be quiet?* and *I just wish you would go to school*). Identify how the treatment procedures eroded and address problems as soon as possible. Parents may need to consider changes in work schedules or ask others to help them bring their child to school.

If a child has clearly increased her misbehavior to force parents to abandon their commands or give up on the set routines and rewards and punishments, help parents develop ways of working through their child's behavior problem to accomplish the treatment goals. To back up their commands, for example, parents may have to physically dress their child and bring her downstairs as she is throwing a tantrum or is becoming "dead weight." In many of these cases, extra support from the therapist is essential. By session 4, parents should know what makes a good command. If they seem uncertain or if extenuating circumstances (e.g., spouse leaving home early) continue to interfere with commands, address these as appropriate.

At this time, start emphasizing to parents the importance of ignoring inappropriate behaviors. Many parents adjust to a child who is constantly striving for attention by attending to her whenever a negative behavior occurs. For example, some parents have a tendency, over time, to leave a child alone when she is playing quietly (*Do not disturb him*) but react immediately when she is disruptive (*Stop that now!*). As the child grows older, she learns that the best way to get parental attention is to misbehave. This needs to be reversed.

When a child is refusing school, a common way of getting attention is to exaggerate physical complaints. This applies especially to vague complaints like headaches, stomachaches, and nausea. Attention-seeking children rarely complain of specific, identifiable symptoms like fever or vomiting. If you are sure a child issues somatic complaints for attention and not because of a medical condition, then ask parents to ignore the complaints. However, any possible medical conditions should be completely ruled out first.

To ignore such exaggerated physical complaints, teach parents different physical and verbal behaviors they can use instead of attending to such complaints. This applies especially to the morning. Examples include lack of eye contact (i.e., looking away when the child complains), using time-out, working through tantrums or excess verbal behavior, paying more attention to well-behaved siblings, and having a conversation with one's spouse. In addition, be sure that, as parents engage in these behaviors, the child does not play one parent against the other to get what she wants. In two-parent families, one parent may ignore a child's inappropriate behavior but the other parent may attend to it. Consistency between parents is crucial for presenting a united front to a child. The child must learn that misbehaviors, including exaggerated physical complaints, will not be tolerated. Conversely, remind and encourage parents to praise and otherwise reward their child when she is not complaining of exaggerated symptoms.

For some parents, ignoring some of their child's behavior, especially complaints of physical symptoms, will be hard. Parents sometimes feel guilty or are concerned about being overly stern with their child, that something might actually be wrong with their child, that they will cause long-term psychological harm to their child, and/or that their child will no longer trust them with personal information. If your clients do feel guilty or have these or other concerns about ignoring misbehavior, discuss these concerns now. In response, provide more information about differences between appropriate parental firmness and inappropriate over-restrictiveness. In addition, assure them, by referring the child for a medical evaluation, that nothing is physically wrong with her.

Assure parents as well that ignoring exaggerated complaints will not cause psychological harm to their child. If parents attend only to realistic and non-exaggerated concerns, the child will respect the parents and may be more likely to confide in them in the future. When parents are in doubt about downplaying child misbehaviors or exaggerated physical complaints, remind them that key goals of treatment are to shift their attention to more positive child behaviors (e.g., going to school without exaggerated complaints) and put them more in charge of their home life. In doing so, repeat examples of positive behaviors toward which parents could focus their attention.

Keep in mind that some parents of this functional group will continue to provide "excuses" for keeping their child home from school. In particular, parents sometimes acquiesce quickly to a child's physical complaints or find some other (often weak) reason to keep a child home from school. In some cases, the reason involves an alleged deficiency with a child's school or teacher (in many of these cases, parent–school official friction is common). This may also involve complaints about you or the therapy program. In other cases, a parent will ask a child leading questions (e.g., *Are you sure you're feeling okay?*) to prompt or induce school refusal behavior (*See? She wasn't willing to go*).

Whatever the reason, a child may be ready to return to school but is actually impeded by a parent. This behavior is sometimes due to extreme overprotectiveness related to insecure parenting styles or some parental psychopathology. These cases will require a broader treatment approach and an initial focus on parental resistance, paranoia, or other factors. In addition, developing a strong therapeutic alliance with these parents is often imperative to maintain their interest in treatment and eventually return a child to school.

Establishing Fixed Routines

As before, review the routine established with family members and discuss changes or deviations that were made. If parents made changes to the daily routine to make it work better, or would like to suggest some changes, listen to and possibly endorse the changes. Emphasize the structure and consistency of routines so a child becomes used to what is happening (or is going to happen) in the morning. Work with parents to develop an appropriate nighttime routine as well. In general, children should have set times for coming home from school, completing homework, eating dinner, playing, and preparing for bed. The order of these activities may change, of course, depending on a family's situation. In addition, you and parents may agree to limit playtime or increase homework time as necessary. If a child is not in school at all, parents should obtain schoolwork from the teacher and have their child work on it at home during the day and/or evening.

By session 4, parents should know what makes up a good routine. Discuss uncertainties they may have. Also, review previous mornings and evenings and indicate areas that could be improved. Have parents discuss extenuating circumstances that interfered with the routines. Common problems include dawdling siblings, lack of energy, increased child misbehavior, constant changes in work and other schedules, and other competing priorities. Address these changes as appropriate.

In some cases, you may want to explore the advantages and disadvantages of having parents suspend their child's social activities at night and on the weekends (e.g., Scouts, soccer practice, dance lessons) until full-time school attendance is obtained. Use this approach if it will have an immediate and positive effect on a child's behavior. However, if you or parents suspect that suspension will lead to more hard feelings and family conflict, then a compromise may be in order (e.g., suspension of activities during the week but greater freedom on the weekend). Moreover, sometimes the threat of such a suspension is enough to prompt compliance with commands to return to school.

Forced School Attendance

If a child is completely absent from school or missing most of school, it may be helpful at this point to start thinking about ways of physically bringing her to school. For many children who refuse school for attention, forced school attendance is effective but must be used with caution. A child may be physically taken to school only under certain circumstances. These circumstances include:

- A child refusing school *only* for attention and without any significant distress or anxiety

- Parents who are willing to take a child to school and school officials who are willing to meet the child at the door of the school building and escort her to class

- Presence of two parents or one parent and another adult who can take the child to school

- A child who understands what will happen if she refuses school

- A child currently missing most school days

- A child under age 11 years

By session 3, you may wish to simply raise this issue with parents and discuss the logistics of how forced school attendance would occur. However, if some urgency exists in getting a child back to school, forced school attendance may be pursued now. *Be sure to remind parents, before they engage in this procedure, to discuss it with you first.* At a minimum, parents must consider whether they have the energy, ability, and desire to engage in this procedure.

By session 4, start thinking about ways of physically bringing the child to school if the circumstances for using this procedure are met. The first step is to discuss with parents the feasibility and desirability of the procedure. In addition, assess whether either parent has substantial guilt or hesitation about the process. If parents (and you) feel able and willing to put forth the considerable effort required, then you may proceed. However, if parents (or you) have any hesitation or guilt, wait before using this procedure or rely more on other techniques in this section instead. Remember that hesitation on a parent's part may be exploited by a child and may make future attempts at school attendance much harder.

Forced school attendance generally involves some physical contact with a child. In most cases, this means getting a child into the car or into the school building. Most children stop their attention-getting behavior once in school, so forced school attendance usually refers to morning behaviors under the parents' responsibility. Also, in most cases, the necessary physical force is usually no more than simply picking the child up and carrying her. We do not, of course, sanction contact that could harm a child.

Forced school attendance typically starts at the end of the morning routine. The child is told to get into the car/bus to go to school and/or to enter the school building once there. Should the child not obey these commands, then parents should give a warning. The warning should be short and clear (e.g., *Go now or we will take you there*). If the child obeys, verbal praise is given. If the child does not obey, parents should pick the child up and carry her into the car or school. School officials should be forewarned and be ready to help if needed. Both parents should be involved in carrying the child and tantrums should be ignored or worked through if possible. Usually, one parent drives the car as the other parent sits in the back with the child to prevent escape. Parents should stay neutral or "matter-of-fact" in their tone and give the child little verbal attention.

Forced school attendance should be stopped if a child is overanxious or if the situation becomes unbearable for parents. Bear in mind that some very strong-willed children are quite resistant to this procedure and are willing to outlast their parents for several days or weeks. The danger in stopping is that a child will learn that parents (and the therapist) will acquiesce if misbehavior is severe enough. Therefore, forced school attendance must be used only *under* the right circumstances and with strong follow-through. Be sure to thoroughly discuss forced school attendance with parents should you and/or they consider this option.

Implementing Punishments for School Refusal Behavior

As before, discuss with parents any past or present information relevant to the design and use of punishments for school refusal behavior. Such information would include past and current disciplinary practices, parent attitudes, and extenuating circumstances. Review how parents used the punishments for the two lowest-severity school refusal behaviors (e.g., screaming and excessive reassurance-seeking). In addition, review the school refusal scenarios since the last session and how parents reacted to them using punishments. As before, try as much as possible to include both parents in the plan.

If parents had problems with the punishments or the punishments had no effect on a child's behavior, then extensively rework how and what punishments are to be given. If the punishments *were* carried out and *did* have some effect on a child's behavior, then link the punishments to the next-highest-severity school refusal behavior. Refer to session 2 and the established hierarchy of problematic school refusal behaviors. From the example used in session 2, crying would be the next-highest-severity school refusal behavior. As before, discuss all relevant scenarios and potential problems that may arise in the days ahead.

Review the punishments used for school refusal behaviors and make changes where necessary. By this time, parents should have a good understanding of which punishments are most and least effective. Review previous mornings and evenings and indicate areas that could be improved. As before, identify and address circumstances (e.g., inconsistent administration of punishments by parents) that erode the effectiveness of the punishments.

If a child's school refusal behavior is particularly severe (i.e., she is missing most days), then daytime procedures should be outlined in more detail. This procedure is sometimes used before, or in lieu of, forced school attendance. If a child is home from school during the day, she should sit in a chair under parental supervision during school hours. This could be done at home or at work if necessary. Verbal or physical attention beyond that which is absolutely necessary should be avoided. In addition, a child's setting should be as dull as possible. Following the end of school hours, normal punishments (e.g., grounded in room doing homework) should be applied. If school refusal behavior continues for the majority of the week, then appropriate punishments for the weekend should be given. Discuss daytime procedures with parents if you and they believe these procedures are a reasonable option.

Special Topic 6.2: A Child Home From School

If a child is home from school because it was impossible to get her in the school building, then she should sit in a chair or on her bed for most of the school day. If the parents had to take the child to work, then she should sit in one spot. *Wherever the child is, she should be in a rather dull place and not have access to fun things such as television, video games, telephone, or computer. In addition, verbal and physical attention toward the child should be kept to a minimum.*

If a child is at home or at a workplace during the day, then she should complete school-work or do other academic tasks such as reading textbooks, finishing worksheets, and writing essays. If others are watching a child, parents should ask them to follow these recommendations. Following the end of normal school hours, say after 3 P.M.., a child should do chores or stay in her room alone. In addition, punishments established for school refusal behavior can be implemented in the evening. If a child missed most of the school week, then restrictions and punishments can be carried out on the weekends. The goal of this approach is to deprive a child of attention when refusing school and to give attention and other rewards when she goes to school.

Discuss with parents any past or present information about rewards for school attendance, including the effectiveness of the rewards, parent attitudes, extenuating circumstances, and new rewards. Review whether the use of rewards from the previous session was effective. Make changes where needed. Ask parents to give rewards to the child for the next appropriate behavior (e.g., absence of crying).

Review the rewards used for school attendance and make changes where necessary. By session 4, parents should know which rewards are most and least effective. Review the previous mornings and evenings and indicate areas that could be improved. As before, identify and address circumstances (e.g., inconsistent administration) that erode the effectiveness of rewards.

Homework

✎ Adjust as necessary the list of commands given to each child.

✎ Implement changes to the morning and evening routines and adhere closely to the routines.

✎ Implement punishments for the next-highest-severity school refusal behavior.

✎ Implement rewards for the absence of the next-highest-severity school refusal behavior.

✎ Engage in forced school attendance and daytime procedures if necessary and according to your recommendations.

✎ Continue to complete the daily logbooks, noting specific issues or situations that may arise during the week.

✎ Gradually increase school attendance. *Read Special Topic 4.6 in chapter 4 to become acquainted with different methods of gradually reintegrating a child to school.* These methods include having a child go to school (1) in the morning for a set period of time and then gradually working forward by adding more time, (2) at 2 P.M. until the time school normally ends and then gradually working backward by adding more time, (3) only for lunch and then gradually adding more school time before and after lunch, (4) only for a favorite class or time of day and then gradually adding more classes or school time, (5) in a school room other than the classroom, such as the school library, and then gradually adding more classroom time.

SESSIONS 5 & 6 *Advanced Maturing of Treatment*

Session Outline

- Continue to review and discuss parent commands, and make necessary changes.

- Continue to work on structuring the morning and evening routines for a child.

In sessions 5 and 6, advanced maturing of treatment should occur. This involves a detailed analysis of what is currently happening in the home and what remains a problem. By this time, all daily procedures (i.e., routines, consequences, forced attendance) should be "up and running" and finely tuned to a family's situation. At this point, you should be quite directive in telling parents what remains to be done and vigorously changing what may be blocking treatment success (this section focuses on some possible reasons). In addition, these later treatment sessions sometimes call for more creativity, and you and family members may need to devise innovative modifications of the techniques described here. For example, you may need to be inventive about how parents can bring their child to school, how parents can extricate themselves from their child's classroom, how parents can address tantrums in public places, or how parents can reward attendance after school without alarming siblings.

In many ways, treatment sessions 5 and 6 may be quite similar, with the latter serving as an extension of the former. The basic techniques of parent training—commands, routines, and consequences—should continue to be addressed in these sessions. Other procedures such as forced school attendance and daytime consequences may be broadened as well. This section discusses extending these procedures and summarizing where things may stand at this point. For children progressing more slowly, a repetition of previous procedures might be appropriate.

Restructuring Parent Commands

Continue to review and discuss parent commands given to their children (use the Parent Commands Worksheet in Table 6.1 as necessary). In particular, examine issues and events that interfere with clear commands and the united front that parents should present to their children. If necessary, examine what may be interfering with parent commands (e.g., distractions) and ask a child if she has difficulties understanding what her parents say. Either you or the parents may use this feedback to make necessary changes in the commands. The following is an example.

Case Vignette

M: Matthew, turn off the television and get ready for school. I want you to put your jacket on and pick up your books now.

C: What? In a minute.

M: Look at me. (Mother establishes eye contact with the child) Thank you. What did I say?

C: Come here?

M: Listen to me. Shut off the television now. (Child does so) Thank you. Look at me. Put on your jacket and pick up your books now. What did I say?

C: Put on my jacket and get my books.

M: Thank you for listening. Go ahead.

Be aware of special circumstances that sometimes erode the effectiveness of parent commands. For example, many children who refuse school for attention are members of a single-parent family. Therefore, no other parent is present to back the single parent or help address other children as a parent focuses on the child who refuses school. In this case, encourage the parent to ask others such as siblings, the ex-spouse, or even school officials to give commands or bring the child to school. This may be difficult for the parent, so do not urge him or her to do anything too uncomfortable (e.g., contacting an estranged ex-spouse). However, parent commands are often more effective if backed by valid promises of consequences (e.g., punishments, forced school attendance) from two parents/adults.

In addition, parent commands sometimes erode when several children in a household refuse school at once. For example, a 7-year-old may start refusing school after seeing her 9-year-old brother refuse school and receive substantial parent attention as a result. You may wish to address the oldest child with school refusal behavior first. In many cases, the older child is the one with the most severe behavior as well as the leader of the household rebellion. In such a case, parents may need to concentrate their best efforts on building and issuing appropriate commands to the older child. A reduction of this older child's school refusal behavior may serve as an appropriate model for younger children to follow. However, parents should be careful not to completely ignore younger siblings who may refuse school. If parents have this situation in their household, identify and discuss with them all relevant family dynamics that may influence treatment (e.g., a younger child idolizing and imitating an older one).

Finally, parent commands will be ineffective, of course, if a parent chooses not to give them. If this is the case, examine family communications and parent moods and attitudes that erode treatment. In some cases, for example, family/parent problems need to be resolved first. Such problems include marital dissatisfaction, family conflict, substance use, financial pressures, and other stressors. In other cases, a parent may deliberately sabotage the treatment process or otherwise fail to follow through on the treatment program. If any of these issues apply to a family, address them as appropriate.

At this point in treatment, parents should be continually and actively reviewing what they say to their child. Parents should be talking frequently with one other (or a single parent with a friend or you as appropriate) to improve the consistency of commands and rely on one another for support. In particular, parents should review commands for clarity, consistency, and effectiveness. Commands given in the morning should be compared with those given in the late afternoon and evening, and parents should be able and willing to identify poor commands and discuss how to change them. They should become gradually more independent at searching for anything that erodes the effectiveness of their commands. Ideally, this review process should occur in evening conversations about the day and before the next morning. Parents should also concentrate on supporting one another during this sometimes difficult process. If necessary and desirable, help parents address communication problems or fights they have during this process.

At this point in treatment, parents should be clear and brief in their morning commands. Commands should be few in number and be given in a neutral manner. Rewards and punishments, already established by this point, should immediately follow compliance and noncompliance with these commands, respectively. For example, if a child appropriately complies with a command, parents should praise the child quickly but not too extensively. The child should realize that attention will be paid to compliance, but it is important not to dilute the value of the attention by providing too much too often. If a child does not comply with a command, then appropriate negative consequences should be given (e.g., time-out, working through misbehavior, ignoring).

At this point in treatment, explore how the child's teacher talks to or otherwise interacts with her at school. If the teacher or other school officials seem to interact with the child effectively, then no intervention is necessary. However, if the child is defiant in the school setting, then include the child's teacher in the therapy process. Of course, this decision ultimately rests with the parents, and all ramifications should be considered. For example, including the teacher may embarrass a family member and harm treatment. An alternative strategy is to meet with the teacher at school (with parental permission). In this way, basic elements of treatment can be transferred to the school setting to reduce a child's behavior problems there. For example, a teacher may be instructed to give a child short, clear commands and send home a daily report to parents. Rewards and punishments based on this report may then be given by parents at night.

Establishing Fixed Routines

As in prior sessions, continue to work on structuring morning and evening routines for the child. By this time, routines should be quite predictable to a child, and parents should be providing immediate consequences for substantial deviations from the routine. You may ask a child what she thinks of the daily routines, but keep this conversation to a minimum. Use this feedback to make changes if necessary, but do not allow a child to dominate this process or negotiate many changes. Remember that parents must ultimately be in charge of routines at home.

Morning Routine

At this point in treatment, a child should be rising at a specific time in the morning and getting ready for school. This should be done even if she is not currently going to school. Specific times for each task in the morning should be set as well. If a child is adhering to the morning routine, then parents should praise her in the morning and evening. If a child is not adhering to the morning routine, then punishments should be given. This may involve an immediate punishment such as verbal reprimand in the morning and a delayed punishment such as grounding in room after school and at night.

During the morning routine, parents should also be ignoring or working through negative behaviors. If a child throws a temper tantrum, for example, parents should try to dress the child and complete other morning tasks as much as possible. If this takes most of the morning, including school time, that is fine. Parents should try to bring their child to school in mid-morning or even mid-afternoon if necessary. The key here is to give the child the clear message that school attendance is mandatory and will be pursued even after school has started that day. This will require substantial effort on the part of the parents and may need to be coordinated with school personnel.

At this point in treatment, a child should be expected to go to school after the morning routine. School attendance may be part-time or involve an alternative classroom setting (e.g., library), but the child should be spending at least part of the day at school. If a child was acting out in the morning but going to school at the start of treatment, then attendance should continue. If a child is not attending school at this point in treatment, forced school attendance may be used if appropriate (see section on forced school attendance).

Many children also complain of physical symptoms early in the day. If you have not yet done so, refer the child for evaluation by a pediatrician or other physician to rule out true physical symptoms. Your case may also have other unique problems (e.g., a child with unrelated medical problems) that may preclude ignoring physical symptoms.

If parents have been ignoring exaggerated physical complaints, they may have noticed that one of two things is happening. First, the child has stopped or decreased her excessive somatic complaints. In this case, parents should maintain what they have been doing. Second, the child may have increased her behavior or started complaining of more serious symptoms to elicit sympathy from parents. In this case, more definitive rules may have to be set. Some suggestions are given here, but implement any procedure *only* after consulting the child's medical doctor.

We recommend requiring school attendance unless a child has a fever of at least 100 degrees or some physical condition that clearly precludes school attendance (see guidelines in chapter 4). Of course, your client's situation may be unique and call for a different approach. Inform the child of these rules and encourage parents to adhere to them closely. Do not be surprised if a child tests the limits of these rules. If a child is legitimately sick and must stay home from school, she should be restricted to bed (not just the bedroom, but bed) for the entire school day. In addition, very little extra verbal or physical attention should be given and the child should be told of the parent's expectation of school attendance the next day (if appropriate). In cases where a child has to miss school for some other reason (e.g., family funeral), she should be told the same thing and attend school as soon as possible.

Daytime Routine

If school attendance is not possible at this point, then daytime routines and consequences should be used. If necessary, have parents make arrangements for their child during the day if the school refusal situation remains unchanged and neither parent can be home. In this case, a parent might bring a child to work and assign her boring tasks or make her sit in a chair all day (with little verbal or physical attention from others), or to a friend, relative, or neighbor who can do the same thing.

In other cases, at least one parent or adult will need to supervise the child while she is at home during the day. During this time, the child should receive no extra verbal or physical attention. In addition, she should be required to sit alone, do boring chores, or complete homework sent home from school. The goal is to deprive children of attention for refusing school but, at the same time, make them expend effort for their disruptive behavior and/or maintain their schoolwork. If possible, parents should get their child to attend school that day, if only for an hour or two. For example, recommend that parents repeat the "*Go to school*" command each hour to the child. Appropriate school attendance rewards or punishments may then follow.

Evening Routine

If a child stayed home for the entire day, then she should not be allowed to enjoy fun activities at night. Some parents allow their children to go out and play after the normal school period is ended (e.g., 3 P.M.). However, this may give a child the impression that all she has to do is "wait it out" to enjoy fun activities. Instead, instruct parents to get their child's schoolwork for that day from the teacher and have her work on it at night. Suspend activities such as television, video games, or other social engagements as appropriate.

Whether or not a child attended school that day, her routine should be set after school hours and at night. After-school activities, homework, and later recreational activities should be set to a specific time and tied to school attendance. For example, if a child eventually attended school but refused to move in the morning for 10 minutes to avoid school, she may be grounded for the evening, required to do additional homework, and/or be sent to bed early. The child may be grounded or made to sit on the stairs or in a corner at night for twice the amount of time she refused school that morning (e.g., 20-minute morning temper tantrum = 40 minutes of grounding that night). Conversely, if a child attended school with no problems, then parents may give substantial verbal attention and spend extra time with her. A child should clearly understand that school attendance is an important part of life. As a result, any missed time will have consequences not just for that morning, but also during the day, night, and perhaps the weekend. For example, some children end up owing their parents a large "debt" of grounding time during the week. This debt can then be paid in grounding or extra chores on the weekend.

When implementing routines and administering punishments for a child with very persistent school refusal behavior, some family members feel a lot of guilt and frustration and find that the home resembles a battlefield. In other cases, family members may feel the treatment procedures described here are too mechanical or foreign to their normal way of interacting. Although pressure on the school-refusing child should continue during the week, the family may need to maintain cohesion and childhood fun. In some persistent school refusal cases, for example, families may need to set aside treatment procedures on the weekend and just enjoy some fun activities together. As the therapist, you will know a family's situation well by this point and will have to make your best clinical judgment as to what is most appropriate.

Forced School Attendance

If parents are physically bringing their child to school, continue to follow the procedures outlined for sessions 3 and 4. If the situation is not improving or is becoming unbearable for parents, then you may need to make changes in the procedure or suggest that parents end it altogether. Remember, however, that stopping the procedure at this point may convey to a child that extreme misbehavior is enough to force parents (and the therapist) to acquiesce. This will damage future attempts at bringing the child to school.

In some cases, parents find it emotionally difficult to force a child to attend school for an entire day. In other cases, getting a child to attend full-time is impossible. In still other cases, the child has some anxiety about attending school all day but the anxiety is not severe enough to justify a full day's absence. In these cases, parents may wish to bring a child to school during the afternoon and let her finish the school day. On subsequent days, the child may be brought to school at earlier and earlier times (e.g., 30 minutes earlier each day until the normal beginning of the school day is reached). An advantage of this approach is that a child may have an easier time going to school at lunchtime or recess when she can be with friends and the separation process from parents is not as tough. In addition, the child knows she has to attend school for only a couple of hours before being home again.

The disadvantage of this procedure, however, is that others may wonder why the child is starting school in the middle of the day and ask the child intrusive questions. A child may need some strategy to cope with this situation. Examples include deflecting the intrusive questions by changing the topic or laughing with peers, declining to answer on the basis of privacy (i.e., none of their business), straightforwardly answering the questions, or referring the questions to someone else.

Another strategy is to have a child stay in a library or other school area before the parents physically bring her into the classroom. This requires cooperation with school officials, who must be consulted beforehand. In some cases, the child may stay at the library and complete schoolwork or chores (e.g., reshelving books) for the entire day. Subsequently, the child should be reintegrated into the regular classroom setting for an initially short (e.g., 1 hour), and then gradually longer, period of time. Behavior problems on the child's part should be conveyed to parents for appropriate consequences that evening.

Another problem with forced school attendance is that school officials may be unable or unwilling to help parents bring a child into school or check the child's attendance throughout the day. In these cases, you and the parents should get to know teachers, counselors, attendance officers, and others who can help to some extent. If absolutely necessary, parents can bring their child into the classroom and monitor her themselves. Parents can then gradually reduce the amount of time they are in the classroom. Keep in mind, however, that parent attendance at school is exactly what many attention-seeking children want, so the procedure must be used with great care. Use this procedure only if you have great confidence that a parent can eventually extricate herself from a child's classroom at a systematic pace set by you. If at all possible, however, avoid this procedure.

Excessive Reassurance-Seeking

In many cases, excessive reassurance-seeking continues to be a problem. Excessive reassurance-seeking may come in several forms, including (1) constantly asking the same questions over and over, (2) attending school but constantly telephoning parents at home or work, and/or (3) attending school but constantly demanding attention from the teacher or deliberately becoming disruptive to be sent home.

Children will sometimes repeat statements or ask the same questions over and over about certain topics. These topics often include:

- Pleas for home schooling or to change teachers, schools, or classes

- Proposed deals to delay school attendance or stop the therapy process (e.g., "I'll go to school next week if you let me go to work with you this week" or "I'll go to school tomorrow if we don't have to go to the clinic anymore")

- Physical complaints and fatigue

- Scheduling of drop-offs and pickups during the day

- Difficulty and scheduling of schoolwork

To address a child who asks the same questions over and over, follow these procedures. If the child asks a question, parents should answer it *one time*. If the question is asked again, the parents should calmly remind the child only once that the child knows the answer. If the parents are asked the question again, they should turn away from the child. For example:

C: Mom, are you going to make me go to school on Monday?

M: Yes, we talked about that in therapy. (Ten minutes or so pass)

C: Are you sure I have to go on Monday? Can't I just start on Tuesday?

M: You know the answer to that question.

C: How about if I do work at home on Monday and then start Tuesday?

(Parent turns away from child. When the child begins to speak about other topics, or continues on a more appropriate discussion regarding school, the parent turns back to the child and continues to give attention.)

You may wish to set a limit on how many times a child can ask a particular question. One rule for young children with highly excessive reassurance-seeking behavior is to allow one question about school per hour. Following this question and an answer by the parent, the child's school-related questions are ignored until the following hour. This period of time is then gradually increased (e.g., 2, 3, 4 hours). Keep in mind, however, that this sometimes requires strong parental stamina and selective deafness.

Excessive reassurance-seeking may also come in the form of children who attend school but constantly telephone a parent at home or work to get comfort about what worries them. Sometimes this is the original problem, and sometimes it develops after a child resumes school attendance. Either way, it is an inappropriate way to get attention and should be changed. In most of these cases, a child should be allowed one telephone call per day to a parent and *only* as a reward for good classroom behavior. In severe cases, this may start with more calls and then be gradually cut back. Of course, telephone calls would have to be established with cooperation of school officials. Excess calls should be linked to punishments at night. Attention-seeking children should not have access to cellular telephones.

Finally, a child may attend school but seek constant attention from a teacher to be sent to the nurse's office or home from school, or to contact her parents. In other cases, a child will simply engage in disruptive behavior to be suspended from school or otherwise be sent home. In these cases, work with parents and the teacher to establish rewards and punishments in the classroom for a child's behavior. For example, a card system may be established so that each rule violation (including inappropriately bothering the teacher with an unimportant matter) results in a card change from green (acceptable) to yellow (warning) to orange (last warning) to red. Upon receiving a red card, the child would be sent to the principal's office for discipline or to complete homework. In cases of older children or adolescents, more age-appropriate methods should be used (e.g., token economy, verbal feedback and reprimands, detention). A key aspect of this plan, however, is to prevent a child from leaving school, which would only serve to reinforce her misbehavior. Therefore, close cooperation with school officials is essential. In addition, a daily report card may be sent home so parents can administer appropriate rewards or punishments at night.

Implementing Punishments for School Refusal Behavior

Continue to review punishments and make changes where necessary. If appropriate, get feedback from a child about the effectiveness of the punishments and use this feedback if desirable. If daytime restrictions on the child's activities are currently used, note their effectiveness and degree of parental attention and make adjustments where needed. Extend punishments to the highest-severity school refusal behaviors (e.g., from session 2, hitting and refusal to move) if appropriate.

Implementing Rewards for School Attendance

Continue to review rewards and make changes where necessary. If appropriate, get feedback from a child about the effectiveness of the rewards and use this feedback if desirable. Extend rewards to the absence of the highest-severity school refusal behaviors (e.g., lack of hitting and refusal to move) if appropriate. Be sure all punishments and rewards are clearly outlined beforehand to the child.

Homework

✎ Adjust the list of commands given to each child. Engage in homework assignments that help prevent ineffective commands.

✎ Continue to implement the morning, daytime, and night routines. Engage in homework assignments that improve adherence to the routines.

Special Topic 6.3: Coming to School Late in the Morning

Many children who refuse school for attention are chronically tardy to school because of morning misbehaviors designed to induce parental acquiescence toward absenteeism. This situation is also common to children with the first functional condition (see chapter 4). These children are generally not missing most of the school day, so the procedures described here are most applicable to them.

In this situation, inform school officials about a child's difficulty entering the school building. In addition, encourage parents to take a child to school even if she is late. School officials can assist by greeting a child at a certain time and place in the morning and escorting her to class if possible. *If a child is willing to be escorted into the classroom by a school official, then parents must allow this to happen and leave quickly.*

If parents can get a child to school but not in the school building, *they should not immediately go home.* Going immediately home reinforces crying and avoidance of school. Instead, parents should stay at the school playground or entrance or sit in their car in the parking lot with the child. Encourage parents not to be angry or critical but rather speak to a child in a matter-of-fact tone. Parents can allow a child to vent whatever she is concerned about, but the child should continue to be told she is expected to go to school. Parents should encourage their child every 15 minutes or so to enter the school building. *Even if this goes on for a couple of hours and the child then enters school, this is better than missing the entire school day.*

A key rule here is no backsliding. Parents should not allow their child to do less than what she has already shown she can do. For example, if a child can enter the main lobby of the school building, then parents should wait with her there as long as possible and encourage her to go in every 15 minutes. If a child can enter a supervised setting such as the guidance counselor's office or school library, then parents should escort her there and have her remain there for some time before entering class. If possible, parents should leave the school building and allow a child to be escorted to class by a school official. Finally, if a child can enter the classroom after some period of time, even if she is late, then she should be allowed to do so.

✎ Implement punishments for the presence of the next-highest-severity school refusal behavior(s).

✎ Implement rewards for the absence of the next-highest-severity school refusal behavior(s).

✎ Continue to complete the daily logbooks.

SESSIONS 7 & 8 *Completing Treatment*

Session Outline

■ Continue to review and discuss parent commands, and adjust if necessary.

■ Finalize commands and provide a summary to parents.

■ Finalize morning and evening routines and provide a summary to parents.

■ Finalize punishments for school refusal behaviors and provide a summary to parents.

■ Finalize rewards used for school attendance and provide a summary to parents.

■ Assign homework.

By sessions 7 and 8, treatment procedures may begin to change in some key ways. First, as the family nears the end of therapy, treatment procedures should more closely resemble what is naturally occurring in a child's environment. For example, a child should be entering school on her own without nudging or coercion. In addition, rewards given to the child should be based more on verbal praise. Also, the strictness of morning and evening routines may be eased if necessary and appropriate. Do not deviate too much from the treatment procedures, however, that led to a child's return to school.

You may also change treatment procedures by extending them to related problem areas if a child's school refusal behavior is fully or nearly resolved. For example, parents may begin to focus more on explicit commands given at other times (e.g., weekends) or for other behaviors that remain a problem. However, do not prematurely extend these treatment practices until a child's school refusal behavior is under control.

In many ways, session 8 can serve as an extension of session 7. As such, treatment procedures can be finalized and termination issues can be discussed. Also, recommendations should be made to parents about how to best address a child and her behavior in the near and distant future. Lists of potential pitfalls to avoid may be developed, and long-term follow-up contact and booster sessions (see chapter 8) may be scheduled.

Restructuring Parent Commands

Continue to review and discuss parent commands (use the Parent Commands Worksheet as necessary). If a child continues to have trouble going to school or understanding her parents, help parents adjust their commands as necessary. Some children, for example, need simpler parent commands or need to be rewarded for compliance one command at a time. To ensure that parents have a firm grasp of good commands, give them a hypothetical example of a child misbehavior and ask them how they would respond. If they do so appropriately, give praise. If not, review material from previous sessions to help parents adjust their commands.

If a child is attending school on a near-regular basis, then parent commands for the morning should stay the same. If other concerns remain, then they can start to be addressed. For example, some children will start to go to school and behave well in the morning because parents have focused so much attention on challenging these behaviors at this time. However, these children may continue to misbehave at night or on the weekends. Such misbehaviors may be addressed now. In addition, some children will start to go to school but continue to show attention-getting behaviors such as excessive questions in other settings (e.g., supermarket). If applicable, talk about parent commands and appropriate responses in these settings as well. Risk of relapse for this population will be lower if parents use treatment procedures for various behaviors in different settings and at different times. Finally, extend these treatment procedures to other children in the family as appropriate.

By session 8, you and the parents may wish to finalize commands given to a child. Give parents a summary of what type of commands seem best for their child. Base this summary on the particular aspects and original problems of the family. In doing so, point out how certain clear commands facilitated a child's return to school. Remind parents of some basic themes regarding commands: simplicity, clarity, consistency, and immediate response to child compliance and noncompliance. If desirable, give parents a written list of appropriate commands and types of comments to avoid, such as question-like commands, sarcasm, and insults.

Warn parents that they may regress to old patterns of behavior. For example, some parents do not practice new command skills once a child is back in school. Whether due to detachment, complacency, or frustration, parents will often "give their all" during therapy but not after therapy. In addition, many children increase their school refusal behavior sometime after therapy to test their parents and induce acquiescence. As a result, maintain contact with parents for some time after termination. Your support and feedback about good commands will help reduce the risk of relapse (see chapter 8).

Establishing Fixed Routines

Continue to work with parents on structuring the morning and evening routines, which by now should be quite predictable to a child. If a child is not complying with the morning routine, then punishments should be given by parents. This may involve an immediate consequence such as a verbal reprimand in the morning or a delayed consequence such as grounding in room after school and at night. If a child continues to have problems going to school, help parents adjust these routines as necessary. For example, some children respond better to more basic routines that involve only a few steps.

If a child is going to school on a near-regular basis, then the morning routine should stay the same. If other areas of concern remain, then they can start to be addressed. For example, some children will start to go to school but still need a lot of structure at school and home or at night and on the weekends. Ask a child for her input as to what routines and activities she prefers, but leave the final structure largely up to parents.

By session 8, you and the parents may wish to finalize routines established for the morning and evening (by this time, if the child is back in school, midday routines may be unnecessary). Give parents a summary of what routines are best for their child. Base this summary on the particular aspects and original problems of the family. In doing so, point out how specific routines facilitated a child's return to school. Remind parents of some basic themes regarding routines: regularity, predictability, and immediate response to child compliance or noncompliance. If desirable, give parents a written summary of the current routines and pitfalls to avoid, such as too much child influence, inflexibility, and failure to respond to deviations from the routine.

As with commands, warn parents that they may regress to old patterns of behavior. Specifically, parents may become lax with new routines once a child is back in school. This is sometimes due to a willingness to give a child some allowance for dawdling or for mild forms of noncompliance, such as excusing minor misbehaviors. Unfortunately, this often leads to a situation where a child gets increased attention for school refusal behavior (the original problem that required treatment). Parents should continue to adhere closely to routines, respond neutrally to their child during these routines, and work through problem behaviors. Remind parents as well to downplay excessive physical complaints and work together to bring their child to school at least part-time on days when she refuses to attend. Maintaining contact with parents for some time after termination will also help prevent recurring problems.

Implementing Punishments for School Refusal Behavior

Continue to review punishments given for school refusal behaviors, which by now should be quite predictable to a child. If a child continues to have problems going to school, focus on what makes the punishments ineffective. For example, some children will respond only to punishments that are stronger, applied more immediately, or applied more consistently. If daytime punishments are currently used, note their effect and help parents make adjustments where needed. At this time, give the parents a hypothetical example of a child misbehavior and ask how they would respond using punishments and rewards. If they do so appropriately, give praise. If not, review material from previous sessions to help parents modify punishments and rewards as necessary.

If a child is going to school on a near-regular basis, then punishments should stay the same. If other concerns remain, then they can start to be addressed. Some children will start to go to school but still require punishments for related behaviors. For example, children who once refused school often continue to require punishments for associated problems like aggression, noncompliance in other settings, failure to complete homework, bedwetting and/or sleeping with parents, tantrums, general disruptive behavior at home or in class, arguing, and yelling, among others. If behaviors such as these remain, address them while the family is in therapy. The risk of relapse will be lower if parents have a firm grasp of punishments and are willing to use them consistently for various problem behaviors.

By session 8, you and the parents may wish to finalize punishments for school refusal behaviors and make changes where necessary (by this time, daytime punishments may no longer be needed). Give the parents a summary of what types of punishments seem best for their child. Base this summary on the particular aspects and original problems of the family. In doing so, point out how specific punishments facilitated a child's return to school. Remind parents of some basic themes regarding punishments: fairness, predictability, consistency, and immediate administration when needed. If desirable, give parents a written summary of the current punishments and pitfalls to avoid, such as giving consequences too long after a specific behavior and inadequate severity of punishment.

Warn parents of the dangers of inadequately administering punishments in the future. For example, some parents stop giving punishments out of old feelings of guilt, shame, general detachment, or nonchalance. Find out why this might be the case and address problems while the family is in therapy. In addition, some parents differ in their responses to a child or to children across different behaviors. Emphasize the importance of, and need for, consistency. Finally, some parents fall into the habit of, or only have energy for, giving severe punishments once in a while instead of consistent, predetermined punishments at all appropriate times. Some parents may use severe physical punishment occasionally to control problem behaviors that accumulate over time or that become crisis-like in nature. Instead, parents should use appropriate punishment every time a child misbehaves. Remind parents of the pitfalls of physical punishment and encourage them to adhere to the treatment procedures outlined in therapy.

Implementing Rewards for School Attendance

Continue to review the rewards used for school attendance, which by now should also be quite predictable to a child. If a child continues to have problems going to school, focus on what makes the rewards ineffective and help parents make changes where necessary. For example, some children respond only to rewards that are stronger, applied more immediately, or applied more consistently. If a child is going to school on a near-regular basis, then rewards should stay the same. If other areas of concern remain, then they can start to be addressed. For example, rewards may be set up for the absence of the school refusal-related behaviors noted in the previous section.

By session 8, you and the parents may wish to finalize rewards used for school attendance and make changes where necessary. Warn parents not to become complacent if their child has returned to school or become lazy in giving rewards in the future. For example, some parents stop giving rewards once their child is back in school, but this will almost always lead to relapse. In addition, some parents begin to take school attendance for granted, become busy and forget to acknowledge a child's behavior, or give big but infrequent rewards. These practices may also lead to relapse. Try to identify and address factors such as parent detachment that might lead to these bad habits.

Remind parents to specifically define other misbehaviors and consequences in the future, and to inform their child of any upcoming changes they decide to make in treatment procedures. Tell parents, "If you need to punish, you do not need to explain, and if you need to explain, you do not need to punish." In other words, all rules, consequences, and unwanted behaviors should be defined beforehand and the child should know them by heart.

Homework

✎ Continue to implement appropriate parental commands. Periodically review the list of pitfalls regarding commands given by the therapist.

✎ Continue to implement the morning and evening routines. Periodically review the list of pitfalls regarding routines given by the therapist.

✎ Continue to implement punishments for the presence of specific and predetermined school refusal behaviors. Watch for potential pitfalls.

✎ Continue to implement rewards for the absence of specific and predetermined school refusal behaviors. Watch for potential pitfalls.

✎ Contact the therapist as needed for support, feedback, answers to questions, long-term follow-up, and booster sessions if necessary.

Chapter 7 | *Children Refusing School for Tangible Rewards Outside of School*

Starting Treatment

Materials Needed

- Sample contracts

Session Outline

- Negotiate a contract between parent(s) and child.

  This section describes initial treatment procedures for a child refusing school to pursue tangible rewards outside of school. Common behaviors in this functional group include secrecy to hide school absences, verbal and physical aggression, running away, spending an excessive amount of time with friends, disruptive behavior to stay out of school, hostile attitude, refusal to talk, drug use, and excessive sleep.

  The major focus of treatment is relevant family members. This is most likely parents and the child refusing school. The major goal is to provide family members with a better way of solving problems, reducing conflict, increasing rewards for school attendance, and decreasing rewards for school absence. Specifically, this will involve:

- Establishing times and places to negotiate problem solutions

- Defining behavior problems

- Designing written contracts between parents and child to address the problem

- Implementing the contracts

This treatment plan therefore involves key elements of a contingency contracting approach. In discussing this treatment approach, these four components will continue to be revisited.

In this treatment plan, you will probably split your time equally between parents (or parent in single-parent families) and child. However, you should ask a child first for his input and negotiate initial contracts separately with him and with parents. Speaking with the child first is sometimes key to getting him "on board" a treatment program. A child should know the therapist is considering his point of view as much as the parents' view. In other words, a child must understand that the therapist and parents are not simply "ganging up" on him. This is especially pertinent to adolescents who are hostile during therapy or those you hope will be more forthcoming and motivated over time in therapy. In addition, a key element of this treatment package will be to ensure that each party is willing to participate and do so in a sincere manner. As a result, you may need to shift your therapeutic alliance among different family members at different times. In this way, one party may feel more empowered and thus more willing to contribute to or maintain a contract.

A key element of contracting is that *everyone* negotiates in good faith. This means a child and parents should try to give a reasonable account of what they are willing to do and what they feel is unfair or unworkable. Probe for anything anyone seems uneasy about during treatment. In particular, ask about each line of each contract to make sure it is satisfactory to a child and parents. Finally, siblings should be informed about procedures that will occur. In some cases, their input is quite valuable and including them may prevent problems on their part during treatment. In fact, in many cases, you may wish to include other children in the contract process so they can help monitor compliance.

Establishing Times and Places to Negotiate Problem Solutions

At this time, structure the problem-solving/contracting process entirely during the therapy session. In this way, you can supervise the contracting procedure, provide detailed suggestions, and address problems immediately. In particular, note communication problems family members may have as well as other behaviors (e.g., sabotage, refusal to participate) that interfere with good problem-solving. If these interfering behaviors are relatively minor, try to address them now. For example, if one family member has trouble expressing what he wants, give suggestions for responding. However, if these interfering behaviors are relatively major (e.g., fighting), you may want to assess them further and address them over several sessions.

Much of the problem-solving/contracting process will initially take place in session, but a child and parents should think about times and places they can talk about problems at home during the week. In later treatment, contracting should take place during these times at home. Ask them to think about times when everyone is home, when other matters are not too urgent, when family members are relaxed, and when no immediate distractions are present. This is often a difficult, if not impossible, task. However, making time for problem-solving is essential if a family's conflict and a child's school refusal behavior are to be reduced. If problems occur in deriving such a time, try to address this in session. An especially common problem is a family member who does not want to participate in family meetings out of fear that other family members will "gang up" on him. Reducing the chances of this scenario, developing rapport with the alienated person, and incorporating him as much as possible in the meeting/therapy process will likely be top priorities.

Defining the Behavior Problem

To acquaint a family with the contracting process, design the first contract around a relatively basic and circumscribed problem. In fact, the first problem to be addressed should have nothing to do with school refusal behavior. Although this may seem counterintuitive, family members should practice appropriate problem-solving on a simpler level at least once. This will help you gauge how fast or slow further treatment needs to be. If a family solves the problem with ease, then treatment may progress more quickly. If family members struggle with solving even a simple problem, then treatment may progress more slowly over several sessions of repeated practice. In addition, setting aside school refusal behavior for the moment may lessen immediate family tension and pressure on a child. If some valid urgency exists in getting a child back to school immediately, then continue with later procedures (e.g., school attendance contracts) with caution at this point.

Choose something that has recently occurred as a minor problem. Examples include not doing chores, not going to bed on time, not checking in with parents, or not completing a homework assignment. Ask the family to address only one problem. Be sure, though, that each family member agrees on the appropriateness of the problem. Avoid unsolvable, long-standing, or overly complicated problems. For example, do not focus on a child's trouble with the law a year ago (now unsolvable), family conflict (which may be long-standing), or family finances (too complicated). Keep it simple.

After choosing a behavior problem, ask each family member to define the problem. You may (or may not) be surprised at the differences in definitions you receive, so bear in mind that some blending of viewpoints may be necessary. For example, a parent might define a problem as "He never takes out the garbage when I ask him," whereas a child might define the problem as "I have to take out the garbage all the time." Each definition is vague, however, and points to a communication problem. As a compromise, you might describe the problem simply as "The garbage is not being taken out on a regular basis." In this case, no one is blamed and the problem is clearly defined.

Designing a Contract

As mentioned above, the first contract should be negotiated separately with a child and parents. In this way, you can engage in "shuttle diplomacy" by working your way back and forth from one party to the other. After the behavior problem is satisfactorily defined, ask the child to describe as many potential solutions to the problem as possible. Include even humorous ones such as "Hiring a maid to take out the garbage." Try to get about 5 to 10 proposed solutions and rank them in order of desirability. Desirability depends on whether a solution is practical, realistic, specific, and potentially agreeable to everyone. Following this process with the child, ask parents to generate solutions and rank them in order of desirability.

Next, choose one proposed solution that is most desirable. Ensure that each family member bargains in good faith and informs you if a solution is acceptable or not. Gently prod each family member into accepting the best solution, but do not counteract strong objections. Focus on compromise. A good solution to the problem presented above might be: "(Child) will be asked to take out the garbage only on Wednesday and Saturday, but must take out the garbage when asked on those days." If each family member agrees to the definition, then you can move to the next step.

The next step involves developing rewards and punishments for completing or not completing the contract. As with defining the problem, speak with each party separately about possible rewards and punishments. Again, focus on those most desirable and agreeable to everyone. The first contract should be quite simple and read something like this:

> (Child) agrees to take out the garbage on Wednesday and Saturday if asked. If (child) completes this chore correctly, then (child) will receive an extra half-hour of curfew on Saturday night. If (child) does not complete the chore, then (child) will be required to be in the house 1 hour earlier than usual.

As mentioned earlier, you or the family may wish to add other children to the contract as appropriate. Close loopholes that might exist in the contract. In this contract, for example, you may wish to define exactly when the child will take out the garbage, what the chore involves, who will decide if the chore was carried out correctly, and what time curfew is supposed to be. In closing loopholes, give more say to parents. Beware that some children will actively seek any loophole to sabotage or scuttle a contract. Identify and address this scenario immediately. In addition, the finished contract should be time-limited—no more than a few days at most. In this way, if problems arise, you can address them quickly.

Implementing the Contract

Once a sample contract has been designed, each party should read it and say whether he or she agrees to it. If not, then renegotiate the contract. If agreement is reached, then ask each party to sign the contract and provide him or her with a copy. Because some family members (including the child) often keep their reservations to themselves during this process, you may need to gently prompt them several times to express reservations and indicate whether they actually agree with the contract. Ideally, once a contract is finalized, ask a family member to display it in an area of the house where it can be read, referred to, and initialed daily by each party. The door of the refrigerator is a good place. Final questions should be addressed at this point.

In addition, give family members a "pep talk" about what has been accomplished (i.e., coming to an agreed-upon solution to a problem) and your confidence that they will carry out the contract. In addition, convey the notion that solving more difficult problems should follow naturally if this contract is successful. Remind a child and parents to contact you should problems arise, and that you will contact them between sessions to discuss outstanding issues. With respect to the latter, contact the family daily until the next session to address problems as quickly as possible.

Special Topic 7.1: 504 and Individualized Education Plans

Parents and children often wonder what the point is in returning to school if make-up work is piled high and a child is at risk for failing the remainder of the school year. We recommend that you and the parents speak to school officials about the possibility of establishing a "504 plan" or an "individualized education plan" (IEP). A 504 plan is named for a federal law that mandates school districts to accommodate students with a condition that interferes with their learning. Examples of interfering conditions include physical problems such as chronic medical illnesses or mental problems such as depression, anxiety, or learning or attention-deficit/hyperactivity disorders.

504 plans may be used to change class schedules, make-up work, credits, or other conditions that might make it easier for a child to attend school. If a child can go to school at least part-time, for example, and complete some schoolwork, then this could be built into the 504 plan. Work closely with school officials to see what options are available. If a child has a developmental disorder such as mental retardation, autism, or Asperger's disorder, then she may have an IEP. An IEP can also be designed to help youths return to school by changing class schedules and other key areas.

Homework

✎ Think about times and places where problem-solving can occur in the future.

✎ Think about problems and potential solutions for the next contract.

✎ Implement the current contract and contact the therapist if necessary.

✎ Encourage general adherence to a regular school-day schedule, even if only in the morning prior to school. This includes early wakening, dressing and preparing for school as if going, and completing school assignments.

✎ Continue to complete daily logbooks. Note specific situations or experiences that arise during the week.

SESSION 2 *Intensifying Treatment*

Session Outline

■ Help parents and child establish times and places for negotiating a solution to a problem by encouraging them to have family meetings.

■ Negotiate a new contract only if the family successfully completed the first contract.

This section describes how to intensify treatment procedures for a child refusing school for tangible rewards outside of school. As discussed before, the major focus of treatment here is relevant family members—most likely parent(s) and the child refusing school. However, other children may be included as well. The major goal of treatment is to provide family members with a better way of solving problems, reducing conflict, increasing rewards for a child to attend school, and decreasing rewards for a child to miss school. Again, this will involve establishing times and places for negotiating a solution to a problem, defining a behavior problem, designing a written contract between parents and child to address the problem, and implementing the contract.

At this time, conduct most of the problem-solving/contracting process in the therapy session. However, family members should begin to meet at regular times at home to talk about the current contract and what changes might be made at the next therapy session. These family meeting times should be marked by little distraction and full family participation. This will give family members some practice discussing important issues and will help the therapy process. In later treatment, contracting will occur during these meetings at home.

For now, schedule one or two home sessions between sessions 2 and 3 where everyone sits and discusses the contract and other relevant issues. At first, this may seem awkward, so limit the meeting to 10 to 15 minutes. Also, ensure family members know that everyone should have an equal amount of time to speak. If four people are in the family, for example, everyone should have 3 minutes to talk about whatever they want. Have someone keep time if necessary. Some other basic rules for the family meeting are:

- Agree ahead of time about who will call the meeting to order. Rotate this job among family members if possible and as appropriate.

- As much as possible, limit family discussion to the contract and complaints or problems each family member may have. Try to adhere to simple statements and avoid tangents. Hurtful comments should also be avoided.

- Allow each person to speak *without interruption*. If one person wants to respond to another, he must wait his turn. Try to minimize questioning.

- Do not allow the meeting to be dominated by one family member, especially a parent. If someone is given 3 minutes to talk and only 1 minute is used, then everyone should think about that person's statement in silence for 2 minutes.

- Encourage family members to stay at the meeting for its entire duration. If a family member does not wish to talk, he can simply sit and listen to others.

- Praise everyone for attending the meeting.

- If the meeting does not go well, end it and schedule another at a later time. Examples of problems include insults and verbal and physical fighting. In extreme cases where family members cannot get along, inform the therapist and discuss these issues in session.

- If the meeting goes well and a healthy discussion occurs, feel free to extend it. However, if one person thinks the meeting is not going well, then you may reschedule the session. An exception may occur if one family member is deliberately sabotaging or disrupting the meeting. In this case, tolerate or include the disruptive person as much as possible, but ask him to leave if necessary. The therapist should be made aware of this disruption to address it as soon as possible. As a general rule, exclusions of this sort should be kept to a minimum.

- Contact the therapist during the meeting if you have questions. (You may wish to discuss with clients your degree of availability and/or your policy for taking certain types of calls at certain times.)

Defining the Behavior Problem

Review with the family the success or failure of the first contract. If the contract failed or other problems arose, investigate at length why this was so. Look for fighting among family members, low motivation, sabotage, or other factors that hurt the success of the contract. Spend considerable time addressing these reasons and re-implement the contract if possible. Keep in mind that some cases take longer than others to resolve and additional practice with simpler contracts is often necessary before advancing to more complicated ones.

If the first contract was successful, give family members ample praise and emphasize the fact that problems can be amicably and effectively resolved. Depending on the severity of the situation, the next contract could involve either more complex problems that have nothing to do with school refusal behavior or introduce school refusal behavior as one component. For extreme or long-standing cases of school refusal behavior or problematic family interactions, the first approach is recommended. In this way, family members will have more opportunity to practice problem-solving on easier issues before tackling difficult school refusal behaviors.

If your case involves moderate to severe school refusal behavior or moderately problematic family interactions, then the next contract may be more complex by introducing a school refusal behavior component such as morning preparation. In addition, discuss what non-school refusal behaviors should be in the contract. We recommend including chores, because later contracts may focus on paying a child for chores if he attends school for some period of time. In the meantime, however, ask what chores, behaviors, or problems family members would like to emphasize. Again, avoid unsolvable, long-standing, or overly complicated problems.

As before, ask each family member to define each behavior and contract condition and develop compromise definitions. The sample contract could be extended to include (1) the "garbage" chore from before, (2) school preparation, and (3) obeying curfew (assuming the latter two are not currently being done). *Define each part specifically.* For example, "preparing for school in the morning" might involve dressing and eating by a certain time in the morning, and "obeying curfew" might involve coming home at a certain time at night. Specific times should be part of any definition.

Designing the Contract

As before, negotiate the new contract separately with child and parents. Each party should describe as many potential solutions to the problems as possible. Again, focus on solutions that are practical, realistic, specific, and potentially agreeable to everyone. Choose one proposed solution most desirable for each problem. With respect to school preparation, for example, a good solution might be to regulate times a child will complete different activities such as eating or dressing. With respect to curfew, a good solution might be to choose a time that is reasonable to parents and the child.

If each family member agrees to the definitions, then develop rewards and punishments for completing or not completing responsibilities. Focus on rewards and punishments that are most appropriate and agreed-upon by everyone. As before, close loopholes in the contract and make sure the contract is time-limited. Finally, a general statement should be added to declare a family's commitment to the therapy process. Following the format from Stuart (1971), a sample contract based on the issues in this section is presented in Figure 7.1.

Implementing the Contract

This sample contract is appropriate *only if* family members successfully completed the first contract, family interactions are not extremely problematic, you are reasonably sure family members can handle the multiple components of this contract, and moderate to severe school refusal behavior is present. If factors in your case are different (e.g., initial contract failure, extreme school refusal and family conflict), then go slower and let family members experience success with an easier contract or re-implement the original one. For moderate to severe cases of school refusal behavior, this sample contract may be appropriate because actual school attendance is not yet required. In many such cases, a gradual buildup to school attendance is more effective than immediately requiring a child to attend school. For milder cases of school refusal behavior, where the child is missing school only part of the time (e.g., certain classes), this sample contract or a more complicated one may be appropriate.

Once this contract has been designed, family members should read it and state whether they will agree to it. If not, then renegotiate the contract. If everyone does agree, then ask each family member to sign the contract and give him or her a copy. Final questions should be addressed at this point. In addition, remind family members about what they have accomplished so far (i.e., coming to an agreed-upon solution to a problem without conflict). Remind them to contact you should problems arise, and that you will contact them between sessions to discuss outstanding issues concerning the contract or family functioning.

Sample Contract

Privileges	Responsibilities
General	
In exchange for decreased family conflict and a resolution to school refusal behavior, all family members agree to	try as hard as possible to maintain this contract and fully participate in therapy.
Specific	
In exchange for an extra half-hour of curfew on weekend nights, (child) agrees to	take out the garbage on Wednesday and Saturday if asked.
Should (child) not complete this responsibility,	he or she will be required to be in the house one hour earlier than usual.
In exchange for the privilege of possessing a radio and television in his or her room, (child) agrees to	rise in the morning at 7:00, dress and eat by 7:40, wash and brush teeth by 8:00, and finalize preparations for school by 8:20
Should (child) not complete this responsibility,	he or she will lose the radio and television and be grounded for one day.
In exchange for the privilege of possessing a compact disc player in his or her room, (child) agrees to	obey 9:00 P.M. curfew on school nights and 11:00 curfew on weekend nights.
Should (child) not complete this responsibility,	he or she will lose the compact disc player and be grounded for one day.

(Child) and his or her parents agree to uphold the conditions of this contract and read and initial the contract 0each day.

Signature of (child) and parents:

_____

_____   Date: _____

Figure 7.1
Sample Contract

A child may agree to a contract because he feels pressured to do so or because he is frustrated and wants to end the therapy session as soon as possible. We recommend contacting a child that night or the next day to see if, upon reflection, he wants to make changes in the contract or make known concerns he has about the therapy process. Often, children are teetering in their support of this treatment approach at this point. You may lose their support if they feel neglected, slighted, or betrayed in some way. Therefore, they must know that their input will be taken seriously. In many cases, you will have to walk a fine line among the interests of various parties and shift your therapeutic alliance deftly to keep everyone involved and motivated in the treatment process. Keep in mind that this sometimes includes the involvement and motivation of *parents* as well as children.

In related fashion, you may have an adolescent who finds the contracting process silly or useless or does not believe his parents will follow through on contract provisions. In cases where a child has given up on the contract process, but not necessarily treatment in general, you may have to rely on different problem-solving strategies or rely more heavily on related procedures for this functional condition (see later sessions). These procedures include communication skills training, escorting a child to school, peer refusal skills training, and improving academic performance. Other family therapy approaches (e.g., structural, strategic, transgenerational, experiential) may be utilized if necessary as well to address problematic dynamics that sap a family's motivation to implement contracts.

Finally, you may come across a child who manipulates the situation to see what he can get or who has no intention of returning to school under any conditions. In these cases, catering too much to a child can alienate parents and weaken your effectiveness. Clarify treatment goals early in treatment and, if possible, have everyone (especially the child) commit to a long-range goal of full-time school attendance. If this is not possible, then you may have to explore whether other goals are acceptable or appropriate, investigate the feasibility and desirability of alternative academic programs, and re-examine whether a family's situation is truly amenable to psychosocial treatment.

Homework

✎ Establish a time and place when a family discussion of issues can occur. Meet one or two times between now and the next session for these informal conversations. Adhere to the rules stated here and record the conversation for the therapist if desired and if all family members agree.

✎ Think about problems and potential solutions for the next contract.

✎ Implement the current contract and contact the therapist as necessary. Write down problems that interfere with the contract.

✎ Continue to complete daily logbooks. Note specific situations or experiences that arise during the week.

SESSIONS 3 & 4 *Maturing of Treatment*

Session Outline

■ Begin communication skills training with family.

■ Teach the child peer refusal skills.

At this point in treatment, contracting should focus more specifically on a child's particular school refusal behaviors. This may also involve ways of addressing a child during the day if he skips school or remains home following disruptive behaviors. You may have a case where you wish to change the family's problem-solving method toward many different child behaviors. However, focusing contracting now on a specific problem like school refusal takes advantage of new family motivation to change, nudges family members to use the technique on an immediate problem, and provides family members with evidence that the procedures have an effect. Early success with school refusal behavior may also increase a family's motivation to extend treatment procedures to other problems in the future.

Special Topic 7.2: Alternative School Placements

When teenagers refuse school, absences can reach a point where full-time school attendance in a regular classroom setting may not be possible or desirable. For other teenagers, the drudgery of high school is so overwhelming that they simply will not attend. In other cases, parental or school support is insufficient to lead to full-time school attendance. For these teenagers, you may have to explore alternative educational placements.

Each school district is different, of course, so if you are considering an alternative educational placement for your client, speak to knowledgeable school officials about where a child is eligible to go. Some school districts have part-time schools that meet only during mornings or evenings or weekends. Other alternatives include vocational schools, programs for home-based and school-based education, and summer classes. If a child is unwilling to attend regular school or you face substantial obstacles from parents and others to pursue a child's full-time attendance in a regular school, then attending one of these alternative settings may be the best option.

Sessions 3 and 4 may be quite similar, with the latter an extension of the former. This section describes the maturing of treatment of children who refuse school for tangible rewards by revisiting components from sessions 1 and 2. In addition, this includes a focus on communication skills training, peer refusal skills training, alternative contract ideas, and what can be done if a child continues to miss classes during the school day.

Establishing Times and Places to Negotiate Problem Solutions

Family members should be meeting at a regular time at home to discuss the current contract and what changes might be raised at the next therapy session. These meetings should occur about once or twice a week. Ask family members how these informal sessions are progressing. Concentrate on whether home meetings have actually been scheduled and held, communications during the meetings, conflicts, points of agreement and disagreement, compliments and insults, silence or nonattendance by certain family members, and general areas that need improvement. If significant problems are occurring, listen to and analyze an audiotape of the meetings and check for hostile communications. In addition, ask family members to change or stop the meetings or conduct more in-depth family therapy in session. If the meetings are going fairly well, ask family members to continue them as before. By session 4, if appropriate, encourage family members to practice negotiating with one another just as you and they are doing in the therapy session. This will enhance problem-solving and communication skills training.

Communication Skills Training

At this stage in treatment, encourage family members to practice negotiation skills that help problem-solving and serve as a basis for communication skills training. In communication skills training, family members are taught to maintain conversations without verbal abuse, hostility, cognitive distortions, interruption, or dismissal of each other's statements. At this point in treatment, communication skills may be taught if family members are experiencing significant conflict or if miscommunications interfere with the contracting process.

Communication skills training is often based on role-play and feedback. At a basic level, this involves having one family member make a statement to, or ask a question of, another family member, who must listen quietly. Following the first person's statement, the second person is asked to repeat or paraphrase what was said to ensure the message was correctly heard and understood. In the following example, C represents the child and F represents the father.

C: I feel like I can't do anything with my friends.

F: It sounds like you feel you want more time with your friends.

During this first step, concentrate on addressing basic problems in communication. Examples of such problems include interruptions of the first person's statement, incorrect paraphrasing, refusal to comply with the task, silence, and escalating negative interactions. Table 7.1 lists some common speaker and listener problems and suggested alternatives (from Foster & Robin, 1997). Intervene as soon as an improper communication is made and give corrective feedback as needed. Afterward, ask the parties to continue.

At this stage, concentrate on having family members give short, clear messages; listen; and paraphrase correctly. Family members can practice these skills in the therapy session and later during family conversations at home. If possible, ask family members to keep a list of major problems that surface in communication.

Defining the Behavior Problem

As before, review with family members the status of the previous contract. If the contract failed, investigate at length why this was so. As before, search for sabotage, problematic family interactions, low motivation, or other pernicious factors. Spend considerable time addressing problems and re-implement the contract if applicable and possible. For example, an adolescent may complain that his parents withheld reinforcement he was entitled to because of misbehavior that had nothing to do with the contract. In this case, all family members should be allowed to comment and be reminded that a contract agreement is binding for a particular behavior. Depending on the situation, the entitled reward may be given that day or the therapist could ask family members to re-implement the contract.

If the previous contract was successful, give family members ample praise and remind them that problems can be peacefully and effectively resolved. As before, depending on the severity of the situation, the next contract could involve either more complex problems that have nothing to do with school refusal behavior or introduce school refusal behavior as one component. As mentioned earlier, the more severe a child's school refusal behavior or the family's problematic interactions, the more likely the first approach should be used.

If a family is progressing fairly well, then the next contract may be more complex and more focused on a child's school attendance. One of the best ways to do this is to link house chores, money, and school attendance. In this way, a child is not directly paid for school attendance but rather earns the opportunity to do chores for money. Obviously, this must proceed with caution and is subject to many factors such as desirability to the parents, a family's financial situation, and whether extra work and rewards are acceptable to the parents and child. With the fam-

Table 7.1. Common Speaker and Listener Behavior Problems and Alternatives

Problematic behavior	Possible alternative
Speaker behaviors	
Accusatory, blaming, defensive statements e.g., "You make me so mad! You don't respect your curfew."	I-statements ("I feel _____ when _____ happens") e.g., "I get angry when you come in after your curfew."
Putting down, zapping, shaming e.g., "You'll never amount to anything."	Accepting responsibility; I-statements e.g., "I worry about your failing grades."
Interrupting	Listening; raising hand or gesturing when wanting to talk; encouraging speakers to use brief statements.
Overgeneralizing; catastrophizing; making extremist, rigid statements e.g., "I don't like it that you never help out around here."	Qualifying; making tentative statements ("sometimes," "maybe"); making accurate quantitative statements e.g., "I don't like it when you don't do your chores."
Lecturing, preaching, moralizing e.g., "I need to convince you of the importance of getting along with your sister. Sibling relationships are very important in families, and without a good relationship with your sister, you can't have that. When I was young . . . ."	Making brief, explicit problem statements ("I would like _____ ") e.g., "I would like you and Susie to fight less."
Talking through a third person e.g., "Doctor, I'd like Susie to clean her room."	Taling directly to one another e.g., "Susie, I'd like you to clean your room."
Getting off the topic	Catching self and returning to the problem as defined; putting other problems on a future agenda for discussion.
Commanding, ordering e.g., "You must be in by 11 on weekends and 9 on weeknights."	Suggesting alternative solutions e.g., "One idea is for you to come in at 11 on weekends and 9 on weeknights."
Monopolizing the conversation	Taking turns; making brief statements

Table 7.1. *continued*

Problematic behavior	Possible alternative
Dwelling on the past e.g., "Last week you didn't do your home- work at all." "That's not true! I did my homework on Monday, and didn't have any after that."	Sticking to the present and future; suggesting changes that will solve the problem in the future e.g., "We need to work out a way for you to get your homework done on time."
Intellectualizing; speaking in abstractions e.g., "The problem is your lack of respect for your parents."	Speaking in clear, simple language that a teenager can understand; talking about the behavior that prompts the abstractions e.g., "I feel hurt and angry when you swear at us when you're angry."
Mind reading e.g., "Mom just wants to spoil my fun."	Reflecting, paraphrasing, validating e.g., "Mom, I feel like you don't want me to have fun. Is that right?"
"Psychologizing" e.g., "I think he talks back to us because he is fundamentally insecure about being adopted	Inquiring about situations that provoke the behavior and about the consequences of the behavior e.g., "Joe, what situations really make you lose your temper? What bothers you about these things?"
Threatening e.g., "If you don't stop lying, I'll send you to live with your father."	Suggesting alternative solutions e.g., "One solution is to reduce your punishment if you tell the truth."

Listener behaviors

Mocking, discounting e.g., "Getting a maid is a stupid idea."	Reflecting, validating e.g., "Getting a maid would solve your problem, but I can't afford it."
Talking in a sarcastic tone of voice	Talking in a neutral tone of voice
Avoiding eye contact	Looking at the speaker
Fidgeting, moving restlessly, or gesturing while being spoken to	Sitting in a relaxed fashion; excusing self for being restless
Using words that say one thing, body language that says another	Matching words with feelings; being direct about feelings
Remaining silent, not responding	Reflecting, validating, expressing negative feelings

ily, develop a list of chores and problem behaviors and use this list to set conditions of the new contract. If family members object to using chores or money, then explore other reinforcers and tasks. Concentrate on tangible rewards most desirable to a child.

During session 4, review with the family the success or failure of this school attendance contract. Because this contract was the first to address school attendance specifically, explore at length problems that prevented the contract from succeeding. As noted before, problems may include fighting among family members, low motivation, sabotage, or other factors.

More specifically, many children are compliant about contracts *until* school attendance is expected. At this point, children may begin to say one thing and do another. For example, a child may agree in your office to attend school but miss school the next day. In related fashion, some children and adolescents claim they went to school when in fact they only became more adept at hiding absenteeism. Remain aware of these possibilities and look for what causes sudden contract failure.

Peer Refusal Skills Training

A common reason for contract failure is peer pressure to skip school. In other words, a child may fully intend to go to school but, once there, is tempted or goaded by others into skipping school. As a result, you may wish to teach the child peer refusal skills he can use to resist such pressure. Peer refusal skills training meshes nicely with communication skills training because the focus is on talking to others in a more constructive way. To start, ask a child to describe what his peers say at school to entice him to skip school. In the following example, T represents the therapist and C represents the child.

Case Vignette

T: Okay, Justin, you're saying you meant to go to school but your friends pressured you to skip yesterday afternoon?

C: Yeah, they found me in the hallway and kept after me to join them off-campus for lunch. Then we just hung out and blew off the afternoon.

T: What did your friends say to you to get you to skip school?

C: I don't know; they just ragged on me. They kept saying we'd have fun and we'd do our work later. They said we'd just have lunch for a couple of hours, but then it turned into the whole day.

You and the child may then create different statements to firmly but appropriately refuse offers to skip school. Use role-play and feedback to discuss different scenarios. Obviously, you must consider a child's anxiety about social rejection and build responses that will not let the child lose face. We have found it helpful for children to blame school attendance on their parents or therapist, thus absolving them (temporarily only) of blame. In addition, a child can talk to peers about his interest in a particular class, the need to finish uncompleted work, potential rewards for school attendance, or lack of desire to skip school. At this point in therapy, you may wish to outline suggested responses to peer pressures and ask a child to try them at school if necessary. For example:

T: Okay, Justin, we've talked about some ways you can avoid being in situations where your friends can pressure you into leaving school. We'll also work, as you agreed, on changing your lunch schedule so you'll eat earlier and see them less. But let's assume your friends do track you down during the day and get after you to skip school. What can you say to them?

C: I don't know; maybe I don't want to or maybe I can't?

T: Okay, you could say that, but you're not giving a definite reason. I'm afraid if you say "I don't want to," they'll think you're thinking about it and keep after you. What are some specific reasons you can give, like focusing on your parents or talking about your schoolwork?

C: I guess I could say my parents are really on my case about school and I should go. Or I could say I have to finish my science project that's due. I guess I could even just say, "Some other time" and walk away.

T: Great! Let's try those in case you do run into friends who ask you to skip school. Let's see how it works over the next few days, and I'll call you to see how it goes.

Peer refusal skills training will likely be most helpful if peer pressure is a main cause of interference with the school attendance contract. In addition, these skills may be helpful for refusing offers of drugs, which may be linked to school absence. However, if the contract is failing simply because the child is giving "lip service" in session to you and his parents, then peer refusal skills may not be helpful and a more intensive treatment alternative may be necessary.

Designing the Contract

As before, focus on negotiation, compromise, and assurances that a contract is acceptable to everyone. Focus on clear and appropriate solutions, effective rewards and punishments, closed loopholes, a limited timeline, and commitment to change. The contract designed in this session should closely mirror the previous contract but with changes as necessary. Also, try to link communication skills training to the problem-solving/contracting procedures. For example, you may wish to bring family members together to form the next contract and practice listening and paraphrasing. A sample contract based on issues discussed earlier (see Defining the Behavior Problem) is in Figure 7.2.

Keep in mind that full-time school attendance does not necessarily have to be pursued at this point. Sometimes asking a child to simply attend a few of his favorite classes per day is a good start. For example, a child may be asked to go to school at 10 A.M. and be allowed to leave at 2 P.M. Setting a foundation for later full-time school attendance, especially for children who have been out of school completely for some time, is usually a palatable option to everyone. You might, of course, have to check with school officials in case special permission is needed for the child to arrive late and/or leave school early.

If parents do not wish to link money to chores and school attendance, then alternative contract ideas may be proposed. Examples of alternative rewards include curfew extension, increased time with friends, fewer required chores, eating by oneself or with friends, shopping, video games and movies, car rides to school, and certain foods, among others.

Sample Contract

Privileges	Responsibilities
General	
In exchange for decreased family conflict and a resolution to school refusal behavior, all family members agree to	try as hard as possible to maintain this contract and fully participate in therapy.
Specific	
In exchange for the privilege of being paid to complete household chores between now and the next therapy session, (child) agrees to:	attend school full-time between now and the next therapy session.
Should (child) not complete this responsibility,	he or she will be required to complete the household chores without being paid.
In exchange for the privilege of possessing a radio and television in his or her room, (child) agrees to	rise in the morning at 7:00, dress and eat by 7:40, wash and brush teeth by 8:00, and finalize preparations for school by 8:20.
Should (child) not complete this responsibility,	he or she will lose the radio and television and be grounded for one day.
In exchange for compensation of five dollars, (child) agrees to:	vacuum the living room and clean the bathroom between now and the next therapy session.
Should (child) not complete this responsibility, or complete the responsibility in an insufficient manner (to be determined by parents),	he or she will not be paid.

(Child) and his or her parents agree to uphold the conditions of this contract and read and initial the contract each day.

Signature of (child) and parents:

_____

_____ Date: _____

Figure 7.2
Sample Contract

Implementing the Contract

This sample contract is appropriate only if you feel the family has progressed satisfactorily to this point. If not, then repeat the procedures from sessions 1 and 2. The initial timeline for this contract should be short and the next therapy session should be scheduled within 3 to 5 days. This will give family members time to implement the contract but also allow you to intervene should problems occur. *In many cases, the first contract that addresses school attendance is the most difficult to implement.* Therefore your support of an feedback to family members is critical at this point. Aspects of previous contracts (e.g., curfew) may also be included if appropriate.

Escorting a Child to School

Despite the contract, you may find that the child is still unable to fulfill his end of the bargain. For example, many children continue to agree to school attendance but skip school anyway without peer pressure. As a re-

---

Special Topic 7.3: Calling the Police

Parents may ask you if they should contact school or regular police if their child leaves the school campus prematurely. For younger children in elementary school, this is certainly necessary. For middle- and high school students, the situation is likely to be murkier and will require clinical judgment. However, we recommend parents contact school and/or regular police if they have no idea where a child is or if a child might be engaged in dangerous behavior such as drug use, unprotected sexual activity, joyriding in a car, or illegal activity.

If parents do have a general idea as to where their child is when she leaves school prematurely, *then we recommend parents find her and bring her back to school if possible.* Depriving a child of the ability to do fun things outside of school during school hours is important. Also, parents should punish this behavior according to contract provisions. If a child continues to skip school, consider having someone escort her to school and from class to class.

---

sult, appropriate rewards from the contract are never given and a child continues to pursue inappropriate rewards outside of school.

In these cases, you may wish have someone escort the child from class to class during the day. School officials are often unable to monitor children during the day, so one of the parents (or another adult they trust) may need to do so. Obviously, this requires substantial effort and time on someone's part. However, the procedure is often effective because it ensures school attendance and allows a child to earn appropriate rewards. At this stage in treatment, you may simply suggest this procedure as an option for your clients (including the child) to consider if the next few school attendance contracts do not succeed. Sometimes the mere mention of escorting prompts a child to adhere more closely to a contract's conditions because of the potential social embarrassment involved. However, if some valid urgency exists in getting a child back to school now, then escorting may be implemented immediately. Remind parents to discuss this procedure with you before starting.

Homework

- Continue to meet informally as a family once or twice between now and the next session. Discuss parts of the current contract that remain a problem and those aspects that are most effective. Also, discuss how family members communicate and what should change. Record the conversation for the therapist if desirable. Practice communication skills as appropriate.

- Think about problems and potential solutions for the next contract.

- Implement the current contract and contact the therapist if necessary.

- Begin to use peer refusal skills and escorting as appropriate.

- Continue to complete daily logbooks, noting specific issues or situations that may arise during the week.

- Gradually increase school attendance. *Read Special Topic 4.6 in chapter 4 to become acquainted with different methods of gradually reintegrating a child to school.* These methods include having a child go to school (1) in the morning for a set period of time and then gradually working forward by adding more time, (2) at 2 P.M. until the time school normally ends and then gradually working backward by adding more time, (3) only for lunch and then gradually adding more school time before and after lunch, (4) only for a favorite class or time of day and then gradually adding more classes or school time, (5) in a school room other than the classroom, such as the school library, and then gradually adding more classroom time.

SESSIONS 5 & 6 *Advanced Maturing of Treatment*

Session Outline

■ Review the family meetings that have been taking place at home.

In sessions 5 and 6, advanced maturing of treatment should occur. This involves a detailed analysis of what is currently happening in the home and what remains a problem. By this time, all daily procedures (i.e., family meetings, contracts, refusal skills) should be "up and running" and finely tuned to a family's situation. At this point, you should be *quite directive* in telling parents what remains to be done. In addition, vigorously change what may be blocking treatment success (this section includes some possible reasons). In addition, these later sessions sometimes call for more creativity, and you and family members may need to develop innovative modifications of the techniques described here. For example, you or family members may need to be inventive about certain aspects of a contract, increasing or enhancing family communication, or helping a child refuse offers to skip school.

Sessions 5 and 6 may be quite similar, with the latter serving as an extension of the former. The basic elements of contracting—defining problems and negotiating solutions—will continue to be addressed in these sessions. Other procedures such as communication skills training and peer refusal skills training may be broadened as well. For children who are progressing more slowly, a repetition of previous procedures might be appropriate.

Establishing Times and Places to Negotiate Problem Solutions

Review family meetings that have been occurring at home. In particular, explore how well family members practiced negotiation during problem-solving. Analyze an audiotape of the meeting if necessary. Check to see if family members were able to listen to one another and accurately repeat or paraphrase one another's verbal messages. As before, check for interruptions, inaccurate paraphrasing, silence, and hostile interactions. Review a family's list, if any, of major problems that surfaced in communication and address them here. If family members struggled with this early step in communication skills training, then refocus your attention on the listening and paraphrasing process described previously. If family members have extreme problems communicating, then more extensive family therapy and exploration of other issues might be appropriate and can supplement the procedures described here.

Advanced Communication Skills Training

Techniques

If family members did listen and paraphrase well over the past few days or sessions, then you may advance to the next step in communication skills training. This might involve practicing conversations without hostility. To start, suggest certain rules about what to avoid in a conversation. Encourage family members to avoid name-calling, insults, sarcasm, inappropriate suggestions, and screaming, among other behaviors. If these behaviors are not a problem, then less serious problems such as lack of eye contact or poor articulation may be addressed.

Conversations between family members should first be short, involve two family members only, and be closely monitored by you. Use the role-play and feedback procedure from before. This might first involve a one-on-one conversation between one family member and yourself before other family members. In the following example, the therapist plays the role of the father speaking to his teenage son. This technique is especially advisable if two family members are having severe problems communicating with one another or have not done so in a long time. The intention is to have the other party (in this example, the father) and other family members model an appropriate conversation.

Case Vignette

C: I just don't understand why I have to go to school. I'm almost 16 years old, but everybody keeps treating me like a little kid.

T: (Acting as father and looking directly at the child). It sounds like you're kind of angry.

C: Yeah, I am. Why can't everybody just leave me alone to do my own thing?

T: Can you be more specific? I'm not sure what you mean.

C: I want to spend more time with my friends. I should be able to go out if I want to.

T: Okay, it sounds to me like you feel confined and feel you do not spend enough time with your friends—is that right?

C: Yeah, why can't I do what I have to do at home and then go out without a hassle?

After this brief role-play, give feedback to everyone about appropriate behavior that occurred during the conversation. Important points to consider are calmness of tone, lack of interruptions, acknowledging another person's viewpoint, correct paraphrasing, and lack of insults or other derogatory remarks. In this example, the therapist/father gathered information from the teenager without judgment or defensiveness. In this way, a problem (i.e., time with friends) could be identified and defined accurately and negative emotions could be vented appropriately.

During this feedback process, address questions family members may have. You may practice this one-on-one conversation with a child to reinforce some important points, such as listening. Later, you may ask these two family members (e.g., father, son) to speak directly to one another in a short conversation. Observe this conversation closely and interrupt and give feedback if problems develop. For example:

C: Well, like I said before, I always get hassled and don't spend enough time with my friends.

F: I don't get it! You're with your friends all the time.

T: Mr. Williams, try to repeat what your son just said.

F: He said he doesn't spend enough time with his friends.

T: Good. Let's find out exactly what concerns your son. (Motions to do so)

F: Okay. What exactly concerns you?

C: I do my chores and homework, so then I should be allowed to see my friends. Now that I have to go to school more, I don't get to see them that often.

F: Okay, how much time do you feel you need to spend with your friends? (Therapist nods to approve of this statement)

C: I don't know; maybe a couple of hours a night. What's the big deal about that?

T: Okay, John, let's stick to answering the question. Leave out statements or questions that are sarcastic or too negative.

C: Okay. I'd like to spend at least a couple of hours a night with my friends. Maybe some more time on the weekends. (Therapist nods)

F: Okay, so 2 hours a night on a school night after chores and homework and dinner are done? Does that sound about right?

C: Yeah.

Introduce different issues in these dialogues between two family members to help them practice appropriate communications. You will likely need to make a recommendation about how long to continue these brief conversations before taking the next step. This next step could involve other one-on-one conversations (e.g., mother and child) or adding more people to a discussion. Once a particular parent–child dialogue is progressing well, for example, the other parent may be added. However, avoid overly strict alliances (e.g., two parents versus one child) that could damage the communication process. Should problems such as hostility occur, gently intervene and give feedback. For example:

Case Vignette

C: When I'm with my friends, I should be able to do what I want.

F: Okay, it sounds like you want more freedom. Is that right?

C: Yeah, I guess so. I'm almost an adult.

F: Well, you're getting there . . .

M: (To father:) Frank, he's not an adult.

F: I realize that, but John seems to feel he's becoming an adult. (To child:) Right?

C: Yeah, and so I should be able to do what I want.

M: Well, you can't do anything you want. Your father and I will discuss what you can and can't do.

T: Okay, Mrs. Williams, let's focus on paraphrasing what John just said and then gathering information about it.

M: Okay, he said he wants to do what he wants. (To child:) What kinds of things do you want to do? (Therapist nods)

If family members have done well listening, paraphrasing, and having short conversations with few problems, then communication skills training may become even more advanced. This might involve practicing extended conversations that are increasingly constructive in nature. As before, this will involve role-play and feedback where you as the therapist first demonstrate an extended, constructive conversation with another family member. As family members practice these extended conversations, closely monitor and address negative communications. In addition, family members may focus more on increasing compliments and other pleasantries. Spend time helping family members reframe comments in a positive way. For example, a statement such as, "You barely finished your homework" may be reframed as, "I really like it when you finish your schoolwork on time."

Potential Problems

Several factors may prevent communication skills training from working quickly or at all. These include pessimism, punishment of one converser, and silence. In many cases of severe school refusal behavior, family members have been fighting for several months or years. As a result, negative patterns of talking are set and family members are pessimistic about change. In this situation, family members should see they can interact well at a basic level and this signals hope for future change. Therefore, extended practice at this level may be necessary, and simple positive conversations may be a realistic final goal. A second problem occurs when one family member continually criticizes another during a conversation. In such a situation, a therapist may act as a mediator by allowing one person to speak, paraphrasing the message himself or herself, and presenting the message to the second person. In doing so, address unresolved family issues that cause hostile conversations between different members. Finally, if silence is an issue, focus on family members who are willing to talk and allow the silent member to watch these conversations. In a one-on-one meeting with the silent member, build rapport, convey the merits of participation, and draw him into the therapy process as much as possible.

Be aware that family members may not be able to completely change all hostile conversations in a short period of time. By this time in treatment, however, family members should know what makes a positive exchange and what prevents a positive exchange. Family members should become skilled at listening to one another and accurately paraphrasing what is said. In addition, family members should use these new ways of communicating in their home meetings and when designing new contracts. If the family is not yet at this point, repeat the procedures described in previous sessions. In addition, continue to explore other issues and family dynamics that prevent family members from having positive conversations using other, or more intense, family therapy procedures.

Defining the Behavior Problem

Review with family members the success or failure of the previous contract. As before, explore at length problems that prevented the contract from succeeding. For example, one factor that often blocks a successful contract is a child's activities with friends outside of school. Activities sometimes powerful enough to overwhelm a contract may range from those that are minor (e.g., eating lunch in a fast-food restaurant for a short period of time) to mid-range (e.g., hanging out in a shopping mall for an afternoon) to major (e.g., day parties, drug use, sexual activity, gambling for extended periods of time). By this time in treatment, you and the parents should know what is generally impeding a successful contract and where a child is during each school day and what he is doing. If not, discuss possible reasons and child activities at length. For example, parents may need to monitor a child's behavior more closely and respond to problems more immediately.

If these activities continue to interfere with school attendance contracts, then more serious steps may need to be taken. These could involve adding to the contract stronger rewards for school attendance and stricter punishments for nonattendance (if all parties agree), increasing parent supervision of a child during the day, and/or legal intervention (e.g., contacting the police to break up an illegal drug party). However, legal intervention of this sort must be used with caution, and all ramifications, including effects on the therapy process, should be considered. If realistic and appropriate, contact your local police and/or an attorney (with permission) for information and advice regarding your particular case. In addition, of course, consider your obligation to report any reasonable suspicion of child maltreatment.

Another child activity that interferes with school attendance contracts is excessive sleeping in the morning or an inability to rise from bed. This is sometimes worse for children who have been out of school for some time and who are not used to rising early in the morning. For many adolescents, difficulty getting up is normal and temporary. In other cases, a child has a medical problem or a true sleep disorder that requires attention (if so, consult a medical doctor or sleep disorders clinic as appropriate for assessment and treatment). Common treatments for sleep disorders in children and adolescents include those in Table 7.2 (from Durand, Mindell, Mapstone, & Gernert-Dott, 1998).

In other cases, a child is simply staying up too late and not getting enough sleep or is feigning fatigue to avoid school. In these cases, you and family members must design innovative ways of getting a child out of bed and ready for school. Try setting regular morning and evening routines and bedtimes (see chapter 6), increasing rewards for rising at a certain time, setting the alarm clock earlier in the morning and having parents constantly remind a child to get up, and allowing a child to get up later and walk to school on his own. This latter option, however, usually requires greater supervision. Some parents try more drastic measures such as pulling a child out of bed or throwing cold water on the bed, but we do not recommend these or any other very coercive procedures. Instead, try to negotiate a solution to the problem with the child and incorporate it into the next contract.

At this stage in treatment, family members should be skillful at defining behavior problems for contracts. Each family member should be giving his or her opinion about how to define a behavior problem (e.g., school nonattendance, lack of time with friends, being late in the morning) as well as appropriate contract rewards and punishments. If this is not the case, repeat the procedures described in previous sessions.

Finally, develop with the family and child some strategies to make up past schoolwork that accumulated during an extended absence and maintain adequate academic performance. This may include after-school programs, extra tutoring, supervised homework time, daily report cards, weekly progress reports, rearrangements of class schedules, and/or teacher meetings to collect assignments. An excellent predictor of ongoing school attendance is often good academic performance. Children who find assigned work appealing or do well in school are more likely to stay in class. As therapy progresses, encourage family members to define different academic problems and solutions and incorporate these into a separate contract.

Peer Refusal Skills Training

By this time in treatment, a child should know how to respond to peers who try to instigate school absence. In particular, a child should know specific phrases and methods of conversation that allow him to refuse such offers without being ridiculed or rejected. In addition, a child should be able to recognize and avoid situations that lead to temptations to leave school.

If peer pressure continues to be an issue, however, then check the child's refusal skills and see whether they were used. If necessary and possible, other coping skills should be emphasized, such as avoiding certain places

Table 7.2. Selected Interventions for Sleep Disorders

Sleep treatment	Description
Bedtime fading	For bedtime disturbances or sleep-wake schedule difficulties, using this intervention the parent establishes a time in which the child consistently falls asleep with little difficulty (e.g., 11:30 P.M.), then systematically makes bedtime 15 minutes earlier until child is falling asleep at the desired time.
Cognitive	This approach focuses on changing the sleeper's unrealistic expectations and beliefs about sleep ("I must have 8 hours of sleep each night," "If I get less than 8 hours of sleep it will make me ill"). Therapist attempts to alter beliefs and attitudes about sleeping by providing information on topics such as normal amounts of sleep and a person's ability to compensate for lost sleep. *More appropriate for older children and adolescents.*
Cognitive relaxation	Because some people become anxious when they have difficulty sleeping, this approach uses meditation or imagery to help with relaxation at bedtime or after a night waking. *More appropriate for older children and adolescents.*
Establishing bedtime routines	Creating a consistent and unchanging routine lasting about 30 minutes just prior to bedtime, including soothing activities (e.g., bath, reading a story), that always leads to bed. *Can be useful for difficulties initiating sleep for children of all ages.*
Graduated extinction	Used for children who have tantrums at bedtime or wake up crying at night, this treatment instructs the parent to check on the child after progressively longer periods of time, until the child falls asleep on his or her own.
Paradoxical intention	This technique involves instructing individuals in the opposite behavior from the desired outcome. Telling poor sleepers to lie in bed and try to stay awake as long as they can is used to try to relieve the performance anxiety surrounding efforts to fall asleep.
Progressive relaxation	This technique involves relaxing the muscles of the body in an effort to introduce drowsiness.
Scheduled awakening	Used for children who wake frequently during the night, this treatment involves waking the child approximately 60 minutes before he or she usually awakens at night. This helps teach children to fall back to sleep in their own while they are aroused from a deeper stage of sleep.

Table 7.2. *continued*

Sleep treatment	Description
Sleep hygiene	Some people's daily habits can interfere with their nighttime sleeping. This approach involves instructing the sleeper about the negative effects of caffeine, nicotine, alcohol, exercise too close to bedtime, certain foods, and medications, on their sleep.
Sleep restriction	This consists of limiting a person's time in bed to the actual amount slept. This is done to help the sleeper associate time in bed only with sleeping, and not with tossing and turning, trying to fall asleep.
Stimulus control	This approach includes instructions to go to bed only when sleepy, use the bedroom only for sleep (not for reading, television watching, or eating), get out of bed when unable to fall asleep, get out of bed in the morning at the same time each day regardless of the amount of time you slept.

at school, not talking to certain peers, and completing homework in the library. In addition, you may wish to use cognitive restructuring procedures to modify erroneous thoughts a child has about his peers and about refusing offers to skip school. For example, children commonly worry that, after turning down offers to skip school, they will lose friends, appear ridiculous, or feel humiliated. If these things are possible, then cognitive restructuring may not be helpful. However, if a child is clearly worried for no legitimate reason when refusing offers to skip school, then cognitive procedures for children with social anxiety (chapter 5) may be helpful.

Designing the Contract

If the previous contract involving school attendance was unsuccessful, explore outstanding issues that block the design of an effective contract. If the contract was successful, you may want to ask family members to renew it. However, changes in the contract may be made at the request of the parents and child if everyone agrees. In addition, family members may design a second contract to address other concerns such as time and activities with friends (Figure 7.3), oversleeping, and academic prob-

Special Topic 7.4: Problems Getting Out of Bed

Some teenagers miss school because they have great trouble getting out of bed in the morning. If your client has this problem, then be sure she is getting plenty of sleep. The following will help:

■ Make sure a child only sleeps in her bed and does not use it for other activities such as reading, watching television, calling people, or completing homework.

■ Be sure a child is in bed *with lights out* at an early time, say 8 or 9 hours before having to rise from bed.

■ Avoid caffeine, nicotine, alcohol, and exercise before bedtime.

■ Practice relaxation methods close to bedtime (see chapter 4).

■ Follow the same routine before bedtime, and begin this routine 30 minutes before lights out.

■ Set curfew for at least 2 hours before bedtime.

■ Have parents consult a pediatrician about sleep medication if necessary.

We recommend parents rise very early and wake their child in stages, much like a snooze alarm. If a child has to be up by 6 A.M., for example, parents can get up at 5:15 A.M. and wake a child at 5:30, 5:40, 5:50, 5:55, and 5:59 A.M. Parents should tell a child how many minutes she has left before having to get up. Set a loud alarm as well across the room. If a child still will not get up, then parents should continue to speak to her every 5 minutes and make sleeping a difficult thing to do. Also, set up contracts to give rewards and punishments for getting up or not getting up from bed. Finally, *parents should not give up and let a child sleep late and miss school completely.* If a child finally gets up and goes to school an hour late, this is better than missing most or all of the school day.

lems. In doing so, define each issue specifically and derive solutions acceptable to everyone.

By this point in treatment, family members should be able to design a good contract for a particular problem. If possible, prompt everyone to practice good communication skills during the contract design process. For example, family members could have short one-on-one conversa-

Sample Contract

Privileges	Responsibilities
In exchange for the privilege of spending two hours per school night (6:30–8:30 P.M.) and three hours per weekend night (7:30–10:30 P.M.) with friends between now and the next therapy session, (child) agrees to:	adhere to all aspects of the school attendance contract and inform his or her parent(s) where he or she will be before leaving the house as well as any changes in where he or she will be when with his or her friends.
Should (child) not complete this responsibility,	he or she will be required to stay in the house for the next two evenings.
(Child) agrees not to engage in any illegal activity during time spent with friends. Should (child) not complete this responsibility,	this contract is terminated and (child) will be required to stay in the house during the evening until the next therapy session.

(Child) and his or her parents agree to uphold the conditions of this contract and read and initial the contract each day.

Signature of (child) and parents:

_____

_____ Date: _____

Figure 7.3
Sample Contract

tions about possible changes in the upcoming contract. Involve as many family members as possible in this process.

Implementing the Contract

Implement the school attendance and/or another contract along the procedures described before. By the end of session 6, family members should be able to recognize problems adhering to a contract and address them accordingly. If not, this skill should be developed further in session because problems in this area can cause future relapse. Talk about anything that erodes a contract. In particular, explore problems of low motivation and parental acquiescence.

If parents are walking their child from class to class during the school day, be sure the child is rewarded for school attendance. In addition, instruct parents to find out whom they should contact if a child leaves school and how they can gradually withdraw from the escorting situation. Having parents do this is a good test of their motivation at this point and increases their independence from you. In general, parents should increasingly rely on school officials (e.g., teachers, guidance counselors, attendance officers, hall monitors) to monitor their child and give daily reports to them about their child. In this way, a child will come to expect that his school attendance is always being checked. As much as possible, parents should reward school attendance or punish school refusal immediately after the behavior.

In some cases of very persistent school refusal behavior, parents find it quite difficult to constantly follow through on implementing contracts, administering punishments, and/or escorting a child to school and classes. In these cases, some family members feel guilt and frustration and engage in conflict. An intense focus on resolving school refusal behavior should continue during the week. However, the family needs to maintain family cohesion and childhood fun. In some persistent school refusal cases, for example, families may need to set aside treatment procedures on the weekend and enjoy some fun activities together. As the therapist, you will know a family's situation well by this point and can use your clinical judgment as to what is most appropriate.

Homework

✎ Continue to meet informally as a family once or twice between now and the next session. Record the conversation for the therapist if desirable. Discuss aspects of the current contract that are problematic and effective. Practice communication skills as appropriate and desirable.

✎ Think about problems and potential solutions for the next contract(s). Follow through on procedures to reduce impediments to contract success.

✎ Continue to use refusal skills as appropriate.

✎ Implement the current contract and contact the therapist if necessary.

✎ Continue to complete the daily logbooks.

SESSIONS 7 & 8 *Completing Treatment*

By session 7, treatment procedures may begin to change in some key ways. First, as the family nears the end of therapy, treatment procedures should more closely resemble what is naturally occurring in a child's environment. For example, a child should be entering school on his own without "nudging" or coercion or parental accompaniment. Rewards given to the child should be made more natural if possible. Also, family members should practice contract negotiations more independently of you. However, family members should not deviate too much from treatment procedures that led to a child's return to school.

Second, treatment procedures may be extended to related problem areas if a child's school refusal behavior is fully or nearly resolved. For example, the development of contracts may be made for other time periods (e.g., weekends) or behaviors (e.g., arguing) that remain a problem. However, do not prematurely extend these treatment practices until a child's school refusal behavior is under control.

In many ways, session 8 can serve as an extension of what was done in session 7. As such, treatment procedures can be finalized and termination issues can be discussed. Also, recommendations should be made to family members about how to best handle child behavior problems and other issues in the near and far future. Lists of potential pitfalls to avoid may be developed, and long-term follow-up contact and booster sessions (see chapter 8) may be scheduled.

Establishing Times and Places to Negotiate Problem Solutions

Continue to review the family meetings that have been occurring at home. In particular, explore how well family members practiced negotiation and communication. Review the family's list, if any, of major problems that surfaced in communication and address them now. If family members continue to have difficulty resolving problems or developing contracts, then review material from previous sessions to help them improve different areas of negotiation or communication.

To ensure that family members have a firm grasp of negotiation and communication skills, give them a hypothetical problem and ask them to discuss it. Check whether certain family members dominate the discussion, whether some aspects of the problem are omitted, whether interruptions or other communication problems occur, or whether family members hesitate to raise certain issues. Be sure to address problems.

If a child is going to school on a near-regular basis, then the family meeting/negotiation/communication process should stay the same. If other areas of concern remain, then they can start to be addressed. For example, some families become good at resolving conflict surrounding school refusal but not other areas. Fighting often continues about marital issues, a child's other behavior problems, extrafamilial activities, finances, and sibling behaviors. If desirable, extend negotiation and communication skills training to these other problems. Inform family members that relapse may occur if they do not appropriately address these other problems.

By session 8, you may wish to finalize your review of the family meetings that have been occurring at home as well as details regarding a family's negotiation and communication skills. Give family members a summary of guidelines about speaking with one another appropriately (e.g., no name-calling, sarcasm, insults; concentrate on listening without interruption, paraphrasing, short conversations). Base these guidelines on the communication problems presented in sessions 3 and 4 as well as particular aspects and original problems of the family. In doing so, point out how certain negotiation and communication patterns facilitated a child's return to school. Remind family members of some basic themes regarding negotiation and communication: simplicity, clarity, respect, and reciprocation.

Warn family members that they may slip into old patterns of communicating once a relatively calm household atmosphere has been restored. In particular, family members may go back to silence or yelling to make their points. Also, parents may start to take good child behaviors for granted, forget to give rewards, or wait for severe behavior problems to occur before giving punishment. To counteract these regressions, ask family members to continue meeting regularly as a group and practice the negotiation and communication skills learned in therapy.

Defining the Behavior Problem

Review with family members the success or failure of the previous contract. As before, explore at length problems that prevented the contract from succeeding. If peer pressure continues to be an issue, then check the progress of the child's refusal skills and see whether they were used. Expand the focus on refusal skills to other coping skills as necessary. If family members continue to have difficulty resolving problems or developing contracts, then help them redefine behavior problems as well as rewards and punishments. If necessary, go back to the point where contracts were simpler and more time-limited. To ensure that a family has a firm grasp of how to define a problem, give members a hypothetical example of a vague problem and ask them to define it specifically. Monitor and address problems as necessary.

If a child is going to school on a near-regular basis, then the contracting process should stay the same. If other areas of concern remain, then they can start to be addressed. For example, many families have other problems not as well defined as school refusal. Concentrating on these other problems now will help a family address them in upcoming weeks. Ask family members to list additional problems that may be addressed. Examples of behaviors related to school refusal include aggression, noncompliance in other settings, failure to complete homework, social withdrawal, tantrums, refusal to move, general disruptive behavior at home or in class, arguing, and yelling, among others. If these or other behaviors are still a problem, ask family members to give specific definitions of them now in case they want to refer to them in the future.

In addition, some parents will still issue vague complaints about their child such as, "*Joshua lacks self-confidence in school,*" "*Sarah shows a lack of respect for others,*" or "*Andrew's just a bad kid.*" Encourage family members to avoid insulting statements and restructure negative statements in a positive and clear manner. In the sentences presented here, for example, the following restatements could be suggested: "*Joshua needs to raise his grades to a 'B' level,*" "*Sarah and her parents need to interact by speaking in a normal tone of voice,*" and "*Andrew needs to get more involved in positive extracurricular activities.*" Remind family members that vague, punishing statements will generally have less desirable effects than specific, positive ones.

By session 8, you and family members may wish to finalize the last set of behavior problem definitions. Give family members a summary of examples and guidelines about defining key behavior problems. Base this summary on particular aspects and original problems of the family. Try to anticipate future problems and provide sample definitions if appropriate. Also, point out how defining problems in a specific way facilitated a child's return to school. Remind family members of some basic themes regarding problem definition: simplicity, specificity, handling one issue at a time, and allowing all members to give their own definitions.

Warn family members that they may slip into old, ineffective ways of defining problems once a relatively calm household has been restored. In particular, family members may start to define a behavior problem specifically (e.g., child needs to be in school) but not completely (for how long?). In addition, family members should consider that children often need ongoing support to resist peer pressure to skip school. Finally, they should remember that a key to preventing future school refusal behavior is to adequately maintain a child's academic performance. To address these issues, family members should continue to practice skills learned in therapy and maintain frequent contact with school officials.

Designing the Contract

As before, help family members design a new contract to fit their current situation. Allow them to be as independent as possible during this process. Extend the contract timeline if appropriate (e.g., to 1 to 2 weeks). Integrate communication skills training during this process and involve as many family members as possible. If family members continue to have trouble designing contracts, then review material from previous sessions to help them.

To ensure that family members have a firm grasp of how to design a contract, give them a hypothetical example of a vague problem and see how well they design a contract. In addition, concentrate on how well family members integrate new communication skills with the contracting process. Try to resolve remaining issues that could erode the effectiveness of future contracts.

If a child is going to school on a near-regular basis, then the family's method of designing contracts should stay the same. If other areas of concern remain, then they can start to be addressed. For example, sample contracts can be drawn up for family members for related problems should they want to use them in the future.

By session 8, you and family members may wish to finalize the last set of contracts. Give family members a summary of examples and guidelines about designing contracts. Base this summary on particular aspects and original problems of the family. Remind family members of some basic themes regarding contract design: agreement by all members, specific and tightly defined conditions, sufficient strength of rewards and punishments, limited timeline, signatures, and daily checking by all members. In doing so, point out how specific contracts facilitated a child's return to school.

Because the contracting process requires time and effort, families sometimes abandon the procedure following therapy. In particular, families may start using "oral contracts" in which some haphazard agreement is made that if a child does "A," parents will do "B." This practice contains two main problems. First, time is often not taken to carefully design the contract, thus leading to possible loopholes, misinterpretation, and forgetfulness. Second, the implicit assumption is that parents will bribe a child for some activity (e.g., school attendance) but not give punishments for the absence of that activity (i.e., school nonattendance). To counteract this, encourage family members to follow the formal contract process.

Implementing the Contract

Family members should implement this new contract using the procedures described previously. If they continue to have trouble implementing contracts, then review material from previous sessions to help them improve compliance. Also, if applicable, ask parents to attend school less and less with their child if they have been escorting him to school or from class to class. Ask parents to rely more on school officials to monitor their child and give daily reports about their child to them.

If a child is going to school on a near-regular basis, then ask family members to implement the contract as before. If other areas of concern remain, then they can start to be addressed. For example, you may wish to add to the contract other behaviors raised by a family member. Do not add too many conditions to the contract, especially if a moderate chance of relapse exists. Finally, remind and encourage family members to read the contract daily.

By session 8, family members should be implementing final contracts designed in session with you. The contracts should be implemented using the procedures described previously. Discuss remaining problems that interfere with the use of contracts. In particular, discuss potential problems that often trouble families once they leave therapy. For example, some families will change the contract midway between the start and end point. If the purpose of this is to close loopholes, that is fine. However, children often pester their parents to ease restrictions and make a contract more favorable to them. In addition, families will sometimes simply continue the timeline of a contract without discussing it further. This may not consider changes in a child's preferences or life, for example, that make the contract obsolete. Therefore, encourage family members to follow through on all contracts and revisit contracts at least once per week.

Homework

Homework assignments after sessions 7 and 8 may include the following:

✎ Meet formally as a family to discuss issues and problems at least twice per week. Practice communication skills. If a family member wishes to raise a problem, have each family member define it as specifically as possible.

✎ During these meetings, formulate a contract for the defined problem if appropriate. Implement the contract for a limited time. Discuss aspects of the current contract that are problematic and effective. Reduce problems that block contract success.

✎ Continue to use peer refusal skills and make up schoolwork as appropriate.

✎ Periodically review lists of pitfalls regarding each of these treatment components given by the therapist.

✎ Contact the therapist as needed for support, feedback, answers to questions, long-term follow-up, and booster sessions if necessary.

Chapter 8   *Slip and Relapse Prevention*

This chapter defines slips and relapse and provides a brief overview of how to help children and families prevent a return to school refusal behavior. As mentioned in chapter 1, long-term school refusal behavior may lead to long-term problems as a child ages. As a result, try to prevent backsliding as much as possible and address new problems that come to your attention as soon as possible. Although some general procedures are described here, more specific recommendations may be necessary for your particular case.

Slips Versus Relapse

A slip is a *single* error or some backsliding following treatment. Slips involve only minor regression toward old behaviors and only a minor amount of interference with a family's daily functioning. Slips may include a missed school day, one or two days of high stress, short-term avoidance of a particular class, or intense but brief acting-out behaviors to stay home from school. Slips are not unusual after treatment and are especially common following long weekends, extended vacations, or, in the case of year-round schools, track breaks.

Relapse, on the other hand, is a return to old problematic behaviors or substantial backsliding to nearly the point when therapy started. In this population, therefore, relapse might involve missing school for several days or weeks, continued high levels of distress, avoidance of many social activities or evaluative situations at school, significant misbehaviors to get attention or tangible rewards, or excessive family conflict about a child's school refusal behavior.

If slips occur, and they probably will as a child "tests" her parents' resolve, then return to the therapeutic assignments listed in this guide and review key aspects of each (see chapters 4, 5, 6, and/or 7). If necessary, review with your client key aspects of exposures, relaxation and appropriate breathing, dispute handles and cognitive restructuring exercises, parent commands, parental firmness and consistency regarding school attendance and refusal, forced school attendance, contracts, communication skills, and other relevant therapy techniques. A good idea is to design, with your client, "relapse prevention sheets" that contain key reminders of what to do in a given situation. These sheets can then be periodically referred to by parents and children.

General sample reminders for each treatment package are listed in Table 8.1. Keep in mind, of course, that this is not an exhaustive or even a necessarily pertinent list. Many relapse prevention reminders need to be specifically designed in accordance with a family's particular history and concerns. Specifically, relapse prevention sheets often involve, among other things, child-based strategies to cope with certain anxiety-provoking situations, procedures for securing homework and attendance records, house rules, contracts, and appropriate family responses to different child behaviors (e.g., what a family should do if a child runs away from school or avoids class).

Tell family members not be too discouraged when slips happen. Some family members mistakenly believe that if a child refuses school again or becomes somewhat more anxious, then the entire therapy process was wasted. This is not true. Slips are usually the result of relaxed efforts and not parent or child incompetence. Instead, have parents and children view the situation as a challenging one that will help them practice the skills they learned in therapy. In addition, be sure parents continue to remain in close contact with school officials to monitor attendance, talk with a child for 10 minutes each night about potential obstacles to school attendance, practice therapy-based methods even during school breaks, ignore minor child complaints about having to attend school, expect school attendance each day except under highly unusual circumstances, and minimize backsliding.

Table 8.1. Sample Relapse Prevention Reminders for Families

For children who refused school to avoid objects or situations that cause general distress/ negative affectivity

1. Practice relaxation and breathing exercises when needed and once per week.
2. Record stressful parts of the day and review them with parents at night.
3. Put aside a safety signal and approach and complete one stressful activity per day.
4. Practice self-reinforcement when appropriate exposure occurs.

For children who refused school to escape aversive social and/or evaluative situations

1. Keep a journal of automatic thoughts during stressful times of the day.
2. Practice changing thoughts to coping, helpful ones when necessary.
3. Approach and have a five-minute conversation with three people per day.
4. Participate in one extracurricular activity per semester.

For children who refused school for attention

1. Review commands given to the child daily.
2. Administer consequences for misbehaviors as soon as they occur in different settings and at different times; work through tantrums in preparing the child for school.
3. Maintain the regularity and predictability of the child's morning routine.
4. Allow the child to ask one question on one topic per hour.

For children who refused school to pursue tangible reinforcement outside of school

1. Monitor the child's school attendance on a daily basis.
2. Contact teachers or other school officials once per week regarding the child's academic work.
3. Schedule one family problem-solving meeting per week.
4. Develop and implement a contract twice per month.

If slips continue, or if parents and the child are increasingly frustrated about renewed school refusal behavior, then you should be contacted. In fact, we recommend you stay in occasional telephone contact with these clients as needed after treatment. This can be done to discuss progress and new issues that may contribute to slips (e.g., changes in class schedule, academic problems, other stressors). However, parents and children should not be too dependent on you for feedback; instead, encourage them to initially solve new problems or slips based on the skills each person learned in therapy.

If Relapse Occurs

In situations where slips are too frequent and a child is relapsing toward regular school refusal behavior, the family should certainly discuss this with you. You may be able to provide some feedback on what to do or schedule the parents and/or family for additional treatment sessions. *Instruct parents not to wait until the following school year to address relapse.* Some parents, if their child starts refusing school again in the late spring, become discouraged and simply wait out the school year or believe there is no point in addressing school refusal behavior at so late a time. However, if a child successfully refuses school during the late spring, then she may be out of school for several months (i.e., spring and summer). This will impede later attempts at reintegration in the fall. A better strategy would be for parents to reintegrate a child to school in late spring (with, perhaps, your help) and pursue summer classes or other strategies to keep her socially active. This strategy will also convey to the child that school refusal behavior will be addressed immediately.

Tell parents not to be too discouraged if relapse happens. Relapses do happen, especially in more severe cases of school refusal behavior. However, perseverance is often as important as any technique in this guide. Inform family members that increased effort is most likely to lead to long-term success. The next section discusses methods of preventing slips and relapse as well as addressing relapse should it occur.

Preventing Slips and Relapse

You may engage in different techniques to prevent slips and relapse. Some techniques can occur as therapy is ending, and others may occur at some time in the future.

Photographs and the Return-to-School Storybook

One method of relapse prevention involves taking photographs during in vivo exposure or desensitization practices. This can be especially effective for children who previously had much distress or social anxiety about school, but it may also be useful for children who refused school for positive reinforcement and who may be in school for the first time on their own. Whatever the reason, pictures are a good way to reinforce a child for her accomplishments. Parents can then display the pictures in a prominent place in their home (e.g., refrigerator or bedroom door), much as they would a report card, drawing, or another of their child's personal accomplishments. In this way, the child can be continually reminded of her progress.

Another family-oriented activity to further reinforce a child's progress is to create a poster, journal, or storybook of the child's accomplishments using photographs of the child's exposures. Common pictures include the child sitting at her school desk, talking with a teacher, interacting with friends, riding the school bus, and giving an oral report before the class. For each picture, parents should help the child write a caption or paragraph description of the scene, including what she is thinking, feeling, and doing in the picture. Combining the photographs with a child's own written words serves as a creative and personal reminder and reinforcer of special moments in the child's therapy program.

Commercial

Another relapse prevention technique is the commercial. Specifically, ask the child's help in producing a video "commercial" aimed at teaching other children how to overcome the problem of school refusal behavior. This is often done toward the end of treatment. Dr. Philip Kendall is the originator of this unique and highly successful idea for preventing slips and relapse. In making the commercial, the therapist serves as the "director" of the project, but the child is the expert on the subject and star of the show. By enlisting the child as an expert in how to overcome school refusal behavior, her self-esteem and feelings of empowerment are boosted.

As the therapist, guide the child's performance, ensuring that all key elements of her treatment are presented in the video. For example, if a child's treatment involved relaxation or breathing techniques, demonstrations of these methods should be in the video. Coach the child to describe the three parts of an anxious feeling (physical feelings, thoughts, behavior) and the ways in which these components build on each other during stressful situations. Cognitive methods (STOP) should also be described, with relevant examples presented by the child. If a portable camcorder is available, ask parents to videotape the child conducting key in vivo STIC tasks such as riding the school bus or eating in the cafeteria.

Some children in our program have devised very creative scripts for these videos. For example, one child acted as the "game show host" as he quizzed family members and the therapist on various techniques for overcoming negative emotions. Another child acted as a reporter who "investigated" the problem of school refusal behavior in which she uncovered negative thoughts and "aggravations from avoidance." Even though this video is developed as a way to teach other children how to overcome their problem, the child keeps this video for her exclusive use. In this way, parents can periodically play the video to remind their child of the program and prevent setbacks during times of high stress or vulnerability (e.g., before the start of school, during standardized testing times).

Structured Activities Outside the Home

Long breaks from school, such as summer vacation or December holidays, can provide enough time for a child to "slip" toward inappropriate habits and anxieties. Children who relapse may have greater tendencies to experience negative emotions and anxiety. Typically, the plans and procedures taught in therapy are forgotten or put aside during this time. There is the tendency to want to "leave well enough alone" and not continue to practice important procedures and skills. To prevent relapse, encourage parents to keep their child as much as possible on a regular "school" schedule during holidays. This means regular waking times and routines in the morning and a regular bedtime at night. This ensures that a child's sleep–wake cycle stays within normal limits and that she gets enough sleep. During the summer, parents should start their child's normal "school" schedule about 3 weeks prior to the start of school. For children who refused school in the past to pursue tangible rewards, gradual restrictions on curfew and time spent with friends may need to start at this time. In this way, a child's day can start to mimic what will need to happen when school starts.

During summer vacation, parents should also try to have their child spend some portion of each weekday outside the home in an organized activity with other children and adults. For example, day camps, volunteer programs, sporting activities, youth groups, and library programs can give children contact with people outside the family. This allows a child to continue to practice and refine anxiety management skills. In addition, especially for attention-seeking children, more independent activities will help prevent backsliding to dependency on parents for moment-to-moment support. If structured programs are unavailable, parents can organize other parents in their community to form play groups or activity programs that may be rotated from house to house. Again, this will gently "force" a child to remain in contact with others and will serve as a natural desensitization and exposure process. For children with separation anxiety, this will help them practice leaving primary caretakers and functioning well on their own.

Booster Sessions

Some therapists and schools provide "booster" programs for children who previously refused to attend school. Booster sessions may be provided in individual or group format. These sessions are usually scheduled at high-pressure times of the year, such as early August before the start of school, during a mid-semester break, or during examination periods. The purpose of a booster program is to review skills and discuss potential problems that a child worries about. By anticipating these problems and intervening before they occur, a child is more likely to successfully re-enter school and engage in school life. Booster programs may be particularly important for children moving from elementary to middle school or from middle to high school. Transition times are difficult for children with a history of school refusal behavior, anxiety, or depression, so some booster program for these children is recommended. Booster programs are usually structured, short-term, and highly individualized to meet a child's needs.

Introduction to a New School

Because many children have trouble coping with changing social and academic scenarios, especially when advancing to a new school (e.g., middle, high school), allow them to explore the new school building before classes begin. This can be done a few days before school starts and may be set up with cooperation from a child's new school counselor (parents should be careful, however, that a child does not view the counselor and his or her office as a safety signal). Of special interest are the location of lockers, specific classrooms, cafeteria, libraries, gymnasia, main and guidance offices, exits, and settings for getting on and off the school bus. Maps are also helpful, but parents should encourage their child to be as independent as possible. Because children with previous school refusal behavior often worry about getting lost and looking foolish, taking them on a tour of their new school building may diminish anticipatory anxiety, increase self-efficacy, and prevent relapse. Children should also receive information on school-based social and sporting groups they are eligible to join. Parents may then gently encourage their child to become socially active in these groups.

Children With Chronic School Refusal Behavior

For children with chronic or extremely severe school refusal behavior, relapse prevention is quite challenging. Follow-up in these cases will generally need to be more frequent and intensive than cases of acute school refusal behavior. Relapse prevention in chronic cases is likely to depend more on various things like reduced family conflict, reduced child noncompliance and disruptive behavior, changes in parent attitudes, a child's participation in extracurricular activities and development of appropriate social contacts, continued motivation to attend school, and ongoing medical interventions if applicable. As a result, tell parents to be vigilant about slips in areas different than those specifically related to absenteeism. You may also wish to remain in closer-than-usual contact with this type of client following the end of treatment.

Keep in mind as well, because children with chronic school refusal behavior are often placed in alternative or part-time curricular programs, that parents should be aware of upcoming changes that could interrupt attendance. For example, a school district with financial difficulties may be forced to eliminate an after-school program that a child was attending. In this case, alternative arrangements may have to be made for attending classes during the day, evening, or summer. In addition, parents may find their child has new behaviors (e.g., substance abuse, depression) that interfere with school attendance. In this case, parents should contact you for feedback, reschedule therapy sessions, or pursue treatment with another specialist, among other options.

Overall, relapse prevention for children with chronic school refusal behavior will depend on a close monitoring of attendance and related behaviors for at least several months. Parents should thus maintain a healthy relationship with you and school officials (e.g., teachers, counselors, attendance officers) who can help identify and address problems as early as possible. In this way, parents and others can lower the chances of relapse.

Other Special Circumstances

You may encounter families with special circumstances other than those described in previous chapters. One special circumstance occurs when parents leave for work in the morning before a child leaves for school. In this situation, parents should arrange to have another adult stay with the child and ensure she arrives at school. If no one is available, a taxi or some supervised ride can be arranged. Parents should ensure their child actually went to school and what went wrong if she did not. If the school attendance problem continues and parents have no one else to take a child to school, then special work arrangements may have to be made so a parent can arrive at work after taking a child to school.

Another special circumstance involves multiple children in a family who are refusing to go to school. This was discussed briefly in chapter 6 but bears repeating here. If parents are faced with two or three children who are refusing school, we recommend concentrating on the child who is missing the most school time or who has the most difficult school refusal behavior. Often this is the oldest of the children refusing to attend school. In this case, use the methods in this guide *and concentrate most on this child.* Other children. ideally, will model the increased attendance of the older child. Even if this is not the case, having the most difficult child go to school frees up parental time to concentrate on other children. Finally, parents must seek help from other adults who can help them complete the morning routine and take children to school.

Another special circumstance involves children with developmental disorders who refuse to attend school. This may include a child with a learning disorder who is frustrated about his schoolwork, but may also include children with more severe developmental disorders such as autism or mental retardation. In these cases, work closely with school officials to design a 504 or individualized education plan (see chapter 7) that includes methods for improving school attendance, such as the ones described in this guide. This is especially important for designing part-time attendance schedules. In addition, consult with school officials often to see what problems at school might be resolved. If a child with a reading disorder feels unmotivated, for example, then some reward-based program at school might be helpful.

Another special circumstance involves families referred to the legal/court system because of a child's absenteeism. School officials may refer a family to the legal/court system for educational neglect (or related statute) should a child miss substantial school time. If this has happened, then get as much information as you can about what is going to happen next. Parents may need to consult an attorney, meet with a juvenile detention officer, or appear at a "truancy" court. Every state is different, so familiarize yourself with the legal process in this type of situation. Our general recommendation is to work closely with parents and school and legal officials to achieve at least a part-time school schedule. In our experience, school and legal officials are generally more concerned with incremental attendance progress than pursuing formal charges and issuing court-based sanctions.

Final Comments

Addressing school refusal behavior can be a trying experience for parents, children, and therapists. Because of this debilitating problem, we have tried to provide some guidelines for identifying key school refusal behaviors and for addressing them in a timely fashion. We hope you find the techniques in this guide useful, and we invite any comments you have about these procedures.

School Refusal Assessment Scale-Revised (C)

Children sometimes have different reasons for not going to school. Some children feel badly at school, some have trouble with other people, some just want to be with their family, and others like to do things that are more fun outside of school.

This form asks questions about why you don't want to go to school. For each question, pick one number that describes you best for the last few days. After you answer one question, go on to the next. Don't skip any questions.

There are no right or wrong answers. Just pick the number that best fits the way you feel about going to school. Circle the number.

Here is an example of how it works. Try it. Circle the number that describes you *best*.

Example:

How often do you like to go shopping?

Never	Seldom	Sometimes	Half the Time	Usually	Almost Always	Always
0	1	2	3	4	5	6

Now go to the next page and begin to answer the questions.

School Refusal Assessment Scale-Revised (C)

Name: _____

Age: _____

Date: _____

Please circle the answer that best fits the following questions:

1. How often do you have bad feelings about going to school because you are afraid of something related to school (for example, tests, school bus, teacher, fire alarm)?

Never	Seldom	Sometimes	Half the Time	Usually	Almost Always	Always
0	1	2	3	4	5	6

2. How often do you stay away from school because it is hard to speak with the other kids at school?

Never	Seldom	Sometimes	Half the Time	Usually	Almost Always	Always
0	1	2	3	4	5	6

3. How often do you feel you would rather be with your parents than go to school?

Never	Seldom	Sometimes	Half the Time	Usually	Almost Always	Always
0	1	2	3	4	5	6

4. When you are not in school during the week (Monday to Friday), how often do you leave the house and do something fun?

Never	Seldom	Sometimes	Half the Time	Usually	Almost Always	Always
0	1	2	3	4	5	6

5. How often do you stay away from school because you will feel sad or depressed if you go?

Never	Seldom	Sometimes	Half the Time	Usually	Almost Always	Always
0	1	2	3	4	5	6

6. How often do you stay away from school because you feel embarrassed in front of other people at school?

Never	Seldom	Sometimes	Half the Time	Usually	Almost Always	Always
0	1	2	3	4	5	6

7. How often do you think about your parents or family when in school?

Never	Seldom	Sometimes	Half the Time	Usually	Almost Always	Always
0	1	2	3	4	5	6

8. When you are not in school during the week (Monday to Friday), how often do you talk to or see other people (other than your family)?

Never	Seldom	Sometimes	Half the Time	Usually	Almost Always	Always
0	1	2	3	4	5	6

9. How often do you feel worse at school (for example, scared, nervous, or sad) compared to how you feel at home with friends?

Never	Seldom	Sometimes	Half the Time	Usually	Almost Always	Always
0	1	2	3	4	5	6

10. How often do you stay away from school because you do not have many friends there?

Never	Seldom	Sometimes	Half the Time	Usually	Almost Always	Always
0	1	2	3	4	5	6

11. How much would you rather be with your family than go to school?

Never	Seldom	Sometimes	Half the Time	Usually	Almost Always	Always
0	1	2	3	4	5	6

12. When you are not in school during the week (Monday to Friday), how much do you enjoy doing different things (for example, being with friends, going places)?

Never	Seldom	Sometimes	Half the Time	Usually	Almost Always	Always
0	1	2	3	4	5	6

continued

13. How often do you have bad feelings about school (for example, scared, nervous, or sad) when you think about school on Saturday and Sunday?

Never	Seldom	Sometimes	Half the Time	Usually	Almost Always	Always
0	1	2	3	4	5	6

14. How often do you stay away from certain places in school (e.g., hallways, places where certain groups of people are) where you would have to talk to someone?

Never	Seldom	Sometimes	Half the Time	Usually	Almost Always	Always
0	1	2	3	4	5	6

15. How much would you rather be taught by your parents at home than by your teacher at school?

Never	Seldom	Sometimes	Half the Time	Usually	Almost Always	Always
0	1	2	3	4	5	6

16. How often do you refuse to go to school because you want to have fun outside of school?

Never	Seldom	Sometimes	Half the Time	Usually	Almost Always	Always
0	1	2	3	4	5	6

17. If you had less bad feelings (for example, scared, nervous, sad) about school, would it be easier for you to go to school?

Never	Seldom	Sometimes	Half the Time	Usually	Almost Always	Always
0	1	2	3	4	5	6

18. If it were easier for you to make new friends, would it be easier for you to go to school?

Never	Seldom	Sometimes	Half the Time	Usually	Almost Always	Always
0	1	2	3	4	5	6

19. Would it be easier for you to go to school if your parents went with you?

Never	Seldom	Sometimes	Half the Time	Usually	Almost Always	Always
0	1	2	3	4	5	6

20. Would it be easier for you to go to school if you could do more things you like to do after school hours (for example, being with friends)?

Never	Seldom	Sometimes	Half the Time	Usually	Almost Always	Always
0	1	2	3	4	5	6

21. How much more do you have bad feelings about school (for example, scared, nervous, or sad) compared to other kids your age?

Never	Seldom	Sometimes	Half the Time	Usually	Almost Always	Always
0	1	2	3	4	5	6

22. How often do you stay away from people at school compared to other kids your age?

Never	Seldom	Sometimes	Half the Time	Usually	Almost Always	Always
0	1	2	3	4	5	6

23. Would you like to be home with your parents more than other kids your age would?

Never	Seldom	Sometimes	Half the Time	Usually	Almost Always	Always
0	1	2	3	4	5	6

24. Would you rather be doing fun things outside of school more than most kids your age?

Never	Seldom	Sometimes	Half the Time	Usually	Almost Always	Always
0	1	2	3	4	5	6

Do not write below this line

1. _____ 2. _____ 3. _____ 4. _____

5. _____ 6. _____ 7. _____ 8. _____

9. _____ 10. _____ 11. _____ 12. _____

13. _____ 14. _____ 15. _____ 16. _____

17. _____ 18. _____ 19. _____ 20. _____

21. _____ 22. _____ 23. _____ 24. _____

Total Score = _____ _____ _____ _____

Mean Score = _____ _____ _____ _____

Relative Ranking = _____ _____ _____ _____

Name: _____

Date: _____

Please circle the answer that best fits the following questions:

1. How often does your child have bad feelings about going to school because he/she is afraid of something related to school (for example, tests, school bus, teacher, fire alarm)?

Never	Seldom	Sometimes	Half the Time	Usually	Almost Always	Always
0	1	2	3	4	5	6

2. How often does your child stay away from school because it is hard for him/her to speak with the other kids at school?

Never	Seldom	Sometimes	Half the Time	Usually	Almost Always	Always
0	1	2	3	4	5	6

3. How often does your child feel he/she would rather be with you or your spouse than go to school?

Never	Seldom	Sometimes	Half the Time	Usually	Almost Always	Always
0	1	2	3	4	5	6

4. When your child is not in school during the week (Monday to Friday), how often does he/she leave the house and do something fun?

Never	Seldom	Sometimes	Half the Time	Usually	Almost Always	Always
0	1	2	3	4	5	6

5. How often does your child stay away from school because he/she will feel sad or depressed if he/she goes?

Never	Seldom	Sometimes	Half the Time	Usually	Almost Always	Always
0	1	2	3	4	5	6

6. How often does your child stay away from school because he/she feels embarrassed in front of other people at school?

Never	Seldom	Sometimes	Half the Time	Usually	Almost Always	Always
0	1	2	3	4	5	6

7. How often does your child think about you or your spouse or family when in school?

Never	Seldom	Sometimes	Half the Time	Usually	Almost Always	Always
0	1	2	3	4	5	6

8. When your child is not in school during the week (Monday to Friday), how often does he/she talk to or see other people (other than his/her family)?

Never	Seldom	Sometimes	Half the Time	Usually	Almost Always	Always
0	1	2	3	4	5	6

9. How often does your child feel worse at school (for example, scared, nervous, or sad) compared to how he/she feels at home with friends?

Never	Seldom	Sometimes	Half the Time	Usually	Almost Always	Always
0	1	2	3	4	5	6

10. How often does your child stay away from school because he/she does not have many friends there?

Never	Seldom	Sometimes	Half the Time	Usually	Almost Always	Always
0	1	2	3	4	5	6

11. How much would your child rather be with his/her family than go to school?

Never	Seldom	Sometimes	Half the Time	Usually	Almost Always	Always
0	1	2	3	4	5	6

continued

12. When your child is not in school during the week (Monday to Friday), how much does he/she enjoy doing different things (for example, being with friends, going places)?

Never	Seldom	Sometimes	Half the Time	Usually	Almost Always	Always
0	1	2	3	4	5	6

13. How often does your child have bad feelings about school (for example, scared, nervous, or sad) when he/she thinks about school on Saturday and Sunday?

Never	Seldom	Sometimes	Half the Time	Usually	Almost Always	Always
0	1	2	3	4	5	6

14. How often does your child stay away from certain places in school (e.g., hallways, places where certain groups of people are) where he/she would have to talk to someone?

Never	Seldom	Sometimes	Half the Time	Usually	Almost Always	Always
0	1	2	3	4	5	6

15. How much would your child rather be taught by you or your spouse at home than by his/her teacher at school?

Never	Seldom	Sometimes	Half the Time	Usually	Almost Always	Always
0	1	2	3	4	5	6

16. How often does your child refuse to go to school because he/she wants to have fun outside of school?

Never	Seldom	Sometimes	Half the Time	Usually	Almost Always	Always
0	1	2	3	4	5	6

17. If your child had less bad feelings (for example, scared, nervous, sad) about school, would it be easier for him/her to go to school?

Never	Seldom	Sometimes	Half the Time	Usually	Almost Always	Always
0	1	2	3	4	5	6

18. If it were easier for your child to make new friends, would it be easier for him/her to go to school?

Never	Seldom	Sometimes	Half the Time	Usually	Almost Always	Always
0	1	2	3	4	5	6

19. Would it be easier for your child to go to school if you or your spouse went with him/her?

Never	Seldom	Sometimes	Half the Time	Usually	Almost Always	Always
0	1	2	3	4	5	6

20. Would it be easier for your child to go to school if he/she could do more things he/she likes to do after school hours (for example, being with friends)?

Never	Seldom	Sometimes	Half the Time	Usually	Almost Always	Always
0	1	2	3	4	5	6

21. How much more does your child have bad feelings about school (for example, scared, nervous, or sad) compared to other kids his/her age?

Never	Seldom	Sometimes	Half the Time	Usually	Almost Always	Always
0	1	2	3	4	5	6

22. How often does your child stay away from people at school compared to other kids his/her age?

Never	Seldom	Sometimes	Half the Time	Usually	Almost Always	Always
0	1	2	3	4	5	6

23. Would your child like to be home with you or your spouse more than other kids his/her age would?

Never	Seldom	Sometimes	Half the Time	Usually	Almost Always	Always
0	1	2	3	4	5	6

continued

24. Would your child rather be doing fun things outside of school more than most kids his/her age?

Never	Seldom	Sometimes	Half the Time	Usually	Almost Always	Always
0	1	2	3	4	5	6

Do not write below this line

1. _____	2. _____	3. _____	4. _____
5. _____	6. _____	7. _____	8. _____
9. _____	10. _____	11. _____	12. _____
13. _____	14. _____	15. _____	16. _____
17. _____	18. _____	19. _____	20. _____
21. _____	22. _____	23. _____	24. _____

Total Score = _____   _____   _____   _____

Mean Score = _____   _____   _____   _____

Relative Ranking = _____   _____   _____   _____

References

Achenbach, T. M. (1991a). *Manual for the Child Behavior Checklist 4–18 & 1991 Profile.* Burlington: University of Vermont Department of Psychiatry.

Achenbach, T. M. (1991b). *Manual for the Teacher's Report Form & 1991 Profile.* Burlington: University of Vermont Department of Psychiatry.

Achenbach, T.M. (1991c). *Manual for the Youth Self-Report & 1991 Profile.* Burlington: University of Vermont Department of Psychiatry.

Achenbach, T. M., & Rescorla, L. A. (2001). *Manual for the ASEBA school-age forms & profiles.* Burlington: University of Vermont Research Center for Children, Youth, & Families.

Albano, A. M., Detweiler, M. F., & Logsdon-Conradsen, S. (1999). Cognitive-behaviorial interventions with socially phobic children. In S. W. Russ & T. H. Ollendick (Eds.), *Handbook of psychotherapies with children and families* (pp. 255–280). New York: Plenum Press.

Beck, A. Ta., Rush, A. J., Shaw, B. F., & Emery, G. (1979). *Cognitive therapy of depression.* New York: Guilford Press.

Beidel, D. C., & Turner, S. M. (1998). *Shy children, phobic adults: nature and treatment of social phobia.* Washington, DC: American Psychological Association.

Benson, H. (1975). *The relaxation response.* New York: Avon Books.

Berney, T., Kolvin, I., Bhate, S. R., Garside, R. F., Jeans, J., Kay, B., & Scarth, L. (1981). School phobia: A therapeutic trial with clomipramine and short-term outcome. *British Journal of Psychiatry, 138,* 110–118.

Bernstein, G. A., Garfinkel, B. D., & Borchardt, C. M. (1990). Comparative studies of pharmacotherapy for school refusal. *Journal of the American Academy of Child and Adolescent Psychiatry, 29* (5), 773–781.

Chorpita, B. F., Albano, A. M., Heimberg, R. G., & Barlow, D. H. (1996). A systematic replication of the prescriptive treatment of school refusal behavior in a single subject. *Journal of Behavior Therapy and Experimental Psychiatry, 27*(3), 281–290.

Church, J., & Edwards, B. (1984). Helping pupils who refuse school. *Special Education Forward Trends, 11*(2), 28–31.

Conners, C. K. (1990). *Manual for Conners' Rating Scales.* North Tonawanda, NY: Multi-Health Systems.

Conners, C. K. (1997). *Conners Rating Scales—Revised.* North Tonawanda, NY: Multi-Health Systems.

Durand, V. M., Mindell, J., Mapstone, E., & Gernert-Dott, P. (1998). Sleep problems. In T. S. Watson & F. M. Gresham (Eds.), *Handbook of child behavior therapy* (pp. 203–219). New York: Plenum Press.

Forehand, R. L., & McMahon, R. J. (1981). *Helping the noncompliant child: A clinician's guide to parent training.* New York: Guilford Press.

Foster, S. L., & Robin, A. L. (1997). Family conflict and communication in adolescence. In E. J. Mash & L. G. Terdal (Eds.), *Assessment of childhood disorders* (3rd ed., pp. 627–682). New York: Guilford Press.

Ginsburg, G. S., Silverman, W. K., & Kurtines, W. S. (1995). Cognitive-behavioral group therapy. In A. R. Eisen, C. A. Kearney, & C. E. Schaefer (Eds), *Clinical handbook of anxiety disorders in children and adolescents* (pp. 521–549). Northvale, NJ: Jason Aronson.

Kearney, C. A. (1995). School refusal behavior. In A. R. Eisen, C. A. Kearney, & C. E. Schaefer (Eds.), *Clinical handbook of anxiety disorders in children and adolescents* (pp. 19–52). Northvale, NJ: Jason Aronson.

Kearney, C. A. (2001). *School refusal behavior in youth: A functional approach to assessment and treatment.* Washington, DC: American Psychological Association.

Kearney, C. A. (2002a). Case study of the assessment and treatment of a youth with multifunction school refusal behavior. *Clinical Case Studies, 1,* 67–80.

Kearney, C. A. (2002b). Identifying the function of school refusal behavior: A revision of the School Refusal Assessment Scale. *Journal of Psychopathology and Behavioral Assessment, 24,* 235–245.

Kearney, C. A. (2005). *Social anxiety and social phobia in youth: Characteristics, assessment, and psychological treatment.* New York: Springer.

Kearney, C. A. (2006). Confirmatory factor analysis of the School Refusal Assessment Scale-Revised: Child and parent versions. *Journal of Psychopathology and Behavioral Assessment, 28,* 139–143.

Kearney, C. A., Drabman, R. S., & Beasley, J. F. (1993). The trials of childhood: The development, reliability, and validity of the Daily Life Stressors Scale. *Journal of Child and Family Studies, 2*(4), 371–388.

Kearney, C. A., Pursell, C., & Alvarez, K. (2001). Treatment of school refusal behavior in children with mixed functional profiles. *Cognitive and Behavioral Practice, 8,* 3–11.

Kearney, C. A., & Silverman, W. K. (1990). A preliminary analysis of a functional model of assessment and treatment for school refusal behavior. *Behavior Modification, 14*(3), 340–366.

Kearney, C. A., & Silverman, W. K. (1993). Measuring the function of school refusal behavior: The School Refusal Assessment Scale. *Journal of Clinical Child Psychology, 22*(1), 85–96.

Kearney, C. A., & Silverman, W. K. (1995). Family environment of youngsters with school refusal behavior: A synopsis with implications for assessment and treatment. *American Journal of Family Therapy, 23*(1), 59–72.

Kearney, C. A., & Silverman, W. K. (1996). The evolution and reconciliation of taxonomic strategies for school refusal behavior. *Clinical Psychology: Science and Practice, 3*(4), 339–354.

Kearney, C. A., & Silverman, W. K. (1999). Functionally-based prescriptive and nonprescriptive treatment for children and adolescents with school refusal behavior. *Behavior Therapy, 30*, 673–695.

Kendall, P. C., Chansky, T. E., Kane, M. T., Kim, R. S., Kortlander, E., Ronan, K. R., Sessa, F. M., & Siqueland, L. (1992). *Anxiety disorders in youth: Cognitive-behavioral interventions.* Boston: Allyn and Bacon.

Kennedy, W. A. (1965). School phobia: Rapid treatment of fifty cases. *Journal of Abnormal Psychology, 70*(4), 285–289.

Kovacs, M. (1992). *Children's Depression Inventory.* North Tonawanda, NY: Multi-Health Systems.

La Greca, A. M., & Stone, W. L. (1993). Social Anxiety Scale for Children—Revised: Factor structure and concurrent validity. *Journal of Clinical Child Psychology, 22*(1), 17–27.

Lazarus, A. A., Davison, G. C., & Polefka, D. A. (1965). Classical and operant factors in the treatment of a school phobia. *Journal of Abnormal Psychology, 70*(3), 225–229.

Leventhal, T., & Skills, M. (1964). Self-image in school phobia. *American Journal of Orthopsychiatry, 34*, 685–695.

Mash, E. J., & Barkley, R. A. (Eds.). (2006). *Treatment of childhood disorders* (3rd ed.). New York: Guilford.

Moos, R. H., & Moos, B. S. (1986). *Family Environment Scale manual* (2nd ed.). Palo Alto, CA: Consulting Psychologists Press.

Ollendick, T. H. (1983). Reliability and validity of the Revised Fear Survey Schedule for Children (FSSC–R). *Behaviour Research and Therapy, 21*(6), 685–692.

Ollendick, T. H., & Cerny, J. A. (1981). *Clinical behavior therapy with children.* New York: Plenum Press.

Patterson, G. R. (1982). *Coercive family process: A social learning approach.* Eugene, OR: Castalia.

Reynolds, C. R., & Paget, K. D. (1983). National normative and reliability data for the Revised Children's Manifest Anxiety Scale. *School Psychology Review, 12*(3), 324–336.

Ronan, K. R., Kendall, P. C., & Rowe, M. (1994). Negative affectivity in children: Development and validation of a self-statement questionnaire. *Cognitive Therapy and Research, 18*(6), 509–528.

Silverman, W. K., & Albano, A. M. (1996). *Anxiety Disorders Interview Schedule for DSM–IV: Child Version, Parent Interview Schedule.* San Antonio, TX: The Psychological Corporation.

Silverman, W. K., & Kurtines, W. M. (1996). *Anxiety and phobic disorders: A pragmatic approach.* New York: Plenum Press.

Silverman, W. K., & Nelles, W. B. (1988). The Anxiety Disorders Interview Schedule for Children. *Journal of the American Academy of Child and Adolescent Psychiatry, 27*(6), 772–778.

Sperling, M. (1967). School phobias: Classification, dynamics, and treatment. *Psychoanalytic Study of the Child, 22*, 375–401.

Spielberger, C. D. (1973). *State-Trait Anxiety Inventory for Children ("How I Feel Questionnaire").* Palo Alto, CA: Consulting Psychologists Press.

Stallings, P., & March, J. S. (1995). Assessment. In J. S. March (Ed.), *Anxiety disorders in children and adolescents* (pp. 125–147). New York: Guilford Press.

Stuart, R. B. (1971). Behavioral contracting within the families of delinquents. *Journal of Behavior Therapy & Experimental Psychiatry, 2*, 1–11.

Wolpe, J. (1969). *The practice of behavior therapy.* New York: Pergamon Press.

About the Authors

Christopher A. Kearney, PhD, is professor of psychology and Director of the UNLV Child School Refusal and Anxiety Disorders Clinic at the University of Nevada, Las Vegas. He is the author of numerous journal articles, book chapters, and books related to school refusal behavior and anxiety disorders in youth, including *School refusal behavior in youth: A functional approach to assessment and treatment; Getting your child to say "yes" to school: A guide for parents of youth with school refusal behavior* (Oxford); *Social anxiety and social phobia in youth: Characteristics, assessment, and psychological treatment; Casebook in childhood behavior disorders;* and *Practitioner's guide to treating fear and anxiety in children and adolescents: A cognitive-behavioral approach.* He is also an author for two forthcoming books from Oxford: *Helping school refusing children and their parents: A guide for school-based professionals* and *Silence is not golden: Strategies for helping the shy child.* Dr. Kearney is on the editorial boards of *Behavior Therapy, Journal of Clinical Child and Adolescent Psychology, Journal of Abnormal Psychology, Journal of Psychopathology and Behavioral Assessment, Journal of Anxiety Disorders,* and *Journal of Gambling Studies.* In addition to his clinical and research endeavors, Dr. Kearney works closely with school districts around the country to improve strategies for helping children attend school with less distress.

Anne Marie Albano, PhD, ABPP, is Associate Professor of Clinical Psychology in Psychiatry at Columbia University/New York State Psychiatric Institute, and Director of the Columbia University Clinic for Anxiety and Related Disorders. Dr. Albano received her doctorate in clinical psychology from the University of Mississippi in 1991 and completed a postdoctoral fellowship at the Phobia and Anxiety Disorders Clinic at the State University of New York at Albany. She is board certified in clinical child and adolescent psychology and a Founding Fellow of the Academy of Cognitive Therapy. She is the President-Elect of the Association for Behavioral and Cognitive Therapies. Dr. Albano is a Principal Investigator for an NIMH multicenter clinical trial entitled "*Child/Adolescent Anxiety Multimodal Treatment Study*" (CAMS) and was a PI for the landmark NIMH-sponsored *Treatments for Adolescents with Depression Study* (TADS). Both trials examine the relative efficacy of CBT, medication, combination treatment, and pill placebo in youth. In addition to the CBGT-A program for adolescents with social phobia, Dr. Albano is the co-author with Dr. Patricia DiBartolo of a treatment manual and parent guide for school refusal behavior and she is the co-author with Dr. Wendy Silverman of the *Anxiety Disorders Interview Schedule for Children,* all published in the Treatments That Work™ series. Dr. Albano conducts clinical research, supervises the research and clinical development of postdoctoral fellows in psychology and psychiatry, and is involved in advanced training of senior level clinicians in the application of cognitive behavioral approaches to diagnosis and treatment.